MARIAN ISZATT WHITE

Collaboration in Public Services

With a foreword by **Denis Desautels**

The Challenge for Evaluation

Collaboration in Public Services

Andrew Gray
Bill Jenkins
Frans Leeuw
John Mayne

Comparative Policy Analysis
Volume X

 Transaction Publishers
New Brunswick (U.S.A.) and London (U.K.)

Library of Congress Catalog Number: 2002042998
ISBN: 0-7658-0183-3
Printed in the United States of America

Library of Congress Cataloging-in-Publication Data

Collaboration in public services : the challenge for evaluation / edited by Andrew Gray ... [et al.].
    p. cm. — (Comparative policy analysis series)
    Includes bibliographical references and index.
    ISBN 0-7658-0183-3 (cloth : alk. paper)
    1. Political planning—Evaluation. 2. Administrative agencies—Evaluation. 3. Intergovernmental cooperation—Evaluation. 4. Public-private sector cooperation—Evaluation. 5. Contracting out—Evaluation. I. Gray, Andrew, 1947- II. Series

JF1525.P6C64 2003
352.5'38—dc21
                                            2002042998

Contents

Foreword

By most accounts, and certainly in my own judgment, the 1990s will go down in the annals of public administration as a decade of very significant and lasting change. Admittedly, in some countries the momentum for change started a few years earlier as was the case in New Zealand when that country faced an urgent financial crisis. It is also true that some of the changes that may have been set in motion in the 1990s will not play themselves out fully for years. Such may be the case for collaborative arrangements, which were put in place in great numbers during that period, although the impact of these structures on governance and accountability was not fully understood and will not be fully mastered for some time yet, if ever. The same holds true, of course, for the evaluation of public programs delivered through collaborative arrangements within governments and between governments—the subject of this very interesting book.

The important reforms that we witnessed in the 1990s were driven by a number of factors. We can point to the huge financial pressures faced by many governments, to political ideology that aimed at reducing the role of government or increasing competition in the provision of public services or to plain common sense, that is, the old ways of delivering public services were simply becoming untenable in a modern world of instant communications and increasingly sophisticated and informed citizens. Whatever the reasons, public management reforms are a reality and all those who have a role to play in the functioning of our public institutions must face that reality. It is true that, even around the notion of collaborative arrangements, there can be some competing philosophies. As one of the authors in *Collaboration in Public Services* describes it, some may see collaboration among partners and institutions as essential in its own right while governments of a more conservative stripe could see such arrangements as an opportunity to promote more competition as the solution to efficient service. Some might therefore be tempted to wait things out and see if these arrangements continue to grow or really last before spending too much energy or intellectual capital on resolving the management and technical challenges that they pose. I personally do not think that this is just a trend or a new label for old practices. On the contrary, as this volume indicates, collaborative arrangements are likely to stay with us and even grow in popularity and, as such, they represent a unique opportunity for practitioners to advance the cause of accountability and results-based management.

Indeed, I am convinced that most people, including politicians and public servants who may find this a burden at times, would agree that enhanced transparency and accountability lead to stronger institutions and more effective government. Clear, timely information on money spent, where it went and what it achieved makes it easier for those outside an organization or program structure to monitor consistency with policy intentions and the effectiveness of public programs. Moreover, I would add that a society or country must be able to criticize itself if it wants its institutions to achieve superior levels of performance. Although there may be certain risks in doing so, namely that we may be too hard or negative on ourselves, self-criticism is essential if a country or jurisdiction wants its institutions to rank among the best in the world. Program evaluation is an essential part of that self-criticism and, as such, has a key role to play with the advent of new collaborative structures. If somehow the challenges and complexities of these arrangements led to a diminution of program evaluation functions, this would lead to a weakening of accountability mechanisms with negative consequences on institutional performance.

However, program evaluation practitioners and the auditing community with which I am familiar must wade carefully through the new governance models that are emerging. These can be highly complex relationships, which have been put together after sometimes extremely difficult political negotiations or negotiations with private sector providers concerned with commercial confidentiality. Public servants who have put these structures together may very well make the point, particularly in partnerships between governments, that compromises were made in order to reach an agreement and that there is a risk that evaluations could aggravate tensions among partners. This danger, in my view, tends to be somewhat exaggerated. And as the chapters in this volume suggest, practitioners must allow for experimentation and evolution in the governance and accountability structures that are put in place. Even as a former auditor general (who would normally insist on clear accountability structures as well as clear performance objectives), I would argue that practitioners should be able at this early stage of collective learning to accept "softer" accountabilities. The partners must work through their inevitable early difficulties and build upon their experiences to continuously improve the arrangements. Although this is not always the case, some arrangements can be so complex that it would be foolish and counterproductive to expect that all of the issues could be nicely circumscribed up front in a written agreement. In the short term, there are bound to be significant differences between the expectations of the partners and the perceived "reality," and timely discussions will need to take place in order to adjust expectations or modify the arrangements. In the longer term, more fundamental changes could be necessary.

The challenges to program evaluation brought about by collaborative arrangements in the delivery of public services are most interesting and program evaluation practitioners must rise to those challenges in order to fulfill their responsibilities in support of accountability and transparency. The editors and the members of INTEVAL who have contributed to this volume are to be commended for sharing their reflections on these important issues and for thus contributing to a timely international dialogue.

Denis Desautels
Center on Governance, University of Ottawa
Auditor General of Canada (1991-2001)

Preface

The International Group for Policy and Program Evaluation (INTEVAL) serves both as a forum for international scholars and practitioners of public policy to discuss ideas and developments and as a community dedicated to enhancing the contribution of evaluation to government. Since the late 1980s it has published through Transaction Publishers a series of books including reviews of country by country developments, the relation of evaluation with budgeting and auditing and with performance management, intergovernmental evaluation, the evaluation of different policy instruments, and its contribution to government learning. From these studies has emerged a common concern with the impact of public management reforms including recently the emphasis on collective and collaborative mechanisms for delivering public policy.

This volume presents some of the Group's initial explorations of collaborative policy delivery. The Group's aim has been to chart some collaborative forms and processes and tease out implications for evaluation. If the intention has not been to develop grand theory there has been an interest in collaboration as a particular form of governance that brings perhaps distinctive relationships with evaluation that may in time be expressed theoretically. The volume is thus provided as a contribution to this expression.

The contributors, a mix of academics, program managers, evaluators and auditors, are grateful for the support of the various hosts and other supporters of their meetings. These include the Instituto de Estudios Fiscales (Madrid), the Institute of Public Administration (Dublin), the University of Durham (U.K.), and the World Bank's Operations Evaluation Department.

The Editors

1

Collaborative Government and Evaluation: The Implications of a New Policy Instrument

Andrew Gray, Bill Jenkins, and Frans Leeuw

The overall objective of this book is to examine, in a variety of different national contexts, the emergence or rediscovery of collaborative mechanisms of policy delivery and implementation. We are therefore less concerned with collaboration per se and its merits as the challenges these developments pose for mechanisms of policy and program evaluation. This opening chapter sets out the background to these developments and discusses some of the salient conceptual issues that are engaged by later chapters. It reviews aspects of the recent debate on policy networks and collaborative government for many of current deliberations (practitioner and academic) are embedded therein. The discussion then explores collaborative government and its mechanisms in greater detail, outlining some of the various contemporary manifestations of these as policy instruments and the problems of transplanting them into different political and social contexts. In all this the merits of collaboration are taken as problematic rather than assumed and some of the costs and benefits of adopting this instrument are assessed. We then turn to examine evaluation and offer some preliminary thoughts on the adequacy of evaluative mechanisms to cope with what many see as new and demanding challenges. Finally, we set out the focal questions explored in different ways by the authors of subsequent chapters.

Policy Delivery Networks and Collaborative Government

In early 2001 a group of senior British civil servants, ministerial advisers, audit officials and representatives of agencies and voluntary organizations held a seminar to discuss better policy design

1

and delivery. Organized by the Performance and Innovation Unit (PIU) of the UK Cabinet Office, this meeting sought to encourage "a more rigorous thinking about delivery issues in government" (PIU 2001: 3). It was pointed out that policy implementation in the "real world" was often radically different from that portrayed by traditional political or management models. In particular, delivery was "a more circular process involving continuous learning, adaptation and improvement." while in the long run it was "more efficient and effective to motivate and empower rather than to issue detailed commands" (PIU 2001: 4). Of particular importance was the concept of *joining up* within government itself and more widely by building up local capacity and community engagement.

Something similar has been evident in the United States. Agranoff and McGuire, for example, argue that public management in the twenty-first century is taking place in a new and complex world where the old models of federalism are no longer adequate. U.S. federalism is a form of government under pressure: "as policy responsibilities between national and sub-national governments have evolved and devolved, governing authority has overlapped to a point where all actors are involved simultaneously to varying degrees" (2001: 671). Such a recognition has led to a focus on intergovernmental management. Practitioners and academics have begun to search for models to explain the new world of twenty-first-century federalism and the way actors seek to cope both by employing tried and tested traditional models (e.g., top down management) as well as new and emergent forms (e.g., networks). Drawing on empirical studies of urban economic development (Agranoff and McGuire 1998a; 1998b) and rural development (Radin et al. 1996), Agranoff and McGuire argue that a new model of governance is emerging characterized by less federal control and more intergovernmental collaboration manifested in increased involvement of state, local, private and voluntary (third sector) agencies (further see below).

In the Netherlands also partnership between governments, private parties and civil society, including grass-roots movements, is becoming a buzzword. Using collaborative arrangements to secure improved standards of education, for example, was the subject of particular parliamentary discussion from May 2000. And partnership extends to communication with stakeholders about the rationale and impact of the collaboration. Simultaneously, the lack of collaboration has been a focus of attention in recent inquiries including of the Enschede disaster (the explosion of a fireworks factory leading to the destruction of a large part of the city of Enschede). Here failures between the layers of government were identified as causes of the disaster.

Some might regard these developments as in striking contrast to the thrust of the past quarter of the twentieth century. During this period a volcano of reform has erupted almost relentlessly against the traditional collectivist values of public service. For some this has been a mission against the scale of government (government as part of the problem rather than as part of the solution). For others, it has been a campaign to bring the functional discipline of private sector management to public services.

It would be an oversimplification to suggest that there has been uniformity in this reforming ideal. Not only have there been important variations in scope and scale between countries, many of the developments have not always been mutually consistent. Nevertheless, there have been common elements either new to public policy or applied in new ways and contexts. These include:

- Market or market type mechanisms designed to provide a demand and supply function and shape resource allocation through contracts;

- Increased regulatory regimes to oversee these mechanisms;

- Disaggregated service organizations characterized by designated agencies;

- Flatter hierarchies and streamlined organizational processes;

- Local rather than national personnel regimes governing contracts, pay and conditions;

- Performance regimes by which agencies and staff work to pre-set targets;

- Financial regimes of cost reduction, external funding arrangements and accruals accounting;

- Emphases on quality of service and consumers as customers.

The manifestation of these reforms has been so evident and widespread that some have labeled them as *New Public Management* (NPM). Here associated patterns of relationships in service provision have suggested a shift towards a system of governance in which economic, organizational, political and technical contexts have forged increasingly mixed economies in the provision of public goods and services. In this, intensifying competition has been a striking characteristic.

Thus, the British PIU exhortation to "join up" government may be seen to question the rise of the competitive ethic in public services and challenge traditions of departmentalism, audit, and accountability. The suggested new key to service delivery is *organizational learning* in which *evaluation* has a key role to play in developing and sustaining the capacity for learning in the policy delivery network. Perhaps this is no more than political opportunism as new labels are found for old practices. On the other hand, the experience of the more competitive emphasis in policy delivery has led some in government to perceive a loss of values of collective provision including those linked to more decentralized and localized capacities. Moreover, intractable problems such as social exclusion, urban regeneration and crime prevention appear to demand systemic or holistic interventions involving a multiplicity of organizations and actors. Thus, the PIU paper may be seen as an attempt to revive collaborative mechanisms as a policy instrument.

If some of the developments discussed above (e.g., in the Netherlands and the UK) share something of a philosophical backing for collaboration, other countries have come to develop collaborative arrangements, or at least focus on them, for somewhat different reasons. In Canada, for example, public sector reform has been sold more pragmatically. Here the thrust for collaborative arrangements has been as much fiscal pressure, political desire (in a federal and multicultural polity) to lock other levels of government into joint efforts or, more simply, recognition that with so much overlapping jurisdiction more formal partnership is administratively functional.

There is a suggestion, however, in these British, American, Canadian and Dutch experiences that genuine collaborative arrangements might constitute a new governance. Such an argument builds on the work of Kickert et al. (1997), Rhodes (1996), O'Toole (1997) and others on network and network management. Put briefly the case is that experiences in the United States, Europe and many other industrial countries point up policy delivery problems (dating from the 1970s onwards) and a frequent loss of control by political authorities. Strategies to overcome such difficulties initially included the new public management devices described above but have recently emphasized networks and interorganizational arrangements. In such systems participants are effectively interdependent and no one actor may be effectively in control. This, in turn, has led to the "hollow state" thesis (Milward and Provan 1993). In such a context governments now have to establish ways to utilize and manage the new collaborative arrangements, many of which challenge traditional ways of political operations (Osborne and Gaeblar 1993; Mandell 1999, 2001).

Thus, collaborative arrangements may involve more of a cultural change than anything seen under the competitive emphases of new public management. This is reinforced by British experience in which "the absence of integrated working is long standing, culturally embedded, historically impervious, obvious to all concerned and deeply entrenched in central and local government" (Stewart 2000: 105). As a result many efforts at collaboration have floundered, trapped in a political maze of entrenched interests and characterized by a failure to learn or transfer knowledge or innovation. Thus, for Stewart, "there needs to be more rigorous thinking about the nature, forms and terms of inter-organizational collaboration" (2000: 107).

So, what is collaboration in service provision and what are its implications for evaluation and the political processes it serves? This volume provides an initial search for answers to these questions. The remainder of this chapter offers an overview of the manifestations of collaboration and evaluation and sets out some of the relationships between them.

Collaboration

In June 2001, Britain's New Labour government secured a second term in office with a massive (and almost unchanged) parliamentary majority. However, the electoral turnout, at less than 70 percent and among the lowest ever recorded, would probably not have surprised U.S. political scientist Robert Putnam, who would argue that this decline in political participation reflects a lack of confidence in government and legitimacy common to many advanced industrial countries reflecting social fragmentation. Putnam's thesis, expressed most recently in *Bowling Alone* (2000), is that in spite (or perhaps because) of a market driven economy and new public management, Western industrial societies, in particular the U.S., have been characterized over the last two decades by politics of disengagement. This disengagement is evident, for example, in sharp falls in group and organizational membership, the erosion of solidarity and trust and a wider detachment from the political process.

The consequence is a decline in state capacity and efficiency and a weakening of civil society (Ashbee 2000).

Key to these developments is what Putnam views as the erosion of *social capital* divided into *bridging* (inclusive groups and networks) and *bonding* (wider networks for developing and mobilizing solidarity). For Putnam "bonding social capital constitutes a kind of sociological superglue whereas bridging social capital provides a sociological WD 40" combining to trigger powerful social effects (Putman 2000: 23). He argues, therefore, that there is a vital link between community capacity and social capital, the latter being crucial to social and political processes thorough developing and sustaining such values as trust, reciprocity and interdependence. The manifestation of this is in powerful social networks and strong self-sustaining organizations.

The debate on social capital is, however, not clear-cut. Different interpretations of the central concept bring different prescriptions from collaboration and democratic enhancement through community empowerment to a case for less state intervention and a building up of voluntary activity (Social Exclusion Unit 2000b: 52-3). There have also been strong attacks on the broader Putnam thesis both for its inaccuracy in analyzing societal developments and in its prescriptions for rebuilding society in the United States and elsewhere (Ashbee 2000).

This debate is important here for offering evidence to support the case of a decline in civic engagement and social communion that may in turn explain some of the difficulties governments face in policy delivery. The increasing emphasis on the operation and language of market mechanisms for determining the content and cost of public service, for example, may have contributed to fragmentation and individualization by eroding organizations and practices based on more socially cohesive mechanisms and values. When the response to such delivery difficulty has been to reinforce central command styles of governance this has been accompanied by further implementation failure, erosion of legitimacy and decline of civic values such as trust. The Putnam solution is to create political capacity by developing social capital. Thus the increased interest in collaborative mechanisms.

For some then, the main issue therefore is less one of democratic governance per se as whether traditional governance structures can cope with changing political, economic and social circumstances.

Agranoff and McGuire (2001), for example, address this issue in conceptualizing the changing forms of interaction between federal, state and local levels in the United States as these relate to the delivery of policies such as urban economic development, health care and environmental protection. They argue that traditional models such as (a) top down federal control or (b) what they term "donor-recipient arrangements" (where policy may be implemented by bottom up negotiation and adjustment) are now mitigated by new forms of interaction that include "jurisdiction based" arrangements and network management. In the former, local managers (i.e., those with a specific jurisdiction) become the strategic hub of policy delivery activities. They manage interdependencies and seek to establish new organizational relationships for the purpose of achieving local goals. Thus, local civic entrepreneurs are the products of the devolved systems. In contrast, the network model is based on interdependency. Here leadership is collaborative and policies emerge as the consequence of collective action where solutions are sought that benefit all parties.

Agranoff and McGuire (2001) argue that network arrangements can be identified in many different policy areas and serve many different purposes. In particular they note their emergence in areas such as human services (often linked to the involvement of not-for-profit organizations), rural development (Radin et al. 1996) and local economic development (Agranoff and McGuire 1998c). But is any one format superior? Agranoff and McGuire's (2001) conclusion would be that this is a misplaced question. They argue that the models operate in different combinations and that the form of these varies with circumstances. Hence, "emergent models do not replace longer standing models" (p. 678). Rather different types of interorganizational management emerge characterized by compliance (top down), two party bargaining (donor/recipient), local leadership (jurisdiction based) and collective strategy building (networks).

So if emergent "governance" models are increasing in importance, is government itself now "just another actor in this array of organizations?" (p. 679). If Agranoff and McGuire are reluctant to yield this point they are convinced that there is evidence that the relationships between government at federal, state and local levels and the wider universe of organizations (private, non profit, etc.) are becoming more asymmetrical involving complex systems of horizontal and vertical linkages that diverge sharply from traditional hierarchical models and market systems. In brief, collaboratives or networks are not alternatives to democratic political arrangements but policy instruments with the potential to change the configurations of government and the political and organizational games associated with these. How far this potential is realized or released is, in itself, a political question (see, for example, Tiesman and Klijn 2002; D. Brinkerhoff 1998).

Thus, collaboration and other network mechanisms are becoming the central aspect of changing governance in many political systems. These have clear costs and benefits on a number of dimensions (e.g., in terms of control and accountability structures) as well as raise problems of evaluation, not least since "there is little agreement amongst organizational and public policy scholars or amongst public administrators about how community based networks...should be evaluated" (Provan and Milward 2001: 415). Hence, the question of whether collaborative or network arrangements work remains difficult to answer and certainly cannot be taken for granted. Indeed, as Provan and Milward go on to argue, it is still premature to conclude that such arrangements "are effective for addressing complex policy problems despite their promise" (2001: 415).

The Rediscovery of Collaboration

It cannot be emphasized too strongly that collaborative arrangements are far from new in the historical sense. For example, several of the countries explored in this volume (e.g., Sweden and the Netherlands) have long and distinguished historical traditions of involving collaboratives in policy design, development and delivery. Moreover, within social science the broader considerations of corporatism and pluralism stand as evidence both to the longevity of the debate and of the importance of viewing collaboration not so much as an end in itself but as a means to specific political and ideological ends (also see Brinkerhoff 2000). Thus, as a sometimes fashionable option of social democratic governments of the 1960s and 1970s, collaboration came under threat in the 1980s and early 1990s from governments of the right who championed competition, targets and contracts to promote clear accountability and efficient service. In this era collaborative strategies were often seen as instruments of a failed ancien regime. A case in point here is British urban policy where a series of community-focused partnerships of the 1970s and 1980s were replaced in the 1990s by competitive initiatives such as

City Challenge and the Single Regeneration Budget (SRB) in which agencies had to bid for resources.

The competitive and differentiating effects of some of these changes, especially those of quasi-markets and disaggregated service organizations were not, however, always welcome. Recently, a number of governments have identified the need to restore or reinvent the collaborative nature of government enterprise. The British Labor government since 1997, for example, has identified a number of policy areas including education, health and social care, in which disjointed provision is seen in part as responsible for policy failures such as social exclusion.

But what are the advantages of collaboration for the participants? Macintosh (1993) identified three distinctive rationales for collaborative or partnership action: (a) *synergy,* where partnership adds value by combining mutually reinforcing interests, (b) *transformation,* where the partnership objective is to transform different views into a ideological consensus, and (c) *financial,* where the maximization of resources provides the motivation to hold the partnership together. This schema helps to evaluate the creation and practice of collaborative mechanisms underlining the importance of the mobilization of partners, the balance of power between partners and the nature of the collaboration itself. Yet collaboratives comprise essentially dynamic, political relationships maintained through a variety of goals and values and, as Putnam would say, the glue that sticks them together is distinctly variable. Thus, for the Social Exclusion Unit, they are "highly contextually specific and come in all shapes, sizes and structures" (Social Exclusion Unit 2000b: 47-8). In brief, social exclusion collaboration is not a panacea or universal fix but a strategy the effectiveness of which is highly contingent on the institutional context (political, social economic) in which it is anchored and has developed?

Manifestations of Collaboration

What, then, is meant by collaboration and what might be its implications for evaluation? References to various manifestations of collaboration are common in academic studies of managing government and the governance of managing. Hence, we read of public private partnerships, partnering, negotiating governments, consortium-based government, networks, covenants and "soft laws."

Of course, as was noted earlier, there is nothing new about the terms themselves; collaborative strategies are historically intrinsic to government. In the Dutch *Polder Model*, for example, government, labor unions, employers' organizations and experts meet to agree, through education, persuasion and negotiation, on their social and policy economic goals and ways to realize them. A recent development of this traditional form of collaborative government brought in stakeholder groups from the environment in order to develop a "Green Polder Model." There is some resemblance with the older Swedish model of negotiation and voluntary coordination so typical of the welfare state in that country. An important difference, however, is that cost-efficiency (including transaction and administrative costs) and de-regulation are shared values of participants in the Polder Model. This consensus building model limits the sense of winners and losers.

Yet a different view of the Dutch experience of collaboration has been provided by Tiesman and Klijn (2002). Here the case study detail is of less importance than their wider observations of the gap between the political *rhetoric* relating to collaboratives and networks compared with the *reality* of relationships as they develop on the ground. The authors argue that while collaboration, in this instance mainly public-private partnerships (further see below), in theory demands new governance arrangements (joint organizational decision making, etc.), in reality developments are governed by existing procedures (hierarchical processes). Thus, traditional top down systems find it difficult to move to more pluralistic forms. In brief, the political demands of network management are difficult to accommodate within hierarchical (command) type government systems and their associated accountability relations. Any arrangements that threaten established power structures are likely to be resisted.

Public private partnerships (PPP) are joint efforts by government entities and private organizations to provide services or facilities directly. Here joint streams of public and private money bring joint responsibilities in service delivery. Found in a wide variety of services such as defense, education, health and highways, a PPP is more than a financial arrangement; it represents a new organizational machinery for delivering public services. Although the collaboration involves challenges for both parties, it has become popular as a way of remedying the chronic shortage of investment in public infrastructure in many countries since the early 1970s. In the UK, for example, both Conservative and Labour governments have championed the Private Finance Initiative (PFI). At its simplest, this allows public authorities to contract with private sector entities for the provision of capital finance and an acceptance of some of the venture's risks in return for an operator's license to provide specified services. The contractor makes its return on investment through the revenue stream arising from the government paying for units of service provision. Examples have included the Channel Tunnel, community care, hospitals, museums, prisons, student accommodation and toll bridges. Contractors, usually in consortia, have included construction firms, banks, and companies in the housing, health care, security and welfare industries.[1]

Less firmly based organizationally but potentially powerful as a way of realizing policy is *network management* related to the emergence of policy networks (see above). Here actors (especially policy initiators) try to influence the structure, the functioning and the outcomes of policy through forging collaborative efforts (Wassenberg 1980). To a certain extent, this is seen as goal-free (though not issue-free) collaboration. Different stakeholder organizations are brought together (sometimes through an incentive such as a subsidy) and then interact to develop joint goals, that is, goals that are agreed upon by administrators and other stakeholders. Network management is seen as especially effective in reinvigorating social and state institutions both in industrialized and non-industrialized contexts. For many developing countries, for example, there is an:

> urgent priority to rebuild state effectiveness through an overhaul of public institutions, reasserting of the rule of law, and credible checks on abuse of state power. Where the links between the state, the private sector, and civil society are fragile and underdeveloped, improving the delivery of public and collective services will require closer *partnerships* with the private sector and civil society." (World Bank 1997:14, emphasis added)

As with public-private partnerships, the perceived attraction to government here is to tap into a source of capital other than its own. The difference from a PPP, however, is that the capital is social and political rather than financial. However, as the next section indicates the effectiveness of such strategies is highly contingent on political, social and economic circumstances.

Transplanting Collaborative Arrangements

As these largely Western developments have become fashionable, in particular with multinational management consultancies and aid organizations, so the appropriateness of exporting Western so-called best practice has been questioned. Straussman (2001), for example, argues in a study of applying new forms of local government to post-Communist regimes (in this instance Hungary) that such transplants often neglect specific historical and contextual conditions and underestimate the importance of local political values and organizational infrastructure. Straussman regards as dangerous the belief that external interventions in post-Communist and Third World states require as a precondition for success the development of some civic capacity. He argues that far from being a quick fix (as per technical assistance) the development of social capital is a long-term process: "building local capacity depends on social capital that is created through civic culture embodied in communal networks" (2001: 517). Moreover, the hollow state thesis (Milward and Provan 1993) may apply as in Hungarian local government any innovative capacity arises not from the traditional administrative systems (weakened by the legacy of their previous history) but through local networks that encompass nongovernmental organizations. In brief, in Hungary, due to weak governmental and administrative systems that characterize "a rejected socialist past" collaborative networks based on interorganizational linkages are emerging as a source of innovation. However, the reasons for this lie in particular historical and contextual conditions.

Similar weaknesses in political and administrative systems may limit governance and delivery mechanisms in Africa and elsewhere. Russell and Byuma (2001), for example, note South Africa's efforts at administrative reform from 1994 onwards have so far been associated with only modest and mixed improvements in service delivery, especially to traditionally disadvantaged communities. This has led to the adoption of alternative delivery mechanisms (ASDs) which include wider partnerships (especially with the third sector) shared service delivery and outsourcing in areas such as transport, criminal justice (young offenders) and welfare. As with the Hungarian case above, collaborations appear to be developing as a "corrective" to a specific set of weaknesses in the traditional administrative infrastructure.

The importance of alternative delivery mechanisms involving nonprofit, nongovernmental organizations is further examined by Henderson (2001) in the context of urban development in Third World countries. Drawing on earlier work (Henderson and Dwivedi 1999), Henderson is critical of efforts to approach urban reform in

Third World contexts principally by market pluralism based on public choice and related perspectives. He considers that such strategies often neglect the potential of non-profit, nongovernmental organizations and other forms of voluntary activity not only in terms of service delivery but also in their potential to enhance civil society. He cites a range of examples from such locations as Latin America, Africa and Eastern Europe to chart a variety of urban service delivery mechanisms that escape traditional bureaucratic command modes through mechanisms that include partnering and collaboration. However, such moves are not without their problems including the fragmentation of delivery structures, self-protective behavior and interorganizational politics and power struggles. In Henderson's view this is also compounded by issues of accountability and transparency that are specific to collaborative arrangements not least since nongovernmental organizations often seek to protect their specific independence and identity. Thus, collaboratives represent one strategy amongst many in escaping from Western bureaucratic solutions. Also as Henderson cautions: "not all are successful and many—perhaps most—are subject to the vagaries of host government and international politics" (2001: 338).

Collaboration and Modes of Governance

The suggestion emerging from this discussion is therefore that different forms of collaborative arrangement display different patterns of interaction and relationship or *modes of governance*. Further the effectiveness of collaboration is highly contingent on context and circumstances. The issue of modes of governance will be covered in this section while the question of contingencies is returned to below.

A mode of governance is a manner by which authority and function are allocated and rights and obligations established and maintained in the collaborative relationship. Gray (1998: 5, 9) has elaborated these modes as command, communion and contract. *Command* is based on the rule of law emanating from a sovereign body and delivered through a scalar chain of superior and subordinate authority. The legitimacy for actions under such governance lies in their being within the bounds prescribed through due process by the institution. The strength of command lies in the efficiency and effectiveness of control and accountability, its weakness in rigidity and conservatism in the face of changing environments. *Communion* is based on an appeal to common values and creeds. The legitimacy for actions lies in their consistency with the understandings, protocols and guiding values of a shared frame of reference. The strength as governance lies in the guidance afforded by its shared values through different environments, its weakness in its insularity from those environments and a consequent failure to adapt its normative order. *Contract* is effected through an inducement-contribution exchange agreed by parties. The legitimacy here derives from the terms of the agreed exchange, that is. the contract, or at least its interpretations. The strengths of contract as governance lie in the pre-determined life of the contract, the motivation to perform up to contract expectation and the consequent high probabilities that planning assumptions will be acted on. The weaknesses can be traced to the reductionist tendency of contracts (i.e., performance conforming only to the standard specified) and the difficulty in the face of changing circumstances in effecting alterations to specification without undue cost.

Expressed in this way, these distinctions are purely analytical. But their combinations in the practical relationships inherent in collaboration are significant for the management and evaluation of the collaborators and their programs as well as the form of collaboration itself. Thus, with the examples cited earlier, they may be used by readers of later chapters as a way of characterizing the collaboration under investigation.

Collaboration and Service Delivery: Benefits and Costs

Whatever its merits the above typology does little to explain either the justification of collaboration as an instrument of government or the implications of such arrangements for evaluation. What follows is thus a set of propositions relating to the costs and benefits of these arrangements and a discussion of the wider implications.

Proposition 1: Collaboration shares information, solutions and learning. If corporate actors voluntarily agree to share information and knowledge and prevent one single actor (government) possessing all, it is believed that there will be fewer negative bureaucratic fights between powers pursuing practices in their own interests with consequent high transaction costs. Also it is claimed that the sharing of information and multiple perspectives enhances the definition of problems (e.g., reducing the budget, increasing environmental quality, improving public housing, etc.) and a more open assessment of different solutions. Shared information, the argument runs, stimulates learning.

Proposition 2: Collaboration builds social capital. Collaborative networks are effective and efficient since such exchange mechanisms can achieve more with less physical capital than one actor alone can. Credit associations, for example, can generate pools of financial capital for increased entrepreneurial activity and job searches can be more efficient if information is circulated in social networks. Networks of civil engagement, such as neighborhood associations, sports clubs and other intermediary or voluntary organizations, are an essential form of social capital, and the denser these networks, the more likely that members of a community will cooperate for mutual benefit. This is so, even in the face of persistent problems of collective action, because networks of civil engagement:

- foster norms of generalized reciprocity by creating expectations that favors given now will be returned later;

- facilitate coordination and communication, and thus create channels through which information about the trustworthiness of other individuals and groups can flow, be tested and verified;

- embody past success at collaboration, which can serve as a cultural template for future collaboration on other kinds of problems;

- increase the potential risks to those who act opportunistically that they will not share in the benefits of current and future transactions (Burt 1992; Leeuw and van Gils 2000).

Crucially, this enhancement of social capital applies not only to voluntary and trust-based collaboration but also to more contractual types of collaboration. Examples include the developmental aid programs stimulated by the World Bank in a variety of contexts such as Africa, the former Soviet Union and Latin America by investing in social and administrative relationships between government actors on the one hand and members of civil society on the other hand (see D. Brinkerhoff 1998). It is collaboration between people or groups of people (with their institutional background and contingencies) rather than the formal collaboration of documents or contracts that enhances social capital.

The World Bank has presented empirical studies showing the importance of social capital in developing contexts such as Africa (World Bank 1997; D. Brinkerhoff 1998). Studies of industrialized countries also show the importance of social capital for effective policy management (Burt 1992; Putnam 1993; Bulder et al. 1996). Putnam, in a study of industrial districts in Italy, showed that for an effective public sector norms of reciprocity and networks of civil engagement were essential: "Networks facilitate flows of information about technological developments, about the creditworthiness of would-be entrepreneurs, about the reliability of individual workers, and so on" (Putnam 1993: 161). Only a civil society that is organized around "horizontal bonds of mutual solidarity," rather than around "vertical bonds of dependency and exploitation," produces trust.[2]

Proposition 3: Collaboration limits the need for formal control and reduces transaction costs. There is some evidence that collaboration increases bonding. The greater the bonding, the less the need for monitoring, auditing, and inspection and thus transaction costs are likely to be lower. Moreover, bonding implies the prevention of shirking not least because when those who have set up partnerships do not live up to their intentions, standards or created expectations, they make future collaboration difficult or even impossible. The other parties will remember this and will refrain from collaboration. This phenomenon inhibits negligence in extant relationships without bringing elaborate control or monitoring.

Yet, as was noted above (Henderson 2001) the effectiveness of collaborative arrangements may be limited by contextual variables relating to political and social institutional structures and processes. Such constraints are further illustrated by recent experiences of AID programs involving agencies such as the World Bank and major national development agencies such as the U.S. Agency for International Development (USAID). Many of these issues are illustrated in a comprehensive and extensively documented paper by D. Brinkerhoff (1998). Here the author notes that development aid programs have moved from a focus on government through an enthusiasm for markets and nongovernmental organizations (NGOs) back to governments, but in a different sense: "government indeed does have an essential role to play but it is not the only important actor." Indeed, as Brinkerhoff notes, decentralization has often been advocated without any critical assessment of its effects while evidence also indicates that "an exclusive focus on extra-governmental actors is insufficient to promote development." Thus, the argument for a "balanced approach that capitalizes on governmental and nongovernmental actors working in conjunction with civil society" (1998: 24-5).

This logic derives from Brinkerhoff's arguments that sectoral policy reform (in the development context) requires strengthening of governance capacity in particular in terms of (a) redefining responsibility, (b) bringing government closer to the public it serves, and (c) changing its behaviors towards citizens. Although cast in a development context this is clearly an extension of the government-governance debate discussed above. However, as Brinkerhoff notes, this shift of governments from a command to an enabler mode is not simply a management issue but is tied in with a more inclusive and pluralistic focus: "an important element of realigned government responsibility can involve the active provision of services to disenfranchised and marginalized social groups, to facilitate their access to economic opportunity and increased well being"(1998: 6). Therefore, in this instance (Brinkerhoff illustrates with examples from land reform in Botswana) redefined government may not be less government since its role may be to foster collaborative enterprise.

The second issue, bringing government closer to the public, is seen to involve decentralization. However, as already noted, this is seen not as an easy solution but rather "a complex process requiring simultaneous attention to capacity building, legal and fiscal reform and the participation and empowerment of beneficiaries to be successful." In particular this involves extending political power sharing to civil society groups while attempting to avoid exacerbating inequalities. Thus, as numerous examples from variety of development contexts indicate, for decentralization of collaborative arrangements to work there is a critical dependence of "some minimum threshold of common interest" (1998: 7).

Finally, in terms of changing the government-citizen relationship Brinkerhoff notes that, in addition to removing undesirable behaviors (e.g., rent seeking and corruption) there is a need for the encouragement of new behaviors, including citizen responsiveness, collaboration and participation. Hence, collaboratives, networks and partnerships are often fragile and may require a sustained and direct effort to initiate and sustain them. This, in turn, can be linked to efforts to develop social capital and a civic capacity.

A feature of the "democratic governance" argument as articulated by Brinkerhoff is therefore the need to strengthen the links between state and civil society that may involve partnerships and collaboratives. Such moves may be justifiable both from a pragmatic (problem solving, policy delivery) and democratic government perspective (promoting transparency and accountability). Yet, in a practical sense such strategies may have costs as well as benefits. Speaking at a seminar on "intersectoral partnering" (USAID 2000), J. Brinkerhoff notes that a fundamental question relating to partnerships and collaborative arrangements is whether "they are a means to an end or an end in themselves." In addition she draws attention to other issues: whether partnering should be seen as a universal good, whether there are situations in which it might be inappropriate and whether the politics of partnerships (power balances and distribution) need to be analyzed more closely. As the above discussion would indicate, a failure to appreciate this political context would ignore the fact that collaboratives may be used for a variety of purposes (and possibly by dominant political or economic elites for their own ends), that certain groups may find themselves excluded from such arrangements (as in many so-called pluralistic structures) and that even when created the sustainability and cohesion of network or collaborative arrangements are problematics rather than matters that can be taken for granted.

What emerges clearly from this and many of the examples discussed above in contexts that vary from the United States (Agranoff and McGuire 2001), Holland (Tiesman and Klijn 2002), post-Communist Europe (Straussman 2001) as well as in other areas such as South Africa (Russell and Bvuma 2001) and Sub-Saharan Africa (Nwankwo and Richards 2001; Mudacumura 2001) is as follows:

1.   Collaboratives, partnerships and networks are being utilized to a greater extent as the inadequacies of hierarchies and markets become apparent;

2.   Their use is linked to perceived problems of service delivery and implementation on one level and attempts to develop social capital and a civic capacity on another;

3.   While partnering and collaboratives may have a role to play in easing some of the above difficulties they demonstrate their own problems in terms of their compatibility with political and social structures and processes;

4.   Part of the problem here (as with previous AID and technology transfer interventions) can be linked both to contextual factors (e.g., corruption, lack of social capital) as well of the demands of the policy instrument itself (high trust, shared goals, transparent information, etc.);

5.   The evaluation of such arrangements is, at best, at an embryonic stage.

Evaluation

The work of the International Group for Policy and Program Evaluation (INTEVAL) has shown that the meanings and interpretations of evaluation can reflect important differences in professional and political cultures (e.g., Rist 1990; Gray, Jenkins, and Segsworth 1993; Furubo, Rist, and Sandahl 2002). Nevertheless, at its simplest, there is agreement that evaluation may be seen as (a) the *ex post assessment* of a policy or program's achievement against objectives. However, some would extend this definition to encompass (b) *ex ante appraisal*, (c) *program monitoring* and (d) *meta evaluation* (the evaluation of evaluation itself).

Although INTEVAL has adopted a broad conceptualization embracing all these meanings, the chapters of this volume necessarily focus on them in different ways. As definitions have become more elaborate so methodologies have expanded. Evaluation has thus become more sophisticated and potentially more useful to both policy makers and representatives as systems of accountable government have evolved. Further, the rapid and complex developments of the recent past have in turn affected the evaluands, that is, those phenomena to be evaluated.

Evaluation and Collaborative Developments

We have seen that in certain circumstances collaboration is postulated as offering a variety of advantages in terms of effecting policy development and delivery. If this is the case, what are the implications for policy and program evaluation?

The design and practice of evaluation is generally not an easy business especially where politics threatens both evaluators and the utilization of their results. However, recent international attention in performance measurement and the search for "evidence based" policy has underlined the importance of evaluation. This has been reinforced by the international work of, among others, the European Union, the Organization for Economic Co-operation and Development (OECD) and the World Bank. Although robust arguments have been made for more "realistic" approaches to evaluation (Pawson and Tilley 1997), the case for a rationalistic perspective has remained strong (Pollitt 1999) and has often been associated with the development of results-based government. The evaluation of collaborative mechanisms has to accommodate these demands and questions including how and why collaborative ventures succeed or fail.

The British Audit Commission (a state auditor of local government and parts of the National Health Service) noted that "making partnerships work effectively is one of the toughest jobs facing public sector managers" (Audit Commission 1998: 5). Drawing on studies of care for the elderly and youth crime, it attributed the high failure rates for partnerships to imposed conflicting strategic objectives, limited powers available to collaborative organizations to address their collective problems and performance management regimes that discouraged collaboration. By way of contrast the Commission argued that effective collaboration required abilities to maintain commitment and involvement, build and sustain trust and harmonize operating and financial systems. Although there was "no blueprint" (1998: 31), the evaluation of collaboratives needed to be designed to assess collective (and agreed) outcomes as well as the health and costs of the partnership itself. This demanded the development of novel sets of cross-cutting performance measures and the recognition that accountability would be more complex both within the partnership and in external relationships with other organizations, service users and the public (1998, Ch.4).

In many ways the Audit Commission's assessment reflects the organization's own internal tensions in trying to reconcile its rationalistic, performance-based model for collaboratives with a recognition of the organizational and systemic difficulties that such structures introduce a problem also reflected in the Dutch experience (see Teisman and Klijn 2002). Moreover, other recent studies on the difficulties of achieving joined up working have indicated that the tensions are generic to the evaluation of collaboration. Stewart et al. (1999), for example, underline what they see as the characteristic features of a "virtuous" system of effective collaboration working as against a more "negative" cycle that characterizes failed or failing collaboratives. The authors specifically point out the difficulties of evaluating complex and independent organizational networks where targets may be shared and systems and programs not always well aligned. Further (as noted above), accountability may be problematic when members of a collaborative are accountable to their own stakeholders as well as to the collective.

Perhaps these difficulties explain why the Social Exclusion Unit in the UK argued that the "evaluation of process (and formative evaluation) are ill developed....and systematic evaluation of joined up working remains to be undertaken" (Social Exclusion Unit 2000a: 61). In developing a capacity and capability in evaluation of collaborative government, some possible responses are unequivocal:

a.   any "new" arrangements can be assessed by traditional methods and evaluators and auditors can make use of their usual toolkits;

b.   the changing nature of relationships between corporate actors in the collaborative society is so pervasive and complex that evaluators and auditors need completely new methodologies; and

c.   evaluators need not to worry about all this because in the new world of collaboration, evaluation is not necessary—trust, commitment and reputation are all around and you do not evaluate such situations systematically without running the risk of undermining the trust itself, with consequent inefficiency and ineffectiveness of the provision of goods and services (Goshal and Moran 1996).

However, there are other less fixed positions that suggest important challenges to the functions and methodologies of evaluation in this context.

Functions of Evaluation

The role of evaluation in policy management as traditionally understood can be undermined by public reform. Market mechanisms (such as those introduced into the British National Health Service in the early 1990s) could be regarded as substitutes for policy and program evaluation as they bring their own intrinsic evaluations—purchaser choices. Similar claims may be made for collaborative mechanisms in which the voluntary support of the parties is itself a check on the merits of the venture. Moreover, the evaluation of a collaborative could be seen as destructive of the social fabric of agreement and consensus: to evaluate is to challenge the consensual basis of the policy or program.

These positions can be challenged. First, evaluation is desirable to check whether the intrinsic mechanisms are working as intended and do not produce perverse incentives or dysfunctional behavior. For regimes of trust, it is similarly desirable to check the costs and benefits of the arrangements. After all there is no a priori evidence that collaborative mechanisms are always cost-effective and do not have unintended side effects.

Second, evaluation is needed to bring order to the potential complexity of collaboratives and networks. Public-private partnerships, for example, sound simple enough but may conceal (like a termite nest) intricate networks of relationships within the parties on each side of the deal (e.g., on both the public and private side the parties may be in fact consortia) and public policy evaluation may need to assess the value of such arrangements. This is particularly so where there are policy management problems arising from new organizational structures and capital is gained in return for substantial revenue commitments for periods as long as thirty years. Evaluation may be used, therefore, to find out the extent to which people and organizations within the arrangements deliver to the agreed standards of outcomes and means.

Third, evaluation can assess collaborative relationships. Logic suggests that transaction costs of highly decentralized collaboration could be high. It may also be possible to develop ex ante evaluative capability to characterize the compatibility of collaborative actors and to inform the design as well as the suitability (ex post) of collaborative structures and procedures.

Fourth, evaluation can be used as action learning to facilitate knowledge building in the collaborative development and inform debates and choices about collaborative alternatives ranging from "simple" retrenchment responses (e.g., privatization or disposal) to the problems of the size of the public sector. Thus, evaluation may assess alternative delivery mechanisms and highlight the costs and benefits such arrangements bring to policy management.

Limitations of Traditional Evaluation Methodology

If collaboration represents a genuine change to the structures, processes and behavior of delivering public goods and services it is likely that not only the evaluands and functions of evaluation will change but that the traditional approaches and methodologies may limit the evaluative products. Such limitations may include the following.[3]

Traditional auditing and evaluation (often) approaches topics under investigation with a *porthole approach*, that is, a compartmentalization of findings, conclusions and recommendations (Barzeley 1996). Problems may therefore arise when a central evaluand is the interlinking of different "portholes." Moreover, the traditional *methodology of the black box*, which focuses on systems, procedures and protocols, may miss the essential interactive nature of the collaboratives and network arrangements overlooking the properties such as trust and reputation that are essential to the functionality of any particular collaboration. Third, both porthole and back box approaches may miss the dynamic of the interrelationship between the complex layers of responsibility. Finally, traditional methodologies may provide no assessment of the value to the end-users of the goods and services provided through these new mechanisms. Stakeholder approaches and the more behavioral and social research methodologies, including case study field investigations and surveys, are more relevant here than procedure-driven studies because there is no a priori certainty that what comes out of, for example, a public-private partnership is effective, efficient or otherwise acceptable.

The implications of all this may be a considerable set of challenges for evaluation as well as for the management of public goods and services. But we are jumping ahead. Our remaining task is to identify the research questions for this volume and the framework for investigating the merging collaborative arrangements and their evaluation.

The Framework of Study

While governments struggle to control budgetary balances and experiment with new collaborative forms of delivery, there is a need for evaluation of both past and prospective policies to inform choices. However, the traditional function of evaluation may be at risk as new market type policy instruments are institutionalized. From these considerations and the conceptualizations presented above the authors in this volume have sought to characterize the changing functions, evaluands, and methodologies of policy and program evaluation associated with developing collaborative service delivery. The primary interest here is in collaboration as a policy instrument. As such the political context of collaboration (i.e., its relationship with democratic governance) is seen as important but as part of a wider perspective that seeks to locate collaboration in a broad social, political and historical (developmental) framework.

Each of the following chapters will therefore seek to contribute to the testing of a set of working hypotheses, namely that evaluation

1.   is being offered new functions, evaluators, evaluands and methodologies by the development of collaborative arrangements;

2.   is being both substituted and complemented by collaborative and associated mechanisms.

Even though these may appear contradictory, they are not designed as mutually exclusive. Rather, they allow for the possibility of a mechanism to support different hypotheses over time, or in different applications.

To test these hypotheses, the following chapters discuss a range of applications. Each chapter is charged with answering the following:

a.   What are the collaborative characteristics of the phenomenon under consideration?

b.   What are the changes in evaluation functions, evaluands and methodologies that have been associated with the collaborative developments?

c.   What are the possibilities for and/or results of the evaluation of collaborative developments?

Each chapter employs a blend of theoretical and empirical approaches in its investigation and in general seeks to draw on more than one country's experience (further see below). The volume's final chapter formulates a general conclusion drawing on these explorations.

Conclusion

This chapter has introduced the central issues of this project. It has emphasized its premise that public sector reforms have changed the structures and processes by which government is delivered and that, in particular, these changes have often been operationalized by the introduction or enhancement of collaborative mechanisms of delivery. The chapters that follow detail some of these developments in Europe, Israel and North America. However, as the discussion above has established, this discovery (or rediscovery) of collaborative mechanisms is not restricted to the contexts of established industrialized countries such as OECD members with well established political and economic systems but also can be detected in a variety of other contexts such as post-Communist Europe as well as in emerging countries such as the new South Africa and in other locations such as Africa and Latin America. Such examples demonstrate clearly the importance of political, social and economic variables (especially institutions) in shaping both the micro and macro political situations in which collaborative mechanisms operate, in turn conditioning their effectiveness (itself a value-laden term in such contexts).

These issues are central, if not crucial, in analyzing the history of collaborative mechanisms in development programs instigated by agencies such as the World Bank and other AID providers and, indeed, such factors are now being more widely recognized by practitioners in the field (see D. Brinkerhoff 1998 and J. Brinkerhoff 2000). This, however, takes one to a wider debate that lies beyond the remit of this book. Rather here we seek to explore the emergence of collaboration as a policy instrument in a number of more highly specified contexts and whether the changes produced by the introduction of collaborative mechanisms undermine or strengthen policy and program evaluation. In particular, we wish to establish whether evaluation can respond effectively to sustain and even enhance its contribution to policy management under these new circumstances.

As will be seen, it appears that many governments view collaboration less as a system of governance (with a subsequent redefining of relationships between itself and other actors) than a way of enhancing or ensuring delivery while retaining control in an established top down sense. This is linked not simply to retaining power balances but also to established perceptions of accountability relationships and the perceived need for policy and services to be delivered in a rationalistic manner. This leads to a particular view of what is desirable in the form of evaluation and evaluation mechanisms. However, a perspective that views government as part of developing networks that together constitute a new governance system may view evaluation in a very different light. The chapters that follow begin to unravel some of these dilemmas, touching on, among other matters, current enthusiasms for partnerships, quality and results-based government. In addition the increasing visibility and utilization of external groups such as third sector organizations are reviewed especially in the light of the difficulties of second sector strategies such as markets.

Collaborative mechanisms therefore add a new dimension to the current debate on the adequacy of political structures and processes to meet what some term twenty-first- century needs and demands. Yet like many policy instruments before them (and no doubt after) they must be seen less as technical fixes (inherently value free) but rather as value-laden variables manipulated by actors or groups of actors to serve different and diffuse agendas. As such they have costs as well as benefits. We return to this issue in our conclusion (Ch.10) where we also seek to integrate and assess the diverse experiences and issues raised by the authors of the subsequent chapters.

Notes

1. A similar approach was used in the 1930s and 1950s. Caro (1975) shows how city planner Robert Moses in New York forged many PPPs for bridge, tunnel and park construction. Caro observes how this developed monopoly powers in a core network at the top of local governance.
2. Note also the anti-corruption programs of the World Bank that through training and education of parliamentarians, journalists and other members of the civic society seek to establish a national integrity system. In fifteen countries the Bank has invested explicitly in social capital by developing trust relationship between the private and public sector (Leeuw and van Gils 2000).
3. These paragraphs draw on Leeuw (1996).

References

Agranoff, R., and M. McGuire. 1998a. "The Intergovernmental Context of Local Economic Development." *State and Local Government Review*, 30(3), 150-64.

Agranoff, R., and M. McGuire. 1998b. "A Jurisdiction Based Model of Intergovernmental Management in US cities." *Publis: the Journal of Federalism,* 28(4), 1-20.

Agranoff, R., and M. McGuire. 1998c. "Multi Network Management: Collaboration and the Hollow State in Local Economic Policy." *Journal of Public Administration Research and Theory*, 8(1), 67-91.

Agranoff R., and M. McGuire. 2001. "American Federalism and the Search for Models of Management." *Public Administration Review*, 61(6), 671-81.

Ashbee, E. 2000. "Bowling Alone." *Politics Review,* 10/1, 30-3, September.

Audit Commission. 1998. *Fruitful Partnerships: Effective Partnership Working*. London: Audit Commission.

Barzeley, M. 1996. "Performance Auditing and the New Public Management: Changing Roles and Strategies of Central Audit Institutions," in D. Shand (ed.), *Performance Auditing and the Modernization of Government*. Paris: PUMA/OECD, chapter 1, 15-57.

Brinkerhoff, D. W. 1998. *Democratic Governance and Sectoral Policy Reform*, Implementing Policy Change Monograph No. 5. United States Agency for International Development.

Brinkerhoff, J. 2000. "Conceptual Overview." Comments in Seminar on *Intersectoral Partnering: Tools for Implementation and Evaluation*. United States Agency for International Development. Dialogue notes. April 12.

Bulder, B., H. Flap, and F. L. Leeuw. 1996. "Networks and Evaluating Public Sector Reforms." *Evaluation*, 2/3, 261-276.

Burt, R. S. 1992. *Structural Holes*. New York: Harvard University Press.

Caro, R. A. 1975. *The Power Broker: Robert Moses and the Fall of New York*. New York: Vintage Books.

Furubo, J-E., R. C. Rist, and R. Sandahl (eds.). 2002. *International Atlas of Evaluation*. New Brunswick, NJ: Transaction Publishers.

Goshal, M., and A. Moran. 1996. "Bad for Practice: A Critique of Transaction Cost Theory. *Academy of Management Review*, 21/1, 13-47.

Gray, A. G. 1998. *Business-like But Not Like a Business: The Challenge for Public Management*. London: Public Finance Foundation: London.

Gray, A. G., W. I. Jenkins, and R. V. Segsworth (eds.). 1993. *Budgeting, Auditing and Evaluation: Foundations and Integration in Seven Governments*. New Brunswick, NJ: Transaction Publishers.

Henderson, K. M. 2001. "Urban Service Delivery in Developing Countries: Escaping Western Bureaucratic Solutions." *International Journal of Public Sector Management*, 14/4, 327-40.

Henderson, K. M., and O. P. Dwivedi (eds). 1999. *Bureaucracy and the Alternatives in World Perspective*. New York and London: Palgrave/Macmillan.

Kickert, W. J. M., E-H Klijn, and J. F. N. Koppenjan (eds.). 1997. *Managing Complex Networks*. London: Sage.

Laumann, E. O., and D. Knoke. 1987. *The Organizational State: Social Choice in National Policy Domains*. Madison: University of Wisconsin.

Leeuw, F. L. 1996. "Auditing and Evaluation: Bridging a Gap, Worlds to Meet," in C. Wisler (ed.), *Evaluation and Auditing: Prospects for Convergence*. San Francisco: Jossey-Bass Publishers.

Leeuw F. L. ,and Ger H. C. van Gils. 2000. "Outputsturing in de publieke sector: voortgang maar traag." *Beleidsanalyse*, 29, 4-12.

Mackintosh, M. 1993. "Partnership: Issues of Policy and Negotiation." *Local Economy*, 7/3.

Mandell, M. 1999. "The Impact of Collaborative Effects: Changing the Face of Public Policy through Networks and Network Structures." *Policy Studies Review*, 16/1, 4-17.

Mandell, M. (ed), 2001. *Getting Results through Collaboration: Networks and Network Structures for Public Policy and Management*. Westport CT: Quorum Books.

Milward, H. B., and K. G. Provan. 1993. "The Hollow State: Private Provision of Public Services." in H. Ingram and S. R. Smith (eds.), *Public Policy for Democracy*. Washington, DC: Brookings Institution, 222-37.

Mudacumura, G. M. 1999. "Building a Network Organization to Foster Participatory Development in Sub-Saharan Africa." Paper presented to participatory development forum, University of Ottawa.

Mudacumura, G. M. 2001. "Networking Development Organizations to Foster Global Economic Development." *International Journal of Economic Development*, 3/1, 17-22.

Nwankwo, S., and D. W. Richards. 2001. "Privatization: The Myth of Free Market Orthodoxy in Sub-Saharan Africa." *International Journal of Public Sector Management*, 14/2, 165-79.

Osborne D., and T. Gaeblar. 1993. *Reinventing Government*. New York: Plume Books.

O'Toole, L. J. 1997. "Treating Networks Seriously: Practical and Research Based Agenda in Public Administration." *Public Administration Review*, 57/1, 45-52.

Pawson, R., and N. Tilley. 1997. *Realistic Evaluation*. London: Sage.

Performance and Innovation Unit (PIU). 2001. *Better Policy Design and Delivery: A Discussion Paper*. London: Cabinet Office.

Pollitt, C. 1999. "Stunted by Stakeholders? Limits to Collaborative Evaluation." *Public Policy and Administration*, 14/2: 77-90.

Provan, K. G., and H. G. Milward. 2001. "Do Networks Really Work?: A Framework for Evaluating Public Sector Organizational Networks." *Public Administration Review*, 61/4, 414-23.

Putnam, R. 1993. *Making Democracy Work: Civic Traditions in Modern Italy*. Princeton, NJ: Princeton University Press.

Putnam, R. 2000. *Bowling Alone*. New York: Simon and Schuster.

Radin, B. A. et al. 1996. *New Governance for Rural America: Creating Intergovernmental Partnerships*. Lawrence: University Press of Kansas.

Rhodes R. A. W. 1996. "The New Governance: Governing without Government." *Political Studies*, 44, 652-67.

Rist, R. C. (ed.). 1990. *Program Evaluation and the Management of Government: Patterns and Prospects across Eight Nations.* New Brunswick, NJ: Transaction Publishers.

Russell E. G., and D. G. Byuma. 2001. "Alternative Service Delivery and Public Sector Transformation in South Africa." *International Journal of Public Sector Management*, 14/3, 241-65.

Social Exclusion Unit. 2000a. *Report of Policy Action Team 17: Joining Up Locally.* London: Cabinet Office.

Social Exclusion Unit. 2000b. *Policy Action Team 17: Joining Up Locally: The Evidence Base.* London: Cabinet Office.

Stewart, M., S. Goss, R. Clarke, G. Gillanders, J. Rowe, and H. Shaftoe. 1999. *Cross Cutting Issues Affecting Local Government.* London: Department of the Environment, Transport and the Regions (DETR).

Stewart, M. 2000. "Social Action to Counter Exclusion: A Research Review." Annex C to Social Exclusion Unit, 2000a, above.

Straussman, J. 2001. "Beyond Markets: The Case of Local Government in Hungary." *International Journal of Public Sector Management*, 14/6, 500-21.

Tiesman, G. R., and E-H Klijn. 2002. "Collaboration Netherlands Style: The Case of Rotterdam Harbor Expansion." *Public Administration Review*, 62/2, 197-205.

Wassenberg, A. 1980. *Netwerken, organisatie en strategie.* Meppel: Boom Pers.

World Bank. 1997. *The State in a Changing World.* Washington, DC: World Bank.

2

Networks and Partnering Arrangements: New Challenges for Evaluation and Auditing

John Mayne, Tom Wileman, and Frans Leeuw

All over the world, a movement towards working together between governments and other public, private and nonprofit actors is
taking place (Atkinson and Coleman 1996; Auditor General of
Canada 1999a; Coleman and Skogstad 1990). Networks and
partnering are becoming common place in the public sector and
there are now a wide variety of such arrangements (OECD 1999).
Public Private Partnerships (PPP), for example, refer to joint efforts
by government entities and private organizations to provide services or facilities directly. Found in a wide variety of policy areas
such as defense, education, health and highways, PPP are more than
financial arrangements. Joint streams of public and private money
bring joint responsibilities in service delivery and represent a new
organizational machinery for delivering public services.

Less firmly based organizationally but as potentially powerful as
a way of realizing policy is network management, a deliberate way
in which actors (especially policy initiators) try to influence the structure, functioning and outcomes of policy through forging collaborative efforts. To a certain extent, the development of networks can
be seen as goal-free (though not issue-free) collaboration. Different
stakeholder organizations are brought together and start to interact.
From then on they develop joint goals, that is, goals that are agreed
upon by the government officials and the other stakeholders, and
joint programs. The role of the government here is somewhat similar to that of a movie director making multiple realities combine.
Sometimes this is also referred to as participatory policy development or goal-development policy. It is believed that by bringing

interested parties together, the social acceptance and effectiveness of subsequent policy instruments will be increased through the joint agreement.

These approaches are not limited to nation-state specific approaches. One of the mechanisms to produce global public goods (such as disease or conflict prevention and the development of a global system of intellectual property rights) is the global public policy network. Reinecke describes these as "loose alliances of government agencies, international organizations, corporations, and elements of civil society such as NGOs, professional organizations or religious groups that join together to achieve what none can accomplish on its own" (Reinecke 1999: 44; Reinecke and Deng 2000). Further, when networks among partners become more formal as represented in written agreements, the resulting collaborative arrangements form the basis for specific action by the partners to achieve common goals (Auditor General of Canada 1999a).

Networks and partnering, that is, consortium-based government, partnerships, collaborative arrangements, networks, covenants and "soft laws," are therefore high on political agendas. Covenants are agreements between parties to work towards realizing goals that the parties have jointly put forward. They are also called "soft laws" because they sometimes are "frontrunners" of real laws and because the structure of covenants sometimes resembles the format of laws. These terms are also found increasingly in government pronouncements as countries throughout the world seek ways of remedying identified dysfunctions in much of the public sector reforms of the past two decades. In a similar vein, this is echoed by the attention given to "good governance" by organizations like the World Bank (1997) and many donors of aid to developing countries.

To a certain extent there is often nothing new about these activities as many collaborative models have existed in the policy world for some time. In the Netherlands, for example, the Polder Model brings together government, labor unions, employers' organizations and experts to agree (through persuasion and negotiation) on social and policy economic goals and ways to realize them. The Polder Model has as an important ideological background in the post World War II years in which central government, corporations, political parties, employers and employees unions and other social groups jointly discussed and developed policy goals, strategies and interventions in an informal way. As of the early 1980s, these negotiating arrangements have had a more formal, public character, while the transparency of the arrangements has also increased.

In the United Kingdom there has been a recent move away from the quasi-markets, agency-development, efficiency-audits and other scrutinies implemented during the Thatcher-years towards what the Blair government calls "modernizing" government. Here solidarity and trust are of central importance and the problem of fragmentation is addressed through joined-up government, that is, integrating vertical functions in common policies and frameworks.

In Canada, too, there is much evidence of government interest in, and use of, networks and partnering. The Treasury Board has expressed the rationale for the use of partnering arrangements as an alternative to the traditional federal structure of departments, agencies and Crown corporations in the following terms:

> The government will cooperate and develop partnering arrangements among departments and with other levels of government and other sectors of the economy. These arrangements will help it create new working relationships, exercise influence and leadership in the national interest, avoid costly duplication and overlap in services, and build on the strengths and capacity of other sectors to provide programs and services that are responsive to the client, innovative and affordable. (Treasury Board of Canada Secretariat 1995)

The Canadian government has also stated:

> There are many alternatives to traditional departmental structures for delivering programs, and the government is vigorously pursuing those alternatives.... Partnerships are an important form of alternative service delivery. Partnering with other governments, voluntary organizations and the private sector helps the federal government reduce overhead costs and duplication, and bring services closer to citizens." (Treasury Board of Canada Secretariat 1997)

The growing use of networks and partnering is therefore evident and while this growth reflects the belief and expectation that these forms of organizing will assist governments in addressing the problems they face, they also bring with them their own sets of problems and challenges. Yet, although they have a long history and have been the subject of much research, networks and partnering are relatively new as phenomena to evaluate and audit. Thus, in order to assess the success of these arrangements, evaluators and auditors need to understand them better. This chapter discusses these aspects of collaborative government highlighting important features evaluators and auditors need to understand if they are to assess these arrangements. The chapter also identifies some of the relevant literature from which evaluators and auditors might benefit. We feel that new approaches are needed to deal adequately with the collaborative nature of these arrangements for working together.

The chapter first presents two examples of networks and partnering in the "real" world, then describes collaborative characteristics of the new developments and what is meant by the concepts of partnering arrangements and networks, including the contribution of the sociology of networks. Prior to drawing conclusions the chapter presents nine collaborative properties for auditors and evaluators to consider when dealing with networks and partnerships.

Two Examples of Partnerships

To give flavor to the kinds of relationships under discussion in collaborative government we offer two examples, one dealing with experiences in Canada and the United States, the other with Europe.

The North American Waterfowl Management Plan, directed at the problem of declining populations of waterfowl in North America, is an international conservation program designed to restore waterfowl populations through managing wetlands and associated habitat. The plan's key strategy is to work through a partnership of stakeholders in the form of joint ventures, which involve federal, state, and provincial or territorial government agencies, nongovernment organizations, the private sector, and landowners, cooperating together across the continent in habitat-management efforts. Within Canada, funding is obtained by the delivery agencies of each joint venture, which make program/project proposals with an offer of partial funding and a request for matching funds primarily from U.S. federal and state governments.

The Partnerships Eures-Cross Border Project (also called Eurest project) is a structured and formal partnership network to facilitate and promote the free movement of workers in the European Union. Eures is a partnership between the European Commission, the national employment services of the member states and organizations representing social partners. It was launched in 1994 and encompasses 450 euro-advisors in seventeen countries who have been specially trained. It is a network approach in which the idea of "coordinated autonomy" is crucial. The activities focused on by Eures cross border concern job vacancies, social security, working conditions, taxation, etc. Directorate General V (DGV) of the EU is responsible for developing and maintaining several databases underlying the activities, coordination of information exchange and for training, animating and promoting the network.

Collaborative Characteristics of the New Developments

In many countries, new public management reforms linked to decentralization and changes in governance structures designed to enhance citizen participation and the quality of service delivery have led to growing use of network-type arrangements (Peters 1996). The use of the terms network, partnership and partnering arrangement to describe such collaborative arrangements between government and nongovernment entities may refer to a wide range of circumstances, and the meanings are often not clear. However, they all involve some form of working together of a number of parties.

So what are the collaborative characteristics of these networking and partnering arrangements? In this chapter we propose to answer these questions in two ways: in terms of the formal characteristics of organizations and from the perspective of less formal relationships between individuals. We see these as two sides of the same coin, both necessary to an understanding of the new developments we are exploring.

What are Networks?

The word "network" is often used with reference to communications and information technology. In social science, sociologists have long used network analysis to examine social relationships, and economists have more recently viewed networks as a form of economic organization. Networks also may be viewed as one of three models of social coordination, the other two being markets and hierarchies. *Markets* are spontaneous forms of coordination between self-interested, autonomous parties. In *hierarchies* the "visible hand" of management supplants the 'invisible hand' of the market, through lines of authority, reporting and decision making from superior to subordinate. The *network*, in contrast, is "light on its feet"—being made up of organizations and individuals engaged in reciprocal, preferential and mutually supportive actions. The key feature of networks is the way cooperation and trust are formed and sustained (Thompson et al. 1991). Network coordination depends on a mixture of factors, including the nature of horizontal and vertical linkages and the development of partnering arrangements of various kinds. The partners have to find ways to coordinate the network effectively, for example, good communication and procedures to resolve differences (Metcalfe 1994a).[1]

This chapter draws on Thompson et al. (1991), Coleman and Skogstad (1990) and Atlkinson and Coleman (1996) in conceptualizing network as a specific type of structured relationship linking organizations (and individuals within these organizations) for a public policy purpose. The organizations are pursuing jointly activities related to public policy concerns, hence the involvement of the government. The three characteristics generally used to describe networks are:

- relationships between organizations
- similarities among organizations, and
- connections between individuals.

In general, therefore, networks have a structure and an identity. The linkages tend to be purposeful, the organizations are not overly dissimilar and the individuals involved have common interests. However, there is a wide range of network concepts to be found in the literature. Without aiming to be exhaustive, we have identified the following principal forms.

Networks as Trust Ties

Establishing trust and confidence among organizations depends on capacities—a belief that other organizations have the skills and resources required—and on commitment—the intentions and good faith in making and implementing agreements (Metcalfe 1994a). Trust is something that in the end exists between people (Coleman and Skogstad 1990). A complementary view is that networks are created because they are economically efficient and effective. They are sustained, however, through the development of trust relationships, based on:

- common values and motivations which facilitate the emergence of trust, often demonstrated by reference to a "track record" or a reputation that has to be protected; and

- an emphasis on the longer term as an essential check against opportunistic behavior (Jarillo 1988).

Trust ties also may be facilitated through connections between individuals based on shared professional training and norms, geographical proximity or other common interests, for example, bilateral networks of like-minded federal and provincial officials involved in regional development programs (Dupré 1985).

Networks as Means of Governance

Several interdependent actors are involved in delivering government services. In such circumstances, governance is defined in terms of "managing networks." These self-organizing, interorganizational networks have the following characteristics:

- interdependence between organizations;
- continuing interactions between network members;
- game-like interactions; and
- a significant degree of autonomy from the state.

Examples include service delivery by autonomous executive agencies in the UK and Sweden (Rhodes 1996).

Policy Networks

These comprise dependent relationships between both individuals and organizations in frequent contact in particular policy areas. A related concept, somewhat broader, is "policy community" which suggests a commonly understood belief system, code of conduct and established pattern of behavior. Examples of policy networks include those devoted to environmental regulation and industrial development (Atkinson and Coleman 1996).

Networks as a Form of Economic Organization

Here individuals (and organizations) are engaged in reciprocal, preferential, mutually supportive actions. The basic assumption is that one party is dependent on resources controlled by another and that there are gains to be had by the pooling of resources, for example, inter-firm agreements, collaborations and partnerships in the automotive and telecommunications industries (Powell 1990). Another perspective is that networks are a mode of organization that can be used by managers or entrepreneurs to move their firms into a stronger competitive position (Jarillo 1988) as observed, for example, in high-growth, adaptive and innovative entrepreneurial firms (Larson 1992).

A Sociology of Networks

But how can one theorize these developments? One solution is to utilize ideas from recent work on the sociology of networks which offers evidence that informal relationships and networks have a significant influence on the performance of organizations. For example, in a recent review article, Flap et al. (1998) summarize the research findings on the relationship between networks and (business) performance and profit: "Most telling to managers is that *informal ties* affect *profit.*" The most convincing evidence here is drawn from two comparative studies on local branches of banks. These provide a near ideal set up for research on the productivity of informal networks, since the institutional context is constant, the formal organization, that is, the prescribed social network, is constant, the size of the local establishments is similar and human capital is not that different. Thus, the only thing that can be held responsible for differences in profit and performance, apart from clientele, is the informal make-up of these local branches.

Similarly, Krackhardt (1994) and Krackhardt and Hanson (1993) in a study of 24 local branches of a large bank on the American East Coast established that a limited hierarchy in the communication network as well as some "slack" in the informal advice network was conductive to higher profit margins. Non-hierarchical branches, those with two-way communication between people of all levels, were 70 percent more profitable than branches with one-way communication between superiors and staff. Some relational slack is productive as it makes the network less vulnerable. Employees are not sealed off from each other if a particular person leaves or is absent.

Perhaps also social networks help an enterprise in the event of an economic setback. Meyerson (1992) studies twenty-nine publicly quoted firms in Sweden, some of which had widespread ownership while others had a stockholder with majority ownership, and analyzed how quickly they recovered after experiencing a drop in stock prices:

> The companies with widespread ownership have a cohesive management team, and weak, non-overlapping external ties. This team is decision competent, able to buy time after a major set back like a fall in stock prices. The management team of a majority owned company is less cohesive and has an external network with overlapping, strong ties, especially to the major owner. This type of team is less well informed and less able to buy time, or to come to a decision and stick to it and less adept in circumventing takeover bids, but it is quicker to recover on the stock market. (Flap et al. 1998)

Other relevant work is that line of sociological research that relates the adoption of organizational innovations to networks. For example, Burt (1987) found that for organizational members, the decision to adopt an innovation is partly dependent upon the decisions of colleagues who occupy a similar place in the organization's informal network. In different studies, Albrecht and Ropp (1984) and Krackhardt (1990) found that in order to adopt innovations, people talk with colleagues to reduce their feelings of insecurity about the value of the innovation. Finally, network studies have also shown that networks of employees are crucial to organizational success when the quality of the products to be delivered is harder to establish or more difficult to describe (Bulder et al. 1996; Krackhardt and Hanson 1993).

The sociology of network is therefore relevant not only in presenting interesting findings but also in indicating a growth of knowledge regarding the types of networks and the methodology required to study them. More and more frequently, three types of networks are charted: communication, task-oriented and friendship-oriented. The first is the occurrence of (day to day) communication between people: to what extent do people communicate and interact with each other? This is operationalized in terms of measuring the "communication network." The second is the embeddedness of officials in networks and is operationalized in terms of measuring and charting the "friendship-oriented or trust" networks. Here the focus is primarily on the emotional support colleagues provide each other with. The third element concerns exchanging information and advice on work-related issues. This has been operationalized in terms of measuring the task-oriented network.

These three types have become a standard in research on networks. For these types of networks, plots are usually made with the use of the multidimensional scaling features of UCINET IV (Borgatti et al. 1992) while graphical representations of network data can be presented by many different programs.[2]

Partnering: Collaborative Arrangements and Partnerships[3]

Some networks are structured and characterized by specific agreements among partners. As in partnerships, these arrangements involve the sharing by government of power, work, support and/or information with others for the achievement of joint goals and/or mutual benefits, while serving a public policy purpose (Kernaghan

1993; OECD 1999). The implication is that there is a cooperative investment of resources (time, funding, materiel, human resources, etc.) and therefore joint risk-taking, sharing of authority, and benefits for all partners.

Where these arrangements have *common objectives tied to a public policy purpose*, *shared governance*, and *written agreements* on *governance and financing,* they exhibit the features of collaborative arrangements, as recently defined by the Auditor General of Canada:

- *Common objectives tied to a public policy purpose.* The collaborative arrangement reflects an involvement of the federal government as well as other parties in the lives of Canadians, within the legal framework approved by Parliament. In this context, the federal government and its partners pursue common objectives and results that have a public policy purpose.

- *Shared governance.* The participating organizations share governance related to public policy as well as to the way in which the arrangement itself is governed. The process for making strategic decisions about collective activities is based on agreement by the participating organizations. They agree on the decisions that matter for the collaborative arrangement and that determine its future course of action. They also share the risks involved in those decisions. There is consultation among the organizations, so that decisions are not taken unilaterally. The way decision making is shared and to what extent will vary considerably with the type of arrangement.

- *Written agreements on governance and financing.* The organizations need to recognize the importance of agreeing on ways to steer the collective effort, as well as the importance of controlling the use of resources. A variety of mechanisms and types of agreements may be used (Auditor General of Canada, 1999a).

Collaborative arrangements may be thought of as the typical, more formal arrangements used within networks. Among the differences between networks and collaborative arrangements are the degree of complexity and formality. Networks may function in a wholly informal way, based on mutual understandings; so, too, may collaborative arrangements, except that there is invariably some form of specific agreement between the parties, usually in writing, specifying mutual obligations. By definition, networks are multiparty relationships, whereas collaborative arrangements may involve two parties of equal standing, as well as multiple parties.

Though less articulated, the concept of "joined-up government" resembles this approach, though probably less attention is paid to the formalization of the agreements (e.g., in the UK). The same holds for the covenants or soft law-approach in the Netherlands. Nevertheless, overall we have a picture of what the world of collaborative governments looks like as it is developing on the ground in several different countries.

Auditing and Evaluating Collaborative Arrangements

As with other public sector delivery approaches, it is necessary to know if networking and partnering are indeed working as intended. What are the issues for evaluators and auditors if they wish or are required to assess collaborative arrangements?

The Auditor General of Canada (1999a) has proposed one framework for assessing these arrangements, shown in Table 2.1. The three basic questions listed there (and the sub-questions) all provide fruitful territory for the evaluator and auditor:

• Is the public interest being served?

• Is there effective accountability?

• Is there adequate transparency?

Given the nontraditional design and structure of collaborative arrangements, we suggest that there is more to be looked at than simply whether the arrangement is meeting its intended objectives. In particular, since traditional mechanisms to ensure public and citizen's rights are often not clearly present, significant attention should be paid to the protection of the public interest and related accountability concerns.

A central question is to what extent the network or partnership has realized its goals and at what (transaction) costs? Though we know that both "market" and "hierarchy" models of managing government (Mintzberg 1996) are confronted with difficulties, there is not a priori evidence that the network or collaborative government approach is *more* efficient and effective.[4]

The questions just raised may also be considered as risks, that is, not paying sufficient attention to protecting the public interest, insufficient transparency, and inadequate accountability. Other risks also deserve attention. These can include the risk of poorly defined arrangements, limiting the chances for success and the risk of partners not meeting commitments to each other or to the common cause (Auditor General of Canada 1999a).

Table 2.1
A Framework for Assessing Collaborative Arrangements

Serving the Public Interest
- Are the objectives being met?
- Is the collaborative arrangement the best way to meet the objectives?
- Are public service values being maintained?
- Are adequate citizen complaint and redress mechanisms in place?
- Are there effective public consultation/ feedback mechanisms?

Effective Accountability Arrangements
- Are the objectives, the expected level of performance and results and the operating conditions agreed to and clear?
- Are the authorities, roles and responsibilities of each partner clear?
- Are the expectations for each partner balanced with its capacities?
- Is there a well-defined management structure?
- Can performance be measured and credibly reported to each partner, Parliament and the public?
- Has adequate provision been made for monitoring, review, program evaluation and audit?
- Are adequate procedures in place to deal with non performance?

Greater Transparency
- Have the information needs of those affected been recognized?
- Is appropriate and sufficient information being disclosed to Parliament and the public?

Source: Adapted from Auditor General of Canada (1999a, 1999b)

Hence evaluation and audit are clearly needed to determine how well these approaches to public sector management actually work. Consequently rather than explore further the evaluation and audit issues listed in Table 2.1, we want to mention briefly a number of factors or conditions that need to be kept in mind when examining collaborative arrangements as they are possible explanatory variables for the success or not of a particular network or partnering arrangement, which are discussed in detail (see Table 2.2).

Table 2.2
Explanatory Variables for the Success of Arrangements

- Social capital in networks
- Goal and outcome differentiation
- The mix of partner organizations
- The pattern of interactions
- The level of available resources
- The structure of the partnering arrangement
- Human resource management issues
- The stability of the partnering arrangement
- The degree of formalization of agreements

Social Capital in Networks

Although the focus in this chapter is on partnering arrangements within and between organizations, it should be stressed that human and social factors are crucial to the success of networks and collaborative arrangements. In particular,

- *People* exchange ideas;

- *people* invest in each other and in each other's networks;

- *people* "create" glass ceilings that reduce upward mobility for certain groups within society due to the mechanism of the "old boys network";

- *people* form (and destroy) friendships within and between organizations; and

- *people* ask and give advice.

Thus, when one evaluates the efficiency or effectiveness of partnering arrangements, it is essential to pay attention to sociological aspects of collaboration and exchange not least since there is strong evidence that informal relationships and networks have a significant impact on the performance of organizations and their collaborations.

In this context social capital concerns the importance of resources which, although possessed by other persons, are available to a given individual through his social relations to these other persons (Flap 1999). The core of the theory and research of social capital is relatively simple:

First, people better equipped with social resources—in the sense of their social network and the resources of others they can call upon—will succeed better in attaining their goals. Second, people will invest in relations with others in view of the perceived future value of the social resources made available by these relations. (Flap 1999: 5)

Thirdly, organizations with more social capital than others will probably be better off. As collaborative arrangements imply "networks and partnerships," there is a logic behind the idea that by focusing on social capital, one can try to make arrangements more effective and efficient.

Coleman and Skogstad (1990) make the important observation that a cohesive, that is, an all-connected network is a resource to its members because it promotes the willingness to cooperate with and provide help to others. Burt (1992) stresses the other side of the coin: an individual has a comparative advantage in competitive situations if those who are connected to him do not have ties to each other. This focal actor, in the words of Flap (1999: 6), "then has a minimum of redundancy between his relationships and can play them off against each other." One can easily understand that what holds for individuals is also true for organizations. In that sense, the position of an organization in a wider (inter-organizational) network appears to be an important factor when evaluating the efficiency and effectiveness of this organization. Bulder et al. (1996) have—with social capital theory as a starting point—analyzed what happens to the public sector when there are re-organizations. Their most important finding is that if one changes the formal structure of organizations, the informal, social networks continue to live on, a phenomenon called "network lag."

Two examples show the importance of the idea of social capital when evaluating governmental activities:

- If British Prime Minister Tony Blair stresses the importance of *joined-up government*, then it is not enough to refer to *organizational requirements* to integrate and de-fragment the current layers of government. It is the people within these "organizations" and governmental layers that have to work together in a more efficient and effective way. Then social capital becomes extremely important in any evaluation that looks into the impact of these activities.

- If the earlier mentioned *Eures-Cross Border "coordinated network" indeed* is effective and efficient (and something more than a number of people irregularly meeting and dining), then commitment to the network and their goals as well as having trust in the EU-regional colleagues are important for realizing the goals of the official regional collaboration. This implies that evaluators and auditors have to dig into the structure of social relations and commitment instead of only looking into the formal arrangements themselves.

Social capital studies are able to present evaluators and auditors with theory and methodology to tackle these problems. This approach goes back to studies in industrial sociology such as the ones conducted by Roethlisberger and Dickson (1939) and Homans (1955). Homans carried out research among cash posters in a factory. He focused on the relationships between the place a girl had in the communication network and the efficiency with which she did her job. He showed that the employees worked harder than the factory required. Homans related this finding to the importance and the pleasure the girls attached to their informal social relations.

Goal and Outcome Differentiation

When networks are managed through structured coordination, that is, managed coordination, they tend to have collective goals, as do, of course, collaborative arrangements. These goals will be different from the goals that each organization would pursue independently (Rogers et al. 1982). In other words, participation in a partnering arrangement may change organizational goals. Given the commonality of interest that helps to create the partnering arrangement in the first instance, the process of goal formation may be expected to reflect those interests, but may proceed in various ways. More precisely defined goals may require some specific arrangements, for example, ensuring that the agreement adequately reflects the expected contribution of each party to intended results. Shared goals may be the glue that holds the partnering arrangement together and helps to secure integration and coordination of activities. As Armstrong and Lenihan see it:

> If the [parties] share the same outcome and adopt the same indicators, a certain level of coordination should automatically follow. First, by seeking the same outcomes, the parties have already agreed to focus their efforts on the same end. Second, in adopting the same performance indicators, they impose the same evaluation standards, and hence the same measure of discipline, on the policies and programs that they may adopt to pursue those ends. (1999: 53)

The example of the North American Waterfowl Management Plan (NAWMP) (see above) includes hunters as well as bird watchers who share a common interest in protecting waterfowl for very different reasons. The partners have set clear and measurable targets to restore waterfowl population to 1970s levels, and to secure, enhance and manage key habitats (Commissioner of the Environment and Sustainable Development, 2000).

The Mix of Partner Organizations

The extent to which partner organizations are similar in various respects, including capacity, size, structure, cohesiveness and accessibility, will determine the potential for coordination. In some partnering arrangements, very different organizations work together in anomalous ways. In Canada, federal and provincial departments may be involved with various private sector organizations that exhibit different characteristics. On the other hand, if only two orders of government, federal and provincial, are involved, some more intricate coordinating arrangements may be feasible. In particular, the capacity of organizations underpins coordination activity. The state of development of the organization will determine its effectiveness as a partner. Here relevant factors include:

- age, maturity, experience of the organization;
- quality of the mission and mandate;
- clientèle and membership size;
- resources and facilities (a different question from *network* resources); and
- internal and external credibility (McDonald 1994).

The Pattern of Interactions

A number of factors relate to the pattern of interactions in a partnering arrangement, including the volume of interactions, the autonomy or interconnectedness of the partners, the intensity of the interactions and the extent to which they are reciprocal in nature. For example in NAWMP, the management structure is complex, involving different levels of government as well as stakeholder organizations. Yet the structure relays information effectively to all partners, and each party's role and responsibilities are clear (Commissioner of the Environment and Sustainable Development 2000, paragraph 7.45-46).

The Level of Available Resources

The allocation of financial, human and physical resources may be critical for the management of a partnering arrangement. The extent to which organizations are funded autonomously, in common or through the partnering arrangement itself determines the potential for leverage through funding. Resources and funding are one of the elements to be coordinated in a partnering arrangement, and one analysis suggests that the institutional level (e.g., governmental), as opposed to other organizations or individuals, is the appropriate level for such coordination to take place (Rogers et al. 1982).

The Structure of the Partnering Arrangement

Diverse structural properties account for a major share of the potential for effective coordination. In theory, a partnering arrangement can function without a coordinator, which can refer to an organization, as well as to the chief executive, board, managers or staff, responsible for coordinating activities. However, a number of studies have pointed to the strategic value of having a coordinator, especially in the form of a "hub" or "core" organization. Metcalfe (1994b: 280-284) noted that the capacity to coordinate begins with a clear understanding of the extent of organizational autonomy, defining the scope for coordination with other partnering arrangement participants. It then proceeds through several levels of competence, gradually improving the performance of coordination, for example, by avoiding conflict, arbitrating differences and establishing priorities. These higher levels of coordination require the involvement of a coordinator. Decision making and enforcement are complemented by well-functioning horizontal communication and information systems aimed at voluntary compliance. Metcalfe's policy coordination scale (Table 2.3) shows the progression in levels of coordination; the higher functions depend on the existence and reliability of the lower ones.

Table 2.3
A Policy Coordination Scale

9	Network strategy
8	Establishing priorities
7	Setting limits on partners' action
6	Arbitration of policy differences
5	Search for agreement among partners
4	Avoiding divergences among partners
3	Consultation with other partners (feedback)
2	Communication to other partners
1	Independent decision making by partners

Human Resource Management Issues

Arrangements for staff from partner organizations to work together on behalf of the partnering arrangement raise various human resource management issues. For example where partners are hierarchical organizations, these arrangements must allow for career development. Assignments also need to be structured to avoid a conflict of duties. In the case of federal-provincial partnering arrangement, where employees of one level of government may report to those of another, clarity of roles and responsibilities will be required. In addition, the employees who work in the core agency will have a frame of reference to deal with partners that is different from that with organizations outside the network. Being the caretaker of the partnering arrangement means devoting special attention to the individuals who are the key players. In Canada, the responsible federal central agency, the Treasury Board Secretariat, has identified several human resource issues, in relation to policies that apply to federal employees involved in partnering arrangement situations, as well as certain other groups, such as volunteers. For example, federal employees continue to be subject to federal laws and policies, maintaining their rights and benefits, in areas such as grievance and redress, employment equity and official languages (Treasury Board of Canada Secretariat 1996).

The Stability of the Partnering Arrangement

The stability of the partnering arrangement relates to its durability over time and its adaptability to change. The stability of the arrangement may depend to a large extent on the conditions prevailing in the external environment. Because partnering arrangements tend to be permeable, with multiple relationships among component organizations and individuals involving other networks or hierarchies, they also tend to be highly reactive to changes in external conditions. One model of network effectiveness suggested that major changes instigated by external forces impacted negatively on common outcomes, advancing the following proposition: other things being equal, the effectiveness of the partnering arrangement will be enhanced under conditions of general system stability, although stability alone is not a sufficient condition for effectiveness (Provan and Milward 1995). Stability may also be determined by the attributes both of the partner organizations and the partnering arrangement itself. If there is a coordinating partner, one of its key tasks may be to see to the continued stability of the network.

The stability-related attributes of partner organizations are the following and all have to do with the extent to which an organization is well established, in terms of:[5]

• The infrastructure of the organization: staff, skills, credibility, facilities, revenues and finances;

• The ability of the organization to use or disburse government-provided funds efficiently and effectively;

• The capacity of the organization to carry out the desired activities in a manner that is satisfactory to the other partners (this may mean satisfactory to the governance or coordinating process in the network) and to the clients (if service to the public is involved);

• Developmental needs that can be addressed through the resources of the network; and

• Good management and understanding of the needs of clients and the other partnering organizations.

The Degree of Formalization of Agreements

It is assumed that there are agreed decision-making rules in operation in a network with managed coordination or a collaborative arrangement. However, the nature of these rules may vary widely. Some of the processes may be largely informal and undocumented. The conditions governing meaningful participation may not be well defined, including the basic question of how an organization first accedes to membership, then moves on to participate fully.

In the case of the North American Waterfowl Management Plan (see above), joint venture partners assumed many responsibilities, based on agreed decision-making processes. The partners established and maintained coordination by establishing site-specific habitat objectives, preparing a joint venture implementation plan, and identifying strategies to achieve the objectives. They coordinated project development, funding, and implementation, tracked habitat accomplishments and evaluated the effectiveness of habitat accomplishments. Consequently, the partners were accountable for the results of projects or habitats managed by them in specific regions, eco-systems or sites.

Conclusions

In many nations, the number, variety and complexity of network and partnering arrangements as means of delivering public policy has increased significantly in recent years. However, their use in this respect is not well understood, whether the arrangements take the form of more structured partnering, or less structured networks. They are complex not only because they lie outside the traditional departmental means of program delivery, but also because they involve informal relationships between individuals that at times may be difficult to discern. Both formal or organizational aspects and informal or sociological factors, such as social capital, require the attention of auditors and evaluators seeking to assess the arrangements.

Given the novelty, complexity and proliferation of network and partnering arrangements, the question of how well they work is increasingly important. At times, these arrangements have been pursued for ideological reasons, or because of the desire to follow a trend. These tendencies add to the need for auditors and evaluators to develop effective analytical tools to assess the arrangements. There is no a priori evidence that network or partnering delivery mechanisms are *more* productive than other arrangements. Neither is the opposite true.

The literature offers some useful lines of enquiry, with the potential to deepen understanding and flesh out approaches that auditors and evaluators may pursue. Thus, viewing networks as a form of economic organization provides insights. Similarly, sociological research has drawn attention to the way in which people communicate within networks, exchange information and secure rewards.

For evaluators and auditors, we believe that it is important to address the *formal* characteristics of partnering arrangement, such as the articulation of the (joint) goals of the collaboration, the level of agreement by the parties involved, the way in which coordination is carried out and the contract's accountability arrangements, However, possibly even more important are the human and social aspects of these arrangements. As has been shown, it is people who close deals, who trust each other, who go for joint accountability (or not). Further behavioral research has put on the agenda that the way in which people communicate within networks and exchange information and rewards are important factors in explaining and predicting a network's performance. Put differently: social capital must be a prime topic for evaluators and auditors in their investigations into the effectiveness and efficiency of collaborative arrangements.

Drawing upon this literature, and considering some real life examples, we have suggested some explanatory factors that may be used to assess network and partnering arrangements. Of particular interest is the need to assess the risks involved when partnering. These risks include inadequate accountability, a failure to protect the public interest and the concerns raised in connection with social capital in networks. In bringing forward these considerations for auditors and evaluators, we recognize that they face a steep learning curve. The fact that network and partnering arrangements often do not fit well within the traditional audit or evaluation frameworks or methodologies means that they require more attention. Evaluators and auditors need to make productive use of the available research, and refine the tools they need to do the job.

Notes

1. This discussion of networks, markets and hierarchies relies on Thompson et al. (1991) and Powell (1990: 301-303). Thompson et al. see these as models of overall social interaction; Powell views them more as forms of economic organization. Mintzberg (1996), however, makes a somewhat more refined distinction between the *machine model* of managing governments where "control" is almost everything, a *network model* where "connect, communicate and collaborate" are catchwords, a *performance control model* where "isolate, assign and measure" are central and a *virtual model* focusing on "privatize, contract and negotiate."

2. See Krackhardt (1990, 1994) and http://www.heinz.cmu.edu/project/INSNA). The latter is the site of the International Network for Social Network Analysis (INSNA) and related subjects. Here you will find Social Networks information, reference sources and links to related home pages. Other information through the Internet is available from: http://www.cpn.org/sections/tools/models/social_capital.html.

3. It has been suggested that the term "partnership" should be avoided because of possible confusion with legal partnership which refers to a relationship among legally distinct entities in which each partner's actions are fully binding on every other partner. Government is reluctant to enter into such legal partnerships because of potential difficulties in holding each partner fully accountable and the risk that it could be held liable for the debts of its partners (Treasury Board of Canada Secretariat, 1996).

4. On the contrary, Kirkpatrick (1999) noted the costs associated with networks because of factors such as the difficult task of building trusting relationships and long-term instability.

5. This is adapted from McDonald (1994).

References

Albrecht, T. L., and V. A. Ropp. 1984. "Communicating About Innovation in Networks of Three U.S. Organizations." *Journal of Communication,* 34, 78-91.

Armstrong, J., and D. G. Lenihan. 1999. *From Controlling to Collaborating: When Governments Want to be Partners.* Toronto: Institute of Public Administration of Canada.

Atkinson, M. M., and W. D. Coleman. 1996. "Policy Networks, Policy Communities and the Problems of Governance," in Laurent Dobuzinskis, Michael Howlett, and David Laycock (eds.), *Policy Studies in Canada: The State of the Art.* Toronto: University of Toronto Press.

Auditor General of Canada. 1999a. "Collaborative Arrangements: Issues for the Federal Government," in *Report to the House of Commons*, Chapter 5, Ottawa.

Borgatti, S., M. Everett, and L. Freeman. 1992. *UCINET IV.* Boston: Analytic Technologies.

Bulder, A., F. Leeuw, and H. Flap. 1996. "Networks and Evaluating Public Sector Reforms." *Evaluation* 2, 261-276.

Burt, R. S. 1992. *Structural Holes: The Social Structure of Competition.* Cambridge, MA: Harvard University Press.

Burt, R. S. 1987. "The Network Entrepreneur." Unpublished Paper, Columbia University, New York.

Coleman, W. D., and G. Skogstad. 1990. "Policy Communities and Policy Networks: A Structural Approach," in W. D. Coleman and G. Skogstad (eds.), *Policy Communities and Public Policy in Canada*, Chapter 1, p. 14-33. Toronto: Copp Clark Pitman.

Commissioner of the Environment and Sustainable Development. 2000. "Cooperation between Federal, Provincial and Territorial Governments," in *Report to the House of Commons, Chapter 7,* Ottawa.

Dupré, J. S. 1985. "Reflections on the Workability of Executive Federalism," in R. Simeon, *Intergovernmental Relations*, Research Report of the Royal Commission on the Economic Union and Development Prospects for Canada. Toronto: University of Toronto Press.

Flap, H., B. Bulder, and B. Volker. 1998. "Intra-Organizational Networks and Performance." *Computational & Mathematical Organization Theory*, 4/2, 109-147.

Flap, H. 1999. "Creation and Returns of Social Capital, a New Research Program." *La Revue Tocqueville* 20, 1.

Homans, G. C. 1955. "The Cash Posters: A Study of a Group of Working Girls." *American Sociological Review,* 6, 724-733.

Jarillo, J. C. 1988. "On Strategic Networks." *Strategic Management Journal*, 9/1, 31-41.

Kernaghan, K. 1993. "Partnership and Public Administration: Conceptual and Practical Considerations." *Canadian Public Administration* 36/1, 57-76.

Kirkpatrick, I. 1999. "The Worst of Both Worlds? Public Services without Markets or Bureaucracy." *Public Money & Management*, 19/3, 7-14.

Krackhardt, D. 1990. "Assessing the Political Landscape: Structure, Cognition and Power in Organizations." *Administrative Science Quarterly,* 35, 342-369.

Krackhardt, D. 1994. "Graph Theoretical Dimensions of Informal Organizations," in K. M. Carley and M. J. Prietula (eds.), *Computational Organization Theory,* 89-111.

Krackhardt, D, and J. Hanson. 1993. Informal Networks: The Company behind the Chart. *Harvard Business Review*, July-August, 14-27.

Larson, A. 1992. "Network Dyads in Entrepreneurial Settings: A Study of the Governance of Exchange Relationships." *Administrative Science Quarterly* 37: 76-104.

McDonald, R. A. 1994. *Intermediaries and the Delivery of Programs.* Ottawa: Industry Canada.

Metcalfe, L. 1994a. "The Weakest Links: Building Organizational Networks for Multi-Level Regulation." in Organization for Economic Cooperation and Development (OECD), *Regulatory Cooperation for an Interdependent World*, Chapter 2, Paris: OECD.

Metcalfe, L. 1994b. "International Policy Cooperation and Public Management Reform," in B. Kliksberg (ed.), Symposium on Redesigning the State Profile for Social and Economic Development and Change, *International Review of Administrative Sciences*, 60/2, 271-290

Meyerson, E. M. 1992. *The Impact of Ownership Structure and Executive Team Composition on Firm Performance*. Stockholm: Almqvist and Wiksell International.

Mintzberg, H. 1996. "Managing Government, Governing Management." *Harvard Business Review*, May-June 1996, 75-83.

OECD. 1999. *Lessons from Performance Contracting Case Studies: A Framework for Public Sector Performance Contracting*. Paris: PUMA/PAC(99)2.

Peters, G. 1996. *The Future of Governing: Four Emerging Models*. Kansas City: University Press of Kansas.

Powell, W. W. 1990. "Neither Market Nor Hierarchy: Network Forms of Organization," in B. M. Staw and L. L. Cummings (eds.), *Research in Organizational Behavior*. Greenwich, CT: JAI Press Inc.

Provan, K., and H. B. Milward. 1995. "A Preliminary Theory of Interorganizational Network Effectiveness: A Comparative Study of Four Community Mental Health Systems," *Administrative Science Quarterly*, 40, 1-33.

Reinecke, W. H. 1999. "The Other World Wide Web: Global Public Policy Networks." *Foreign Policy*, 117, 44-57.

Reinecke, W. H., and F. Deng. 2000. *Critical Choices. The UN, Networks and the Future of Global Governance*. Ottawa: International Development Research Center.

Rhodes, R. A. W. 1996. "The New Governance: Governing without Government." *Political Studies*, XLIV, 652-667.

Roethlisberger, F., and W. J. Dickson. 1939. *Management and the Worker*. Cambridge, MA: Harvard University Press.

Rogers, David L., David A. Whetten, J. Benson, Kenneth Halpert, P. Burton, and Charles L. Mulford. 1982. *Interorganizational Coordination, Theory, Research and Implementation*. Ames: Iowa State University Press.

Thompson, Grahame, Jennifer Frances, Rosalind Levacic, and Jeremy Mitchell (eds.). 1991. *Markets, Hierarchies and Network: The Coordination of Social Life*. London: Sage Publications.

Treasury Board of Canada, Secretariat. 1996. *The Federal Government as "Partner": Six Steps to Successful Collaboration*. Ottawa.

World Bank. 1997. *The State in a Changing World*. Washington, D.C.

3

Quangos, Evaluation, and Accountability in Collaborative Government

Bill Jenkins, Frans Leeuw, and Sandra Van Thiel

In 1999, the UK New Labour government launched a comprehensive program for the reform of public service delivery. This program, set out in its policy document, *Modernising Government* (Cabinet Office 1999), was described by Prime Minister Tony Blair as a significant step forward in changing how government really works. It sought to improve three main areas of operations: policy formulation, service delivery and the way other functions of government were performed. The focus was on better policy, more responsive and quality public services and an information-age government. This required policymaking that was more joined-up and strategic, a focus on public service users rather than providers and high quality and efficient service delivery.

The emphasis on joined-up government emerged from a concern that institutional fragmentation historically worked against efficient and effective public services. In the words of *Modernising Government*, policies were needed that optimized inclusiveness and integration. This required new structures dealing with problems in "a joined-up way, regardless of the organizational structure of government." and focusing on groups (older people, youth unemployment) or areas (Health Action Zones, Education Action Zones) (Cabinet Office 1999, Ch. 3). Further, there was a need to reform audit regimes since current practices often helped stimulate organizational specific performance stress which, in turn, limited public service organizational capacity for cohesion.

In addition to institutional weaknesses, *Modernising Government* highlighted those in governmental processes of policymaking, imple-

mentation and evaluation. It spoke of policy needing to be "a continuous learning experience" rather than a series of on-off initiatives. Further, it advocated a more systematic use of policy and program evaluation: "we will ensure that all policies and programs are
clearly specified and evaluated and the lessons of success and failure communicated and acted upon" (Cabinet Office 1999, Ch. 2).
The government thus called for the modernization of evaluation
standards and tools particularly to deal with cross cutting issues.
However, it acknowledged that this might require a new audit culture and approaches to overcome barriers caused by established
systems of audit and accountability (Cabinet Office 1999, Ch. 4).
The message of *Modernising Government* was therefore one of institutional innovation and cultural change. High on the reform agenda
were new flexible organizational arrangements subject to fewer re-
strictions, drawing in external groups (both public and private), and
willing to take risks and promote change.

Yet such organizations, in particular quangos (quasi-nongovern-
ment organizations), were previously viewed with suspicion as
sources of patronage and clientelism, lacking in accountability and
transparency and often threatening good government. Before the
election New Labour promised to address the issue of the "appointed
state." In government it issued a consultative document that rehearsed
the arguments often raised against quangos, real or perceived: they
were unelected and unaccountable, secretive, unresponsive, under-
pinned by unfair appointments systems and had grown in number
and power without commensurate increases in scrutiny. It asked
whether quangos were needed and if so whether their openness,
responsiveness and accountability could be improved (Cabinet Office 1996; 1997).

This concern with quangos as a *political* problem had its origins
in their use by the previous Conservative administrations of the 1980s
and 1990s as a way of delivering government policy independently
of local elected bodies and outside the normal scrutiny mechanisms
of Parliament and audit. This led to two major criticisms: first, that
the government was bypassing the political process and creating a
new magistracy of appointed rather than elected bodies and, second, that this led to a democratic deficit as quasi-governments and
quasi-markets eroded established governmental mechanisms especially at a local level (Stewart 1994). However, these doubts are not
shared by all. Indeed some have advocated the devolving of respon-

sibilities to decentralized structures and the freeing up of controls and formal rules to promote more efficient and effective public sector performance (Holmes and Shand 1995; OECD 1995). Such a shift provides for a search for quality at affordable prices, a greater interest in goal-driven management, more public-private partnerships and a reconception of government as a people-focused business.

Such arguments may, however, side step the accountability questions of quasi-government raised not only in the UK but also in countries such as the Netherlands and Scandinavia (Algemene Rekenkamer 1995; Weir and Beetham 1999; Greve 1996; Weir and Hall 1994). Quangos therefore represent a major organizational strategy in the armory of those who seek to reinvent governments. This strategy is not new but what may be new is the extent to which it has been employed recently to redesign governmental operations. So is it less that quangos should be the focus of criticism than the way they are deployed in particular sets of circumstances? Can quangos provide a mechanism for better policy-making, service delivery and citizen involvement in government? Previously, it has often been argued that far from contributing to good governance the growth of quangos has posed severe questions for the design and operation of mechanisms of accountability and evaluation particularly in parliamentary systems. In response to this it would appear that quangos (possibly in a new form) are now seen as a means of advancing collaborative government, a strategy that in turn may require new systems of audit and evaluation.

These issues will be discussed in this chapter. First, we will sketch out the origins of quangos, explore their growth in the Netherlands and the UK and discuss their effects. We will then consider their role in collaborative government and their audit and evaluation. Finally, we will assess the strengths and weaknesses of new collaborative mechanisms in which quangos now play a part, especially the design and effectiveness of evaluative and accountability systems.

Quangos: What and Why?

Taken at its simplest quango is the acronym for a quasi-autonomous non governmental organization that is (a) publicly funded, (b) appointed rather than elected, (c) operates at arms-length from government, and (d) accountable to its funding agency rather than the wider public (Skelcher 1998, Ch. 1; Weir and Hall 1994: 1). Quangos constitute the appointed (in contrast to the elected) state. The use of such bodies is hardly new. Many owe their origins to a historical combination of political ideology and pragmatism (Skelcher 1998). However, it was their explosive growth in the 1980s, when they became a favored governmental tool of service delivery at local levels, that fuelled concerns. These developments also coincided with the doctrines of new public management which, combined with a political ideology that sought to shrink and fragment the state, viewed quangos as "an appealing and managerial efficient way of governing a complex society" (1998: 2).

Quangos have been controversial particularly in the UK where throughout the 1980s and 1990s critics claimed their numbers were increasing sharply (Hall and Weir 1996; Stewart 1995; Weir and Hall 1994) while governments retorted that the problem had been exaggerated (Hunt 1995; Waldegrave 1993). As writers such as Hogwood (1995) note, the term "quango" was introduced to categorize UK bodies which, although essentially private, were instruments of government policy delivery (Barker 1982). However, within a short period, the term expanded to encompass all bodies to which governments make public appointments but outside the line management of central departments of state. This, in turn, led to a debate on the number and influence of quangos and, in 1980, to the rejection of the term quango by the then UK government and its substitution in official language and statistics by Non Departmental Public Body (NDPB) (Pliatzky 1980). Since that time UK governmental discussions and counts of quangos have been based on this categorization (Cabinet Office 1997) and although the definition of NDPBs has been refined and extended, the view of critics is that it remains, perhaps deliberately, too restrictive. As Skelcher observes, "the search for a definition is an intensely political activity" (1998: 7). Yet, whatever the underpinning rationale, a consequence of this narrow categorization has been that UK official statistics have failed to recognize the dramatic changes in governance structures that quango growth has brought and its effects on accountability at central and local levels.

This proliferation of appointed bodies led critics such as Weir and Hall to challenge the adequacy of official definitions arguing that what was required was a definition of "all explicitly executive bodies of a semi-autonomous nature which effectively act as agencies for central government and carry out government policies"

(1994: 8). They therefore offer the term Extra Governmental Organization (EGO) to include (a) non-departmental public bodies as defined by UK government; (b) national health service bodies; and (c) "non recognized" executive bodies operating at local level. This allows one to concentrate on "all explicitly executive bodies of a semi-autonomous nature which effectively act as agencies for central government and carry out governmental policies" (1994: 8).

Do definitions matter? For some it remains *the* key issue since it is argued that without a clear definition generalizations are difficult to sustain and key differences between quangos may be ignored (Cole 1998; Hogwood 1995). Yet this should not prevent the development of arguments that seek to explore the consequences of the growth of the appointed state for systems of governance and accountability. In its analysis this chapter will define quangos as "part of the public sector by virtue of their collective purpose, underlying accountability to governmental authority, lack of direct and indirect board election and primary resourcing from the public purse" (Skelcher 1998: 13).

In the Netherlands, quangos are defined as bodies that form no part of established ministries but rather are independent organizations with their own board of management (Algemene Rekenkamer 1995). Some have existed for several centuries. These bodies have public authority to make decisions that are binding on citizens as well as for profit and nonprofit organizations. They are financed directly through government bodies or through levies. As in the UK such organizations carry out a diverse range of activities: financial transfers like issuing grants and subsidies and collecting fees and tariffs, supervision, control, inspections and quality assessments. Dutch examples include public universities and may be found in legal aid, students' loans and youth health and welfare.

Yet why have quangos been employed and how can one explain their growth? Historically, they can be seen as devices used not only to widen *governmental capacity* but also to enhance *governance* by: (a) allowing diversification of activities; (b) drawing in outsiders to assist the governmental process; and (c) protecting sensitive areas by allowing a degree of operational autonomy. Consequently one interpretation of quangos is as an organizational form that allows better governance by widening state strategic capacity without extending the mechanisms of control (Stone 1995). Another interpretation would be that governments have developed a variety of centralizing and bypassing strategies to circumvent political inertia (especially at local levels) in which quangos play an important part (Jenkins 1996).

Such sweeping interpretations, however, may oversimplify the complex history of quangos. As Skelcher observes, successive UK governments continued "to view quangos as a legitimate means to achieve policy objectives" although in many cases an overarching motive behind their creation appears to be their use to depoliticize situations by removing functions from directly elected bodies. Yet how can one explain the growth of UK quangos, especially the apparent sudden increase of their numbers in the 1980s? As we shall observe later, Skelcher favors an explanation in which quango growth is seen as a historical continuum characterized by distinct phases. The emergence of different quango types can be understood as the product of different combinations of ideological and managerial forces set within regulatory contexts. More generally the growth of locally appointed bodies may be seen as a strategy designed to regulate tensions between central and local government by creating new organizations that operate according to a centrally determined agenda (Payne and Skelcher 1997). However, while reducing pressures on central government such developments bring with them their own problems.

In the Netherlands, argues Aquina (1998), differing rationales have been offered to explain and justify the growth of quangos and these often neglect hidden or unstated agendas. Hence public pronouncements that the development of quangos will increase government efficiency and the quality of services may conceal different ideological agendas varying from an aversion to state interference in private life (Catholic and Protestant religious groups) through a fear of bureaucratization (social democrats) to a preference for market mechanisms (liberals).

Quangos are therefore part of governmental strategies of public sector re-design. While in the UK and the Netherlands the commitment to articulated theoretical positions and agendas has never been as strong as in (say) New Zealand (Boston et al. 1991), there can be no doubt that quangos have played an increasing role in reinventing government. This has, in turn, led to a growing interest in collaboration as a means of drawing together an increasingly fragmented governmental system. This is highlighted by Painter et al. (1997) in their work on the changing role of UK local government bodies in the 1990s. Noting that central policies successively eroded local authorities' powers and functions, these authors argue that local *government* has been replaced by a system of local *governance* where the role of authorities is essentially that of network management and where they can only succeed by developing collaborative strategies. For local authorities the achievement of objectives "depends as much on relationships with external agencies as what they can do directly" (Painter et al. 1997: 230-1). This involves collaboration with a variety of organizations, in particular quangos. Hence, the quango state is in part the collaborative state. Before returning to this issue, we examine briefly some statistics on quango growth.

Quangos in the UK and the Netherlands: Some Facts and Figures

Although data on quangos are rare (due perhaps to their lying outside the ambit of official statistics), we offer here some information on quangos in the UK and the Netherlands. The authoritative study, for example, by the Algemene Rekenkamer, the Netherlands Court of Audit (1995), revealed 545 quangos at the national level in 1993 employing more people (c. 130,000) than central government (c. 120,000). Between 1987 and 1993 the staffing of quangos in the Netherlands increased annually by an average of 30 percent. In 1993 the government spent over 38 billion DFL (18 percent of the total expenditure of the Dutch government). In the same year quangos spent approximately 160 billion DFL on running and program costs (Algemene Rekenkamer 1995: 15). A wider historical perspective also reveals that, until the 1980s, the growth of quangos in the Netherlands was paralleled by an increase in the size of central government bureaucracy, measured as departmental bureaus by Carasso et al. (1994) (see Figure 3.1). Since 1982 growth of bureaus has decreased, in line perhaps with the thesis of smaller government and slimming the state. However, what this data also demonstrates is that, similar to the situation in the UK, the use of quangos by the Netherlands government demonstrates a history that goes back over decades. Although, categorization and other problems mean that these figures need to be treated with caution, they reveal something of the scale of the quango state.

The work of Weir and others (Weir and Beetham 1999, Ch. 8; Weir and Hall 1994; Hall and Weir 1996) is the most detailed available on the state of UK quangos. Using the term Extra Governmen-

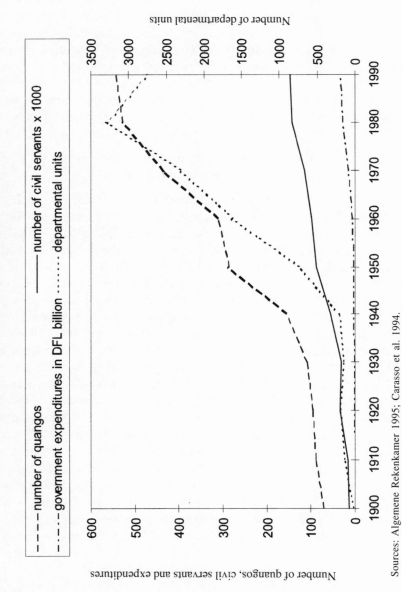

Figure 3.1
Development of Quangos in the Netherlands 1900-1990

– – – number of quangos ——— number of civil servants x 1000
·–·–· government expenditures in DFL billion ······· departmental units

Number of departmental units

Number of quangos, civil servants and expenditures

Sources: Algemene Rekenkamer 1995; Carasso et al. 1994.

tal Organizations (EGOs) as "executive bodies of a semi-autonomous nature that act effectively as agencies for central government and carry out government policies" (Weir and Hall 1994: 4), they list over 4,500 EGOs in 1994 and 1996 (see Table 3.1). Weir adds that a full count of quangos should include advisory and quasi-judicial bodies, central government agencies and police authorities—and would bring the total to nearly 6,500.

Table 3.1
Executive Quangos in the United Kingdom 1994 and 1997

	1994	1997
Executive Non Departmental Public Bodies (NDPB)	350	309
Northern Ireland Executive NDPBs	8	9
National Health Service bodies*	629	681
Local pubic spending bodies	4534	4682
Comprising:		
Career service companies*	-	91
City technology colleges*	15	15
Further education corporations*	557	560
Grant-maintained schools*	1025	1103
Higher education corporations*	164	175
Housing associations*	2668	2594
Local Enterprise Companies (Scotland)	23	22
Training and Enterprise Councils	82	81
Police authorities*	-	41
Total Executive Quangos	5573	5681

* Local authorities previously controlled or were represented on these
Source: based on Weir and Beetham 1999: 202

The value of the work of Weir and others lies not simply in the figures but also in the identification of the paucity of official information of the quango world. Official statistics, for example, claimed a reduction in NDPBs in the period 1979-1993 (from 2,167 to 1,389) (Greer and Hoggett 1995) and did not recognize 83 percent of Weir and Hall's EGOs, although the latter comprised nearly 70,000 appointed and self-appointed persons. Thus, Weir and Hall's analysis reveals the "new magistracy" (1994) of quango appointments and compares it with that of elected local government councillors (see Table 3.2). Yet more telling perhaps is the financial implication of these developments. Using longitudinal data, Hall and Weir (1996) argue that spending by EGOs increased by 45 percent in real terms during the period 1978/79-1994/95 (see Table 3.3) and represented nearly 30 percent of total government expenditure in 1992/93, far in excess of the official picture of £12 billion that "the government owns up to" (Weir and Hall 1996: 9).

Table 3.2

EGOs, the New Magistracy and Elected Councillors in the UK

	Executive NDPBs	NHS bodies	Non-recognized EGOs	Elected Councillors	Local Magistracy
England	234	557	3,981	20,852	51,148 - 55,953
Scotland	47	23	304	1,977	3,324 - 3,843
Wales	23	33	158	1,682	1,707 - 1,967
Northern Ireland	54	16	91	582	1,117 - 1,357
Total	358	629	4,534	25,093	57,296 - 63,120

Source Weir and Hall 1994: 10

Table 3.3

Expenditure by Government EGOs in the UK, 1978-95

	1978 1979	1984 1985	1989 1990	1994 1995
Executive quangos	17,940	12,710	14,870	20,840
National Health Service bodies	22,580	27,900	24,260	33,100
Other Extra-Governmental Organizations	1,120	1,180	1,109	6,462
Total	41,640	41,790	40,239	60,402

Source Hall and Weir 1996: 7

Analysis of the study of the Netherlands Court of Audit reveals that the growth of quangos in the Netherlands varies considerably between policy areas (see Figure 3.2). In 1993 the areas with the largest number of quangos were social affairs, justice, agriculture, welfare, housing and planning and education. In contrast, areas with the smallest number of quangos included governmental finance and home affairs. Between 1993 and 2000 the total number of quangos declined, mainly due to policy changes and definitional issues. The rate of establishments, however, accelerated: over 50 percent of all quangos in 2000 were established after 1993 (Van Thiel and Van Buuren 2001).

To facilitate a comparison with the number of quangos in the UK, Figure 3.3 shows the number of UK quangos at national level, in this case mainly executive NDPBs, per policy field in the UK in 1994-96. Although the sources indicate different numbers of quangos, they agree that the policy fields that have the largest numbers are the Scottish Office, Environment, Agriculture, National Heritage and the Welsh Office.

While the information outlined above on the growth of quangos in the Netherlands and the UK is not strictly comparable, both the financial and organizational importance of quangos as an instrument of government policy is clear. In particular, the 1990s were characterized by a significant change in the way quangos were employed by government making them, as Weir and Beetham (1999) argue, the politicians' "flexible friend." In 1997, in response to a growing general concern with standards of public life in the UK, which included the operation of quangos and the perceived patronage systems attached to these, reports by an independent committee (the Committee of Standards in Public Life 1995, 1996, 1997) made a number of recommendations concerning the accountability and corporate governance of quangos especially those operating at local level. Official responses to these reports (Cabinet Office 1996, 1997, 1998) acknowledged the need for action but argued that "the new diversity of quangos" was not only noteworthy for contributing to the flexibility of government but also offered a network of "smaller, more dedicated, organizations" that provided a more responsive and efficient service than local authorities or other more centralized bodies (Weir and Beetham 1999: 196-7). But this presumes that the effectiveness of quangos is being evaluated and that the fragmented state is, ipso facto, a good thing in terms of service delivery and policy implementation.

Such propositions remain to be tested. Further, what also requires examination is the effect on the state of quango growth in terms of policy delivery and the effectiveness of governance itself. We turn to this in the next section as we examine the moves towards collaborative government in the context of quango development particularly at local level.

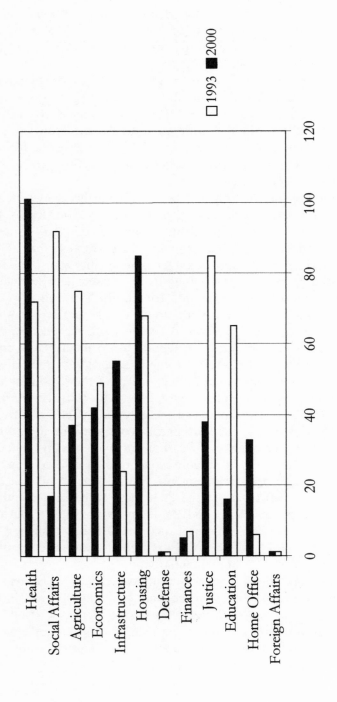

Figure 3.2
The Number of Quangos per Policy Field in the Netherlands, 1993 and 2000

□ 1993 ■ 2000

Source: Algemene 1995; Van Thiel and Van Buuren 2001

Quangos, Governance, and Collaboration

As was noted above, the use of quangos by national governments is far from new and they have been employed at different times, to assist a variety of political goals. What is new (or at least different) is the *growth* in their use, especially over the last two decades. An effect of this has been to redefine both the central and local state apparatus leading to a new system of governance. In the UK this is illustrated centrally by the creation of executive agencies, privatization strategies and the bypassing of elected local authorities (often via the creation of quangos) leading to what Rhodes (1998) has called the "hollow state" with its emphasis on network management. Meanwhile, the local state has been redefined with reduced functions for elected bodies and a proliferation of appointed quangos. Similarly, in the Netherlands the Polder Model indicates how social policy and economic goals have been achieved via new collaborative mechanisms that involve various agencies and arms of government and a wide variety of stakeholder groups. In these arrangements not only is the coordinative agency itself a quango but many, if not most, of the involved organizations are also quangos in their own right.

The emergence of appointed quangos has therefore redefined local political arenas, initially fragmenting them but leading to renewed efforts to design collaborative mechanisms that differ from traditional hierarchical command and control systems. Consequently, an unintended byproduct of the quango state, may be a greater reliance on collaborative mechanisms between quasi-autonomous bodies (Payne and Skelcher 1997; Skelcher 1998). But why have quangos emerged? As Skelcher notes, traditionally the creation of executive quangos reflected a trade-off between democracy and enterprise as governments sought to pursue objectives efficiently and with minimal resistance (e.g., public corporations). In other instances quangos were designed to facilitate policy implementation by locking in stakeholders with different perspectives (e.g., the former Manpower Services Commission in the U.K. which brought together government, industry and unions) or effect policy as though it was a business (e.g., the U.K. Training and Enterprise Councils). Yet, such descriptors hardly begin to explain quango growth. In an effort to provide greater explanatory power, we draw on Skelcher's ideological, managerial and regulationist perspectives.

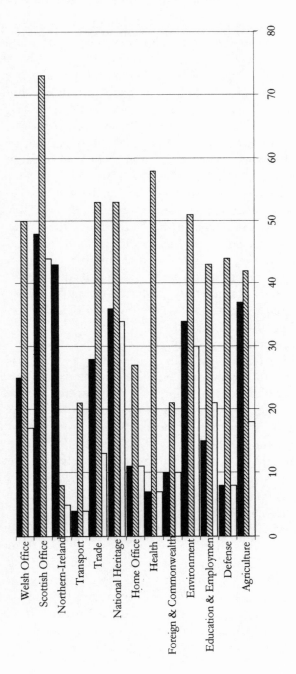

Figure 3.3
The Number of Quangos per Policy Field in the UK, 1995-96

☐NAO   ▨PERC   ■Hall & Weir

Sources: National Audit Office 1995; McConnel 1996; Hall and Weir 1996

An ideological interpretation of quango development views them as devices used by governments of the right to bypass problems, particularly those caused by elected bodies. In addition quangos can be seen as a way of strengthening state influence by appointment and patronage (e.g., in areas such as education). The managerialist thesis can, in part, be coupled with an ideological interpretation (indeed managerialism *is* an ideology) in the attachment to business-like and market mechanisms as an antidote to the perceived inefficiencies of public organizations dominated by monopolistic and vested interests (e.g., professionals, trade unions). However, managerialism has also had a broader attraction. Osborne and Gaeblar's (1993) reinventing government thesis, for example, conceptualized a smaller central state steering a differentiated set of entrepreneurial organizations sensitive to public service consumers rather than producers. Here quangos can be seen as devices that enhance managerial efficiency, focus more tightly on specific client groups and provide greater choice and accountability through markets (Waldegrave 1993).

Against such ideological and managerialist interpretations of quango growth, regulation theory offers a more complex set of explanations (Payne and Skelcher 1997; Skelcher 1998, Ch. 3). Briefly, regulation theorists argue that economic and political stability (the regime of accumulation) is sustained in various political and economic systems by the emergence of particular systems of regulation that stabilize the system and defuse points of pressure and protest. Generally, this perspective is offered as a macro-level interpretation of the changing pattern of Western economies and polities (e.g., the transition from Fordism to post-Fordism) and the survival of capitalism against successive economic and political shocks. However, it has been applied more particularly to UK local government by Stoker and Mossberger (1995) and by Skelcher (1998) in relation to quangos. Hence, Skelcher argues that the emergence of Urban Development Corporations (control of local economy) and TECs (control of the labor market) can be seen as regulatory mechanisms helping to sustain a central state in which "workfare" has replaced "welfare."

In the final analysis, Skelcher's assessment of these competing explanations of quango growth is that while none alone provide adequate accounts, combinations of ideological and managerialist approaches within a regulationist framework offer good interpretative possibilities (Payne and Skelcher 1997; Skelcher 1998, Ch. 3). This is linked to his argument that the development of quangos in the past forty years in the U.K. falls into three phases: first, pluralism and tripartism (1960s and 1970s) and, second, an ideological regime of competition (1980s) which was bolstered in the 1990s by the rise of managerialism that helped consolidate previous changes. Hence, in terms of a regulationist perspective, quangos are seen as part of a strategy to diffuse pressures on, and tensions in, the central state apparatus "by isolating the governance and management of public service from local democratic processes and hence developing a local state that was more aligned with emerging modes of regulation" (Skelcher 1998: 54). But, as we noted earlier, this solution provides a further problem—how to manage the fragmenting state. Thus, the development of quangos has frequently led to an increasing need for collaboration.

These issues of collaborative forces acting on the quango state emerge clearly from the work of Painter et al. (1997) on UK local government and non-elected agencies (NEAs). Drawing on extensive research into UK local authorities Painter et al. note that the decade of the 1980s saw the stripping away of many local authority functions via bypassing or privatization strategies and produced a system in which the capacity of local authorities to achieve objectives "depends as much on relationships with external agencies as what they can do directly" (1997: 230-1). Such restructuring of the local state and the proliferation of quangos has reshaped the politics of collaboration as both elected and unelected agencies find themselves part of a system of networked organizations. Although quangos have emerged in different areas and arenas (e.g., education, local economic development, health, housing), Painter et al. note that this disparate group of organizations have in common "their intimate involvement in the delivery of public services, pursuit of public policy goals and spending of public money" (1997: 230). Consequently, UK local government has found itself with decreasing control over its environment and, crucially, the resources (fiscal and otherwise) it requires to achieve its objectives. It is therefore forced into a set of inter-dependent relationships more detailed and complex than experienced before.

Yet while local authorities may be forced into collaborative relationships with appointed bodies the latter may need to link with other organizations in a search for legitimation and to achieve their goals. As we shall see, quangos, especially those of recent origin, are often performance-driven. Their centrally imposed targets and objectives bound in quasi-contractual agreements promote a tightly circumscribed view of the world. However, goal achievement is dependent on the cooperation of other agencies in a shifting and fluid local state. The problem for evaluation includes the habit of fragmented agencies attempting to evaluate activities in a particularistic way and leading to "a Babel of evaluative languages" (Day and Klein (1987: 206). Thus the growth of the quango state has produced a highly differentiated political order in which networks and the management of influence replace old certainties of hierarchical control. Central to this order are mechanisms of collaboration which raise their own questions of evaluation, especially that of cross-cutting activities in a results driven and highly differentiated world.

The work of Skelcher (1998) and Painter et al. (1997) deals with the emergence of UK local quangos in the 1980s and early/mid 1990s. This period is also the focus of the studies of Weir and others (Weir and Beetham 1999; Weir and Hall 1994; Hall and Weir 1996) on the nature of quango growth and the problems seen to arise from this (lack of transparency, accountability, patronage, etc.). Public concerns with the latter problems in the U.K. were partially responsible for the creation of the Committee on Standards in Public Life and its reports on the governance of quangos (1995, 1996). The then Conservative government reacted to this with efforts to democratize quango appointments and enhance the mechanisms of audit and accountability (Cabinet Office 1997).

The New Labor commitment was similarly to "open up" quangos (Cabinet Office 1997, 1998). Yet it did not attack the conception of quangos as a mechanism to promote political ends. Indeed, its efforts to attack wicked issues (social exclusion, health inequalities, community safety) brought a new breed of quangos (e.g., health action zones, education actions zones) to join-up government. However, recent research confirms that the design of collaborative mechanisms needs to identify problems with audit systems poorly equipped to take on board a cross-cutting agenda focusing narrowly on inputs rather than broadly conceptualized outputs (University of Birmingham 1999). Other research for the UK Department of Environment, Transport and the Regions (DETR), dealing specifically with "joined-up" activities in local government, identifies continuing tensions between stakeholders and evaluation systems dominated by short-term monitoring rather than long-term, comparative methodologies that connect with local client groups (University of the West of England/Office of Public Management 1999). More specifically, in a preliminary assessment of problems facing health action zones, Maddock (1999) has argued that crude performance measures threaten the modernization process in the absence of indicators of partnership and collaboration. This is seen to arise from governmental pressures (often exerted via civil servants) for individual organizations to focus on specific short-term targets and indicators. This leads to a neglect in developing cross-cutting measures of collaborative practice and partnership: "at present no government monitoring of best value services assesses collaborative, inter-departmental or inter-agency work" (1999: 8).

Hence, quangos, once seen as part of a problem of governance, are, in the UK at least, being employed as an agent of modernization in assisting collaborative government. Yet, despite their capacity to overcome some problems, quangos bring their own, including a particular perspective on how evaluation should be conducted and a danger of compromising accountability as the price for increased efficiency.

Auditing and Evaluating Quangos

When Sir John Bourn, head of the UK National Audit Office (NAO), gave evidence to the Nolan Committee investigating standards in UK public life, it emerged that the NAO did not audit over one-third of UK non-departmental public bodies due to limits on its terms of reference. As a consequence, an increasing area of UK public life was being excluded from the mechanisms of parliamentary accountability, audit and value-for-money evaluation (Bourn 1995a, 1995b). Bourn's arguments underline a dislocation in audit and accountability mechanisms that results directly from the fragmenting state. More fundamentally, they also point up executive-legislative problems of control in parliamentary systems. Audit and evaluation are part of a system of checks and balances on executive government. However, if audit can be circumnavigated or redefined, or evaluations cast in different terms the balance of power between executive and legislature can be shifted.

Dutch developments illustrate something of this problem. In 1990, the Dutch government prepared a position paper on functional de-

Table 3.4
**Compliance with Accountability Requirements of Quangos
at National Level in the Netherlands in 1993**

requirement	requirement in % of quangos (545)	Compliance in % of quangos (545)
to send annual report to department	63%	47%
to send annual account to department	49%	44%
to send accountant's audit of annual account to department	36%	34%
to send budget to department	44%	33%
to send annual plan to department	12%	11%
to send performance data to department	25%	20%
to send evaluation report to department	4%	1%

Source: Algemene Rekenkamer 1995

Table 3.5
**Openness and Accountability of Executive Quangos
in the United Kingdom: 1993 and 1997**

Obligation:	NDPBs 1993 %	NDPBs 1997 %	NHS 1993 %	NHS 1997 %	Local 1993 %	Local 1997 %	TOTAL 1993 %	TOTAL 1997 %
Publish annual report	56	69	39	100	41	87	42	88
Publish annual accounts	53	67	39	100	100	99	99	98
Full public audit*	53	81	100	100	22	44+	33	47
Subject to Ombudsman	35	49	100	100	0	1	14	14
Subject to Code of Openness	35	68	0	100	0	5	2	20
Public access to Register of Members' Interests	6	20	0	100	1	83	0	74
Public attends board or Committee meetings	6	12	46	18	0	1	5	3
Public access to agendas	0	0	20	19	40	40	35	31
Public access to policy papers	0	0	0	0	0	0	0	0
Public access to minutes	1	0	46	1	38	40	36	30
Public meetings	1	7	50	78	2	3	7	11

All figures refer to statutory or mandatory provisions of regulations, codes of practice, etc.
* by National Audit Office or Audit Commission
+ In addition in 1997, 2,498 registered housing associations were subject to partial public audit
[The authors have the impression that more of these bodies have become subject to the obligations listed: e.g., all NHS bodies provide public access to meetings, agendas and minutes.]
Source: based on Weir and Beetham 1999: 208

centralization that set out a number of important issues requiring regulation of new autonomous administrative authorities. In 1991, the Second Chamber of the Netherlands Parliament called for all such bodies to be reviewed in light of this framework. However, the study of quangos by the Algemene Rekenkamer (1995) demonstrated that significant departures from the government position paper in, for example, (1) establishing the case for task decentralization, (2) setting out a statutory basis for the performance of public tasks, and (3) regulation of funds according to parliamentary rules. Only 30 percent of the quangos delivered satisfactory evaluative reports, in other cases supervisory powers for requesting information were limited, and at least a third of the bodies were not obliged to submit an annual report. The Algemene Rekenkamer concluded that central regulation of such agencies needed to be tightened, that more information should be made available, and that the evaluation of the operations, performance and effectiveness of autonomous administrative authorities should be regularized. The government promised to study the findings and indeed acted upon them.

Both the UK NAO and the Netherlands Court of Audit therefore demonstrate common concerns with the consequences of fragmenting governmental systems in terms of systems of the scrutiny and operational transparency of many autonomous agencies. Tables 3.4 and 3.5 show the findings of the Algemene Rekenkamer (1995) and Weir and Beetham (1999) on national mechanisms for scrutiny and redress. Traditional scrutiny mechanisms are defined as a quango's exposure to public audit via official bodies such as the NAO or the Audit Commission or to the attention of the Ombudsman. Accountability and "openness" of quangos are assessed using a variety of criteria ranging from the publication of annual reports and accounts, through exposure to full audit, to various public entitlements to access and information.

Tables 3.4 and 3.5 suggest that in both countries scrutiny has been "fitful and inconsistent" with citizen redress limited and audit powers constrained. However, some progress may have been made in the UK following the reports by the Committee for Standards in Public Life (1995, 1996). As Weir and Beetham (1999) note, the Conservative government set out recommendations to improve standards of openness and accountability (but not public access!) to executive quangos. These included greater powers for the NAO and requirements for executive quangos to be reviewed on a regular basis. In addition, Citizens Charter criteria, including the requirement to develop regular systems of performance indicators were extended, if uneasily. While welcoming such moves, Weir and Beetham nevertheless argued that prior to the coming to power of the New Labor government in 1997 "there remained no uniform or adequate structure for auditing quangos large or small, national or local" (1999: 209-11). In the Netherlands, the study of the Netherlands Court of Audit led to an entire program to restore the primacy of politicians. New guidelines were published and all quango legislation and statutes are still being changed to meet these guidelines. Moreover, in 2001, the Dutch Cabinet presented a framework law on quangos to Parliament.

Aside from the wider questions of accountability two specific questions can be asked: do quangos deliver improved performance (i.e., are they evaluated and if so how?) and does the emergence of the quango and collaborative government pose new challenges for the nature and methodologies of program evaluation? In the UK, the first of these questions has been addressed by Skelcher (1998, Ch. 7) with specific reference to urban development corporations (UDCs), grant-maintained schools (i.e., those receiving funding directly from central government rather than through local authorities) and training and education councils (TECs). He notes that in terms of the overall challenges any evaluation of quangos faces difficult methodological problems such as establishing cause and effect and rigorous measurement of performance. Perhaps the greatest evaluative challenge, however, stems from the need for many quangos to forge collaborative relationships: "such an interactive environment produces a complex evaluative task and raises questions about the availability and adequacy of data on outputs and outcomes" (1998: 131).

Although there have been clear efforts in the U.K. to evaluate quango performance, most specifically in the case of TECs, where detailed sets of performance indicators have been developed to assist comparative assessment of effectiveness, the design of these measures and the interpretation of their results continue to be controversial. In part this arises necessarily where a quango's capability to deliver jobs, for example, may be determined by factors outside its control. This may include dependence on collaborative relationships. As a result, "it is perhaps more appropriate to consider the overall performance of the system—the particular arrangement of agencies, processes and relationships, than to try and isolate one individual component" (Skelcher 1998: 144).

This leads into a debate on the question of whether or not quangos may require new methods of evaluation especially as part of collaborative government. As we noted earlier, problems here include the inadequacy of conventional audit systems and the narrow focus of performance-driven evaluation systems designed to chart results in single organizations (e.g., TECs). There is also a wider issue in that certain collaborative arrangements are meant to act as developmental organizations adding value to services in a particular area over time. In this context, conventional evaluation mechanisms may be inadequate to deal with the dynamics of collaboration requiring instead the use of innovative evaluation methodologies such as the "realistic evaluation" approach (Pawson and Tilley 1997). Evidence of the need for this emerges in recent efforts to evaluate cross-cutting initiatives involving multiple participants in the UK such as health action zones (Judge et al. 1999). This will be examined in greater detail in the next section.

Evaluating Quangos as Collaboratives: New Challenges

In 1999, the New Labor government began to intensify its reform of the UK National Health Service and especially the abolition of the internal market introduced by the previous administration. The replacements included the system of General Practitioner Fundholders by Primary Care Groups (PCGs). The former were primary care practices of usually less than ten doctors that were allocated budgets for purchasing health care on behalf of patients. PCGs, however, are much larger groups of doctors, community nurses and social workers who are responsible for providing a more comprehensive service for populations of about 150,000. The change of policy is interesting for its (a) establishment of another cluster of quangos (the PCGs), (b) commitment to evaluation, (c) advocacy of collaboration and network management, and (d) implied shift from *command* and *contract* to a *communion* mode of governance.

A criticism of the British internal health care market in the late 1980s was its deliberate protection from evaluation on the grounds that the market was its own evaluator. The internal market had developed its own quangos including the health authorities that purchased care, yet, while accountable in traditional ways (through ministers) and made more transparent through mechanisms such as the Patients Charter, remained removed from much public scrutiny. This condition was remedied in part by the New Labor government in 1997 (Weir and Beetham 1999) that has been more willing to expose policies to evaluative scrutiny. Hence, the program of Primary Care Groups has been subjected to pilot studies while other initiatives (such as Health Action Zones, on which more below) are linked to broad ranging evaluations.

UK health care also illustrates moves towards collaborative government. The latter emerges from a perception of the need to join-up previously fragmented sectors of public life and from a belief that policy development and implementation will be enhanced by the synergies provided by cross-cutting organizations and programs in health, education and employment action zones. Current initiatives therefore appear to emphasize *communion* as a mode of governance and limit *contract* as represented by quasi-market mechanisms. Even if the contract state has not entirely been rejected (e.g., public-private partnerships) and there remain tensions as government seeks to retain controlling powers despite its rhetoric of collaboration, there is evidence of a growing move towards collaborative forms of government in which quangos, old and new, play a part. This shift appears to be influenced by (a) a belief that collaboration builds social capital, (b) that new organizational forms will share information and encourage joint learning, and (c) new forms will reduce the need for controls and reduce transaction costs. Thus, UK Health Action Zones, designed to attack problems of local health inequalities and social exclusion through multi-agency collaboration (Judge et al. 1999; Maddock 1999), reflect an assumption that such arrangements will energize communities to take responsibility for their own health care by developing flexible and responsive organizations that will adopt a whole systems approach. In theory, Health Action Zones are therefore meso-level quangos that draw together a variety of organizations (public and private) in a collaborative effort to maximize social capital and develop organizational leaning.

But what place does evaluation have in this new world? We have already noted that in the old *contract* and *command* cultures evaluation was either ignored or developed in a highly specified and formularized way that focused on inputs and targets determined by central policy mandates. However, the rhetoric of collaborative government with its advocacy of learning and policy development appears to require different evaluative procedures. In collaborative government the *function* of evaluation needs to change. Further, it would also appear that the *collaborative mechanisms* may require new methodologies to assess them, that is, modes of evaluation designed for the fragmented state are unlikely to be adequate to deal with collaborative arrangements. Thus, if we are concerned with the role of quangos in the new joined-up world it is necessary to examine the differences in evaluative systems that characterize the move from *contract* and *command* to *communion* modes of governance as these relate to the development and utilization of quangos.

British solutions to the problems of evaluating quangos before 1997 included strengthening performance audit to reflect the "true" performance of quango operations and developing systems to assess the effectiveness of quangos within a wider public sector performance framework that determines how activities relate to the broad scope of public policy and strengthens or weakens public accountability mechanisms (Leeuw 1995). However, even these measures may be inadequate to meet the challenges posed by the emergence of collaboration exemplified by *Modernising Government* as embracing policy as learning, the use of evidence in policy development and more rigorous evaluative processes (Cabinet Office 1999, Ch. 2). *Modernising Government* offers collaboration as a means of producing responsive and quality public services. Here traditional evaluative and audit mechanisms are seen as inefficient: individual agencies' performance targets and budgets can get in the way of them working together while audit and inspection processes may hinder cross-cutting working. Rather, an approach is required to focus on "assessing improvements in the effectiveness and value for money of whole systems, such as the criminal justice system, not just the constituent parts" (Ch. 4).

The rhetoric of such a *communion* mode of governance requires (a) the redesign of traditional evaluative systems to turn them into learning frameworks and (b) the reshaping of traditional audit regimes. In the UK this latter challenge is reflected in the activities of the Public Audit Forum, an independent body made up of the heads of the four national audit agencies which is cooperating with government to promote innovation in public service delivery. Noting that the move to collaborative government represents a significant change in the public service environment, the forum has committed itself to designing audit approaches that combine the search for value-for-money with a commitment to accountability. This will require new ways of working and new forms of accountability (Public Audit Forum 1999).

But what of quangos in the new collaborative arrangements? While there have been criticisms of the way quangos developed and were used under the *command* and *contract* modes of government, the quango form has not been rejected. Indeed, with the advocacy of collaborative government, quangos appear to have been redeemed and rejuvenated as a new meso-level agency designed to promote joined-up-government (e.g., Action Zones). Further, the effectiveness of the new quango is being evaluated by the establishment of national evaluation programs. Yet "traditional evaluation approaches are unlikely to provide completely satisfactory ways of learning" (Judge et al. 1999). Health Action Zones, for example, are intended to be catalysts for policy development, acting as learning organizations which have a responsibility not only to achieve health-related change but also to communicate results to and promote understanding in local communities (Judge et al. 1999).

The use of quangos to promote social capital and learning poses challenges to traditional evaluation mechanisms, their methodologies and criteria. In recent years the evaluative literature has reflected an increasing interest in stakeholder evaluation in situations such as this although writers such as Pollitt (1999) have issued warnings in going too far in this direction. In the case of the evaluation of HAZs, however, Judge et al. (1999) argue that traditional evaluation approaches do not reflect the complexities of collaborative government, arguing instead for the adoption of methodologies based on models of "realistic evaluation" (Pawson and Tilley 1997) and the "theories of change" approach promoted by the U.S. Aspen Institute (Connell et al. 1995). Only then will the complex relationships between national and local policy contexts and the dynamics of organizational learning that characterize this initiative be understood (Judge et al. 1999).

It would be premature to read too much into the case of Health Action Zones. It offers particular insights from which it may be dangerous to generalize. It does suggest, however, that quangos may be emerging from a state of disgrace to one of redemption as they are utilized to advance the cause of collaborative government. How we can test that through evaluation is another matter.

Conclusion

Although quangos may have the potential merit to redefine accountability in a clearer fashion and sharpen evaluative capacity (e.g., through a focus on clients and customers), there appears very little evidence so far that such potential has been realized. Indeed, until the mid/late 1990s, the development of quangos in the two contexts examined, the Netherlands and the UK, more frequently eroded evaluation mechanisms by effectively privatizing relationships, that is, quangos were used to remove activities from highly visible political arenas and the gaze of a variety of publics including audit and scrutiny bodies. Yet such problems are not inevitably the fault of quangos per se but a reflection of how these institutions have been utilized in the wider political system primarily to serve political goals on the basis of efficiency defined by central executive elites.

This set of tensions is recognized clearly by Skelcher (1998, Ch. 9) in his creation of a balance sheet listing quangos' strengths and weaknesses. In their favor they permit a focus on specific policies or tasks, allow greater expertise to be brought into government and have the potential to allow various groups of stakeholders to be incorporated into the policy process. Against this their use results in loss of representation (the democratic deficit), raises questions about accountability and reduces the transparency of state operations. In addition, Skelcher argues, they lead to the congested state: "an environment where high levels of organizational fragmentation combined with plural modes of governance require the application of significant resources to negotiating the development and delivery of public programs" (1998: 181-2). The resulting obscurity of the state is compounded not only by the frequent protection of quangos from the attentions of external audit bodies but also by problems of evaluation criteria and the "Babel" of evaluative languages arising from the lack of an agreed approach and methodology.

The congested state is also characterized by institutional fragmentation that symbolizes the shift from simple command structures to more complex networks of delivery (i.e., a shift from government to governance). In this, quangos, old and new, are perceived to have a place in the search for joined-up government as a way of enhancing social learning and increasing social capital. This role is a distinct challenge to audit and evaluation systems designed for more limited purposes, in particular unitary organizations with vertical accountability structures, narrowly defined results-based cultures that focus on single entities, and sectional producer interests. But, at the start of a new century this role does appear to be a feature of both the Netherlands and the UK and is enhancing a *communion* form of governance at the relative expense of *command* and *contract* as the hollow state requires a more skilled management of networks (Rhodes 1998).

As the Introduction to this volume points out, collaborative mechanisms offer opportunities for greater sharing of information, the building of social capital and crucially social learning. However, this may involve institutional design where transaction costs (in, for example, creating and maintaining networks) are in fact increased and where competing ideologies may lead to organizational politics that threaten attempts to fashion *communion* modes of governance. In this world, the quango, often the object of severe criticism, is being reinvented as a mechanism of policy integration. Yet such developments take evaluation into uncharted waters as evaluation's competing and conflicting functions may include ordering complexity, checking whether arrangements are working, action learning or the assessment of collaboration itself. Thus, there are dilemmas facing evaluation's functions and purposes aptly illustrated by debates over stakeholder evaluation (Pollitt 1999) and the objectives of action zones (Judge et al. 1999). However, these are not simply technical matters. Rather, as Skelcher has observed, they reflect wider political problems, especially the tensions relating to control and autonomy, that separate out *command* and *communion* modes of governance. Thus, the quango question illustrates some of the general problems underlying evaluation in collaborative government. Understanding these may require a closer examination of competing modes of governance and their power relationships.

References

Algemene Rekenkamer. 1995. *Zelfstandige bestuursorganen en ministeriele verantwoordelijkheid*. Tweede Kamer, vergaderjaar 1994-5, 24130, nr 3. Sdu, Den Haag.

Aquina, H. 1998. "The Netherlands," in T. Modeen and A. Rosas (eds.), *Indirect Public Administration in Four Countries*. Finland: Abo Akademi Press, pp. 281-99.

Barker, A. (ed.). 1982. *Quangos in Britain*. London: Macmillan.

Boston, J., J. Martin, J. Pallot, and P. Walsh (eds.). 1991. *Reshaping the State: New Zealand's Bureaucratic Revolution*. Auckland: Oxford University Press.

Bourn, Sir John. 1995a. (Chairman: Lord Nolan), *Standards in Public Life: First Report of the Committee on Standards in Public Life, Volume 2: Transcripts of Evidence*, pp. 214-19. Cm. 2850 II. London: HMSO.

Bourn, Sir John. 1995b. In evidence to Committee on Standards in Public Life (Chairman: Lord Nolan, Supplementary memorandum from the Comptroller and Auditor General, *Standards in Public Life: First Report of the Committee on Standards in Public, Volume 2: Transcripts of Evidence*, pp.513-23. Cm. 2850 II. London: HMSO.

Cabinet Office. 1996. *Objective Setting and Monitoring in Non-Departmental Public Bodies*. London: HMSO.

Cabinet Office. 1997. *The Governance of Public Bodies: A Progress Report*. Cm. 3557. London: HMSO.

Cabinet Office. 1998. *Quangos: Opening the Doors*. London: HMSO.

Cabinet Office. 1999. *Modernising Government*. Cm. 4310. London: HMSO.

Carasso, L. C., J. M. P. Koopmans, J. C. N. Raadschelders, and I. F. J. Voermans. 1994. "Organisatiedifferentiatie bij de rijksoverheid in historicsh perspectief," *Bestuurswetenschappen*, 6, 483-95.

Cole, M. 1998. "Quasi Government in Britain: The Origins, Persistence and Implications of the Term "Quango."" *Public Policy and Administration* 13(1), 65-78.

Committee on Standards in Public Life. 1995. *Standards in Public Life: First Report of the Committee on Standards in Public Life* (Chairman: Lord Nolan). Cm. 2850. London: HMSO.

Committee on Standards in Public Life. 1996. *Local Government Public Spending Bodies* (Chairman: Lord Nolan). Cm. 3270. London: HMSO.

Committee on Standards in Public Life. 1997. *Review of Standards of Conduct in Executive NDPSB, NHS Trusts and Local Public Spending Bodies* (Chairman: Lord Nolan). London: HMSO.

Connell, J. P., A. C. Kubisch, L. B. Schorr, and C. H. Weiss (eds.). 1995. *New Approaches for Evaluating Community Initiatives: Concepts, Methods and Contexts*. Washington DC: The Aspen Institute.

Day, P., and R. Klein. 1987. *Accountabilities*. London: Tavistock.

Greer, A., and P. Hoggett. 1995. "Non-elected Bodies and Local Governance," 17-53 in Council for Local Democracy (CLD), *The Quango State: an Alternative Approach*. Research Report No.10. February.

Greve, C. 1996. *Quangos in Denmark and Scandinavia: Trends, Problems and Perspectives*. PERC Occasional Paper No. 14. Sheffield: University of Sheffield.

Hall, W., and S. Weir. 1996. *The Untouchables: Power and Accountability in the Quango State*. The Democratic Audit of the United Kingdom. London: Charter 88 Trust.

Hogwood, B. W. 1995, "The 'Growth' of Quangos: Evidence and Explanations." *Parliamentary Affairs*, 48(2), 207-25.

Holmes, M., and D. Shand. 1995. "Management Reform: Some Practitioner Perspectives on the Past Ten Years." *Governance*, 8(4), 551-78.

Hunt, D. 1995. "Worthwhile bodies." *Parliamentary Affairs*, 48(2), 192-206.

Jenkins, S. 1996. *Accountable to None*. Harmondsworth: Penguin.

Judge, K., L. Bauld, M. Benzeval, and M. Barnes. 1999. *Health Action Zones: Learning to Make a Difference*. Personal Social Service Research Unit, University of Kent. Report submitted to Department of Health.

Leeuw, F. 1995. "Performance Auditing, New Public Management and Performance Improvement: Questions and Challenges." Paper presented to OECD symposium, *Performance Auditing and Performance Improvement in Government*, Paris. June.

Maddock, S. 1999. "Managing the Development of Partnerships and Modernisation." Paper presented to Public Administration Committee (PAC) Conference, Sunningdale, Civil Service College. September.

McConnel, H. 1996. *Quangos: Why do Governments Love Them?* Position paper, Workshop 3. PERC Quango Project, University of Sheffield.

Ministerie van Financien and Binnenlandse Zaken. 1997. *Doorlichting zelfstandige bestuurorganen*. Den Haag.

Organization for Economic Co-operation and Development (OECD). 1995. *Governance in Transition: Public Management Reforms in OECD Countries*. Paris: OECD.

Osborne, D., and T. Gaeblar. 1993. *Reinventing Government: How the Entrepreneurial Spirit is Transforming the Public Sector*. New York: Plume Books.

Painter, C., K. Isaac-Henry, and J. Rouse. 1997. "Local Authorities and Non-Elected Local Agencies: Strategic Responses and Organizational Networks." *Public Administration*, 75(2), 225-46.

Pawson, R., and N. Tilley. 1997. *Realistic Evaluation*. London: Sage Publications.

Payne, T., and C. Skelcher. 1997. "Explaining Less Accountability: The Growth of Local Quangos." *Public Administration*, 75(2), 207-24.

Pliatzky, Sir Leo. 1980. *Report on Non-Departmental Public Bodies* (Cmnd.7797). London: HMSO.

Pollitt, C. 1999. "Stunted by Stakeholders? Limits to Collaborative Evaluation." *Public Policy and Administration*, 14(2), 77-90.

Public Audit Forum. 1999. *The Implications for Audit of the Modernising Government Agenda*. London: Public Audit Forum.

Rhodes, R. A. W. 1998. *Understanding Governance: Policy Networks, Governance, Reflexivity and Accountability*. Buckingham: Open University Press.

Skelcher, C. 1998. *The Appointed State: Quasi-government Organizations and Democracy*. Buckingham: Open University Press.

Stewart, J. 1994. *The Rebuilding of Public Accountability*. London: European Policy Forum.

Stewart, J. 1995. *Reforming the New Magistracy: Choices to be Faced and Criteria to Guide*. Council for Local Democracy (CLD), *The Quango State: An Alternative Approach*. Research Report No. 10, pp. 5-16.

Stoker, G., and K. Mossberger. 1995. "The Post-Fordist Local State," in J. Stewart and G. Stoker (eds.), *Local Government in the 1990s*. Basingstoke: Macmillan.

Stone, B. 1995. "Administrative Accountability in Westminster Democracies: Towards a New Conceptual Framework." *Governance*, 8(4), 505-26.

University of Birmingham School of Public Policy. 1999. *Cross Cutting Issues in Public Policy and the Public Service*. University of Birmingham School of Public Policy.

University of the West of England and The Office of Public Management. 1999. *Cross Cutting Issues Effecting Local Government*. University of West of England and Office of Public Management.

Van Thiel, S., and M. W. Van Burren. 2001. "Ontwikkeling van het aantal zelfstandige bestuursorganen tussen 1993 en 2000: zijn zbo's 'uit' de mode?" in *Bestuurswetenschappen*, 55(5), 386-404.

Waldegrave, W. 1993. *The Reality of Reform and Accountability in today's Public Sector*. London: Public Finance Foundation.

Weir, S. 1995. "The State, Quasi Governments and Accountability." Paper presented to the UK Public Administration Committee (PAC) annual conference. September.

Weir, S., and D. Beetham. 1999. *Political Power and Democratic Control in Britain*. London: Routledge.

Weir, S., and W. Hall. 1994. *Ego Trip: Extra Governmental Organizations in the UK and their Accountability*. Democratic Audit of the United Kingdom. London: Charter 88 Trust.

4

The Politics of Evaluating Government Collaboration with the Third Sector

Robert Schwartz

Collaborative government entails changes in management and accountability relationships that affect the nature of ties among citizens, politicians, government officials, service providers and consumers. Over the past thirty to forty years evaluation has emerged as an important tool for enhancing the management and accountability of government programs. Yet political considerations have been shown to impede the efficacy of evaluation. This chapter explores the effects of government-third sector collaboration on the politics of evaluation. Is collaboration with third sector organizations likely to make evaluation more or less attractive for various players? Do politics of evaluation arguments gain or lose strength when addressing collaborations between government and third sector? What are the consequences of collaboration for the potential of evaluation to enhance management and accountability relationships?

The exploration of the implications of government-third sector collaboration is progressive. It starts with general issues of evaluation in the third sector, continues with issues in evaluating general collaborative efforts and finally looks at what happens to evaluation when government collaborates with third sector organizations. The conceptual analysis is bolstered with empirical evidence from Israeli and international experience.

Evaluation theories tell us that evaluation is not a particularly attractive activity for most players, under most conditions. The politics of evaluation literature strongly suggests that public sector managers will not willingly assess the execution and outcomes of their programs. The politics of evaluation theory has been set down most

83

notably in the 1970s and 1980s in Aaron Wildavsky's classic, *The Self-evaluating Organization* (Wildavsky 1972), in numerous publications by Carol H. Weiss (Weiss 1970, 1973, 1988) and in Dennis Palumbo's book, *The Politics of Program Evaluation* (Palumbo 1987). Recently, Eleanor Chelimsky has observed increasing political pressures aimed at preventing the conduct of an evaluation, moderating evaluation questions and even softening or deleting particular conclusions (Chelimsky 1995).

Briefly, theory postulates that administrators' interests in organizational stability, budget maximization and the promotion of a favorable image contribute to a general desire to refrain from conducting evaluations that might show agency programs in a bad light. The politics of evaluation literature further tells us that the preponderance of political appointments at senior agency levels and the resulting short tenure of top management officials diverts attention to short-term opportunities for political gain and away from long-term issues which might be addressed through program evaluation (Weiss 1973; Bowsher 1991).

Yet program evaluation is a growing endeavor in many countries and in many supernational organizations—notably the World Bank and the European Community (Rist 1990; Gray, Jenkins and Segsworth 1993; Leeuw, Rist and Sonnichsen 1994; Chelimsky 1995). This growth appears to contradict Wildavsky's contention that there can be no such thing as a "self-evaluating organization." However, much of this growth can be attributed to regulations that require government agencies and grant recipients to evaluate their programs. Schwartz (1998) notes further that much of the evaluation effort in Israel tends to be internally focused, technocratic, isolated from senior decision makers, from central executive agencies and from legislative oversight. These evaluations may indeed improve the functioning of government programs, but they generally ignore root questions about program impact.

It has been suggested that provision of public services through third sector organizations may be the best way to resolve what has been called the crisis of accountability in modern government. Several commentators note that a general perception of government being out of control has resulted in a crisis of accountability, potentially endangering the fabric of contemporary democratic government (Normanton 1966; Smith 1971; Crozier et al. 1975; Janowitz 1976; Yates 1982). Among the responses to this perceived crisis of accountability have been efforts to shrink the public sector, privatizing, and enlarging the third sector. There have also been efforts directed at mechanisms of accountability, such as performance reporting, program evaluation, improved legislative oversight, and strengthened state audit.

Problems associated with the politics of accountability mechanisms (i.e., oversight and evaluation) (Wildavsky 1972; Rosen 1986; Palumbo 1987; Weiss 1988; Jenkins and Gray 1990) have led to suggestions for downward accountability, where local communities of service users would hold accountable community organizations (Day and Klein 1987; Smith and Lipsky 1993; Taylor 1996). A recent initiative in the UK—the Voluntary Sector Compact—seeks to implement these suggestions. Ross and Osborne (1999) delineate the rationale behind the program: local government partnerships with voluntary and community organizations (VCO) are seen in government policy documents as essential to the development of communities in which citizens participate positively in the democratic process and policy is formed in a "bottom-up" rather than a "top-down" manner.

One critic, however, takes much of the air out of the argument that third sector organizations can provide meaningful downward accountability:

> Both the Right and Left, however, usually fail to distinguish between different forms of voluntarism: between volunteers as unpaid staff, and as peer self-help, and between mutual aid associations, neighborhood or community-based organizations, and service bureaucracies staffed by professionals. This confusion is part of the mystique of voluntarism, in which its virtues are exaggerated and contrasted with what are believed to be the inherent vices of government or the market. (Kramer 1993:10)

An immediate implication of using the third sector as an alternative to top-down accountability mechanisms is that there ought to be less demand for program evaluation. Where local communities of citizens are actively involved in policy formulation and execution, by way of voluntary community organizations there might be less perceived need for formalized accountability-oriented evaluation. Indeed, the literature suggests that without top-down requirements, effectiveness evaluation will not likely be done. Hans-Ulrich Derlien, suggests, for example, that unless the conduct of evaluation studies becomes institutionalized, their occurrence and then certainly their use tends to be random (Derlien 1990).

This chapter explores these and related implications for evaluation of different types of collaboration between government and the third sector. First, however, it is necessary to set out an idea of what we mean by both "third sector" and by "collaboration" with it.

The Third Sector and Collaboration

Terms used to describe third sector organizations include voluntary, not-for-profit, charitable, eleemosynary, quasi-governmental, nongovernmental and tax-exempt. The purported meaning of third sector is that the bodies are somewhere between the private and public sectors. The medley of terminology parallels the variety of organizational structure, as well as relations with clients, sources of funds, and mechanisms of supervision and control. Expectations, perhaps romanticized, are that these bodies provide opportunity for self-help, creativity, effectiveness, and efficiency, as well as passing to some other body responsibilities that might otherwise fall upon already strained officials and financial resources of government (Salamon and Anheier 1992).

Salamon et al. (1998) have wrestled with the problems of collecting data about the ill-defined third sector. Their measures show that third sector employment (not including volunteers) accounts for an average of 4.9 percent of total employment in twenty-two countries. Israel's third sector employs 9.3 percent of all workers placing it fourth on the list following Holland (12.4 percent), Ireland (11.5 percent) and Belgium (10.5 percent). Following Israel are the United States (7.8 percent), Australia (7.2 percent) and Britain (6.2 percent). The definition of a "not-for-profit" is also problematic, especially as the concept is applied cross-nationally. According to data collected by Israel's Central Bureau of Statistics, the value of not-for-profit services in Israel increased by 5.5 percent annually during the 1990-96 period, and amounted to about 10 percent of gross domestic product in 1996 (Central Bureau of Statistics 1998).

Salamon (1995) attributes the increasing significance of third sector activity to several political, social and economic developments over the past two decades: the failure of the Welfare State in the West and the downfall of socialist regimes in Eastern Europe and in the Third World; the rise of new social forces, especially organized self-expression; recognition of the inadequacy of the neo-liberal free market in solving various economic and social problems. Recent public management reforms, which have inter alia promoted market or market-type environments for public service provision, have encouraged third sector organizations to compete alongside private sector enterprises and government agencies for contracts. A significant proportion of third sector activity has come to involve some sort of collaboration with government.

The nature of government-third sector collaboration can be seen as running on a continuum ranging from that of principal-agent relationship to that of communion type partnership. Collaboration in the framework of new public management takes the form of principal-agent relationship in which the government maintains control of the policymaking process and uses third sector organizations as service providers (Grutch 1990). More recent initiatives, such as the "third way" of the current Labour government in Britain, seek to develop communion type partnerships between government and third sector organizations. The Voluntary Sector Compact launched by the British government in November 1998, "seeks to establish 'undertakings' for both government and the VCO sector which will provide the basis for real partnership in the formulation and implementation of public policy" (Ross and Osborne 1999).

Government-third sector relations in Israel run the gamut of the collaboration continuum. Principal-agent type relations characterize a growing tendency to contract-out much service provision to third sector as well as private sector organizations. A subset of principal-agent relations is the highly developed system of grants. If in contracting arrangements, the government maintains control of policymaking and relinquishes its role as service deliverer, in grants arrangements the government often relinquishes even much of its policymaking role and has much less control over service delivery.

Partnership arrangements are not new to Israel. Voluntary organizations played a central role in providing services prior to Israel's independence. Gidron (1992) calls this the "collaborative-partnership" era and Kramer (1981)—"the close partnership" era. For various reasons the new state opted to leave large areas of services in the hands of these organizations, including: most health care; pre-schooling; much of secondary education; ultra-orthodox education; universities; settlement activities; and many welfare services for the aged, the handicapped and the chronically ill. Government offices collaborated with these organizations, in varying degrees, in both policy formulation and program execution. Over the years, the government has engaged in numerous additional collaborative arrangements in areas such as: nature education, culture and road safety.

In Israel, collaborative arrangements of the communion type vary in the degree of formalized collaboration-shared governance, and written agreements on governance and financing (Auditor General of Canada 1999). For example, formalized collaborative arrangements guide policymaking, governance and funding of universities. In many other cases collaboration is rather implicit and indirect as when voluntary organizations such as the Histadrut Sick Fund were controlled by the political party that dominated government (Gidron 1992, 1997).

Evaluation in the Third Sector

Several characteristics of third sector organizations suggest substantial obstacles to the conduct of evaluation. Not all third sector organizations display all of these characteristics. Overall, however, one or more of these characteristics will apply to most third sector organizations.

Many third sector organizations are shoestring operations, operating on minimal—hand-to-mouth—budgets with little or no resources for such "staff" work as performance assessment, evaluation and research. Much third sector activity is with human service provision (Salamon et al. 1998). Such organizations tend to "repel" evaluation for at least two well-documented reasons: their performance is difficult to evaluate; and their staff tend to be of the "giving" type, rather than the analytical-economic type (Schwartz 1998).

Altruism has traditionally been a defining characteristic of the third sector. Donors tend to support third sector organizations because of the worthiness of the cause that they serve and because of the voluntary nature of their work. They often see no need for performance measures and feel uncomfortable about holding committed staff and volunteers to account. In other words, the prestige of being a donor to a valued cause gets in the way of looking closely at the activities being supported. Brett (1993), in exploring altruism as a motivating factor argues that it should reduce, although not eliminate, the need for surveillance of voluntary agencies. Lipsky and Smith contend that the perceived worthy missions of voluntary agencies limit the exercise of both external and internal accountability mechanisms:

> The mission orientation at times tends to be matched by disregard for organizational control mechanisms. Historically, accountability systems in nonprofit organizations have been crude or nonexistent. Performance indicators were lacking. Executive direc-

tors were in relatively weak positions to monitor their organizations' financial status; administrative functions tended to be underfunded. Trustees tended to be intrusive, but not excessively worried about organizational efficiency. (1989-90: 642-3)

An Israeli study of accountability in the third sector lends support to these claims. Interviews with representatives of Diaspora-based foundations (i.e., Jewish organizations outside Israel) and the agencies they fund revealed several issues concerned with the politics of accountability. Donors like to feel good about their contributions. They want to believe that their money is being used by good people for good purposes. Often they decide to support an organization because of its reputation, because of the persuasiveness of people who represent the organization, or because of impressive brochures. Donors provide continuing funds based on unaudited reports which rely on anecdotal evidence of program success. Some foundations that have started conducting evaluations of program operation find that reality is quite different from image. Yet one foundation representative noted that speaking truth to blinded donors does not always change their funding decisions (Schwartz and Sharkansky, 2000).

If foundations have trouble using evaluation, recipients of their funds may have even better reason to forego the pleasure. One recipient of funds from a large overseas foundation complained bitterly of her experience with evaluation. Naively, she initiated formative evaluations of four funded programs. When the evaluation results showed serious deficiencies in program design and accomplishments she justified her desire to "moderate" the report saying that she needed to compete for funds with many other program providers, none of whom had evaluated their programs. It would be unfair, for her to lose funds just because she had initiated an evaluation which in the end made her programs look bad to foundation representatives.

Some empirical evidence of the limited extent of evaluation efforts by donors comes from a 1996 study of 170 donor organizations in Britain (Ashford and Clark 1996). This study found that 28 percent of donor organizations collect no information at all once grants were given and another 30 percent never or rarely conduct evaluation of information collected. Even those donors who do evaluate tend to focus their evaluations on ensuring that grants are used for requisite purposes, finding out about work funded and identifying wasted resources; little impact of evaluation was found.

Plantz, Greenway and Hendricks (1997) note that in the United States the nonprofit sector has been measuring certain aspects of performance for twenty-five years or more. During that period, the scope of performance measurement has expanded to address such issues as financial accountability, program products or outputs, adherence to standards of quality in service delivery and client satisfaction. By 1990, the nonprofit sector was commonly measuring all of these aspects of performance except client satisfaction (Taylor and Sumariwalla 1993) and these measures yielded critical information about the services that nonprofits were providing. Increasingly, however, there has been recognition that, while such measures show how much effort has been generated for how many individuals, they reveal nothing about whether this effort has made any difference—whether anyone is better off as a result of the service.

Evaluation of Collaborative Efforts

Toulemonde et al. (1998) delineate some key issues facing evaluation of collaborative efforts. They note that obstacles to evaluation stem foremost from the fact that in collaborative efforts, program objectives are based on fragile compromises between partners with different political, social and economic aims. As a result it is difficult for evaluators to find clear and simple evaluation criteria in official documents and to get partners to clarify their objectives.

In collaborative arrangements, it is generally a nongovernmental agency that actually provides services. Sharkansky (1979) has suggested that accountability of agencies at the margins (contractors and special authorities) tends to be weak. Where the actual service deliverer is an agency at the margins of the state and/or not controlled by the government, it may not be clear who ought to be responsible for evaluation and oversight, and such activity may be overlooked. The relative autonomy granted to agencies at the margins reduces legislative access to evaluative information necessary for oversight. Where such agencies are partially controlled by nongovernment entities, the legislature may leave oversight responsibility in their hands or in the hands of the program's board of directors.

A number of empirical studies support Sharkansky's contention that evaluation of collaborations with agencies at the margins will be less prevalent than evaluation of programs provided directly by government agencies. Reagan (1975) demonstrated that grant-in-aid programs funded by the federal government and provided by states or local authorities were less subject to accountability than direct provision programs. Friedberg (1985) found that the incidence of state audit is lower in government corporations and in local authorities than in government ministries. And Schwartz (1998) assessed the incidence of evaluation for 39 direct provision and 24 indirect provision programs in four social service agencies. The mean incidence of evaluation was 2.4 for direct provision programs and 1.2 for indirect provision programs, conforming with the expectation that programs delivered collaboratively with agencies at the margins exhibit a lower incidence of evaluation.

Where funding and provision are separated there is a chance that it may not be clear who is responsible for the program. The local service provider may assume that the program funder has assessed the effectiveness of the program—otherwise why would it provide funding? The funder of the program may feel that it is the responsibility of the service provider to evaluate the service provided. Research on third sector accountability has suggested that collaborative efforts are often characterized by multiple providers of funds or organizations with formal responsibilities for oversight (Taylor 1996). As a result, each provider may rely on the other to perform oversight, with the result that little oversight occurs. A survey of foundation-funded organizations working in the field of promoting religious pluralism and Jewish identity revealed that they have numerous sources of funds. One organization listed nine sources for its $200,000 budget. In these cases each source provides a relative small proportion of the overall organization budget, and thereby has little incentive to concern itself with evaluation (Schwartz and Sharkansky 2000).

Evaluation of Collaboration with the Third Sector

Evaluation of government-third sector collaborations faces the obstacles encountered by evaluation of third sector activity, evaluation of collaborative efforts in general and some "value-added" (or value-subtracted) obstacles when these two are combined. Important in this exploration are the reasons behind establishing the collaboration. Two modes of reasons might be distinguished: positive and negative. The positive includes civil society arguments and the negative avoidance of regulations governing government work. The obstacles to evaluation in the latter are obvious. Often collaborative arrangements are set up particularly to avoid regulations governing government work. Collaboration provides opportunities for misuse, abuse and cronyism—in which few, if any, have an interest in evaluating. The obstacles in the case of positive reasons for collaboration concern the altruism argument as will be shown below in the example of SPNI (Society for the Protection of Nature in Israel). This shows that speaking truth to power is difficult when it comes to perceived "do good" organizations.

Contracting

Ostensibly contracting arrangements provide ample opportunity for evaluation based on performance measures specified in contracts. Moreover, competition among service providers is thought to ensure efficient and effective performance of contractors. Those who do not meet performance objectives stand to lose their contracts. Yet several studies note significant obstacles to evaluation in contracting arrangements—obstacles that are particularly salient to contracting with third sector organizations. Kettl (1993: 171) notes, for example, that, "most social service contracts tend to be negotiated, not put up for bids. It is difficult to design performance contracts for evaluating the work of social service contractors because their goals tend to be hard to define and results hard to measure. Contracts tend therefore to focus on input or process measures."

Government agencies often seem unwilling to invest in evaluating the performance of contractors (Lipsky and Smith 1989-90; Sharkansky 1979) for a number of political reasons. Contracts may be given to providers with close family or political ties with agency heads. Political agency heads are more interested in quick program start-ups than in monitoring the performance of existing contracts. And government agencies sometimes face contractors who hold a monopoly in providing certain services. Smith and Lipsky (1993: 198), for example, illustrate how the monopoly of the "High Street Boys Club" restricts the flexibility of public officials to critically assess performance or cut funds, "the need to retain a capacity to treat certain classes of clients creates an incentive to continue contracting with important providers.... When they consider cutting funds for the Boys Club, public officials also must confront the political pressures, particularly from powerful community supporters."

Perhaps as a result of these political considerations, government capacity to evaluate the performance of contractors is quite limited.

Kettl (1993: 174) reports that because there are few staff member or other resources devoted to monitoring social service contracting in American state and local governments, "oversight is virtually non-existent." Smith and Lipsky (1993: 200) summarize the situations as follows:

> Even if the public agency could know what it wanted, it would be defeated in monitoring the providers. While government contracting for services has vastly increased in volume, the program auditing capacity of the public sector has not kept up. Contractors typically file reams of reports which, except for basic fiscal information, are ignored. There is little independent auditing of the accuracy of program numbers submitted, and hardly any capacity to assess the effectiveness of contractors' programs. Thus the public sector may not know what it is purchasing even when it can define what it wants.

Similarly, a 1997 General Accounting Office (GAO) report on performance monitoring found that key impediments to successful performance monitoring include: resistance by contractors to spending money on data collection; deliberate misreporting; and difficulties in ascertaining the quality, completeness and comparability of data.

The following example, from the Israeli experience, demonstrates some of the obstacles to evaluation in contracting arrangements with third sector organizations. The Ministry of Labor and Social Affairs contracts with a third sector organization to provide ambulatory services for treating alcoholics. A 1994 State Comptroller's Report found that: the contract did not specify what is included in the treatment; the ministry did not carry out professional inspection and evaluation of the quality of treatment; detoxification was not medically supervised. Furthermore, the contractor did not collect data on dropout rates from the treatment program, on hospitalization rates or on recidivism. In the absence of such data, notes the comptroller, the ministry is unable to evaluate the effectiveness of treatment (State Comptroller 1994). This not atypical example of government-third sector contracting illustrates how basic trust in well-respected third sector contractors combined with an undeveloped government capacity for monitoring makes evaluation a difficult, if not impossible, task.

Grants

Grants arrangements are a subset of principal-agent type collaboration in which the principal is at an even greater evaluation disadvantage than in contracting. Principal-agent theory contends that the extent of a principal's stake in an organization will determine the extent to which the principal will invest in surveillance of the agent. In a number of grants arrangements, government agencies generally have a relatively small stake in the activities of any given grantee for two reasons. The government agency gives a large number of relatively small grants to a large number of grantees. And the government grant constitutes a relatively small proportion of the income of each grantee. Under these circumstances, the willingness to invest in evaluation will be small.

Additional characteristics of many grants arrangements further decrease the likelihood of evaluation. Needy organizations lack basic resources for conducting evaluations. Do-good grantees are perceived as not being in need of evaluation. And some organizations receive grants, not because of their capacity for effective performance, but to support family or political cronies.

Israeli government attempts at instituting effective monitoring and evaluation of grants have met with limited success. The Knesset enacted directives in 1992 for the orderly provision of government grants to third sector organizations. The directives require that government ministries: set objective criteria for making grants; establish grants committees responsible for equitable distributions; and oversee grantees to ensure that they fulfil grant conditions and use the grant for the intended purpose (State Comptroller 1998: 256). Despite these directives, State Comptroller and newspaper reports are rife with descriptions of how grantees abuse funds. Common practices include: hiring family members and political cronies and paying them high salaries; withdrawing large sums from the bank and making cash payments that cannot be traced; obtaining funding from two or more government agencies for the same activity; and lying about numbers of participants and activities.

In 1997, a ministerial committee issued directives requiring the grants committees of the ministries to hire accountants to check the financial affairs of grantees and internal auditors to conduct operational audits of the use of grants to achieve objectives. The results of this directive are not yet apparent. One study of the decisions taken by these committees suggests a flaw in their structure. "The clerks who serve on grants committees report to the minister and rely on him for their advancement. Their ability to protest the favoring of an association depends on their willingness to endanger their standing in the ministry" (DeHartog 1998: 98).

Evaluative information that demonstrates ineffective operations often reveals the need for additional funding. In a country where many public services suffer from chronic under-funding this may act to decrease the propensity to evaluate. In 1984, for example, the Ministry of Education stopped conducting national achievement tests because it was unable to fund improvements needed in underachieving schools (Razel 1996). Ralph Kramer (1993: 21) finds that similar rationale may be behind the lack of evaluative information about grants in Israel: "Some of the dilemmas in securing accountability were epitomized for me in the reply of an official to my question as to why the government seemed to require so little information from the VNPOs it funded: 'If we knew more, we'd have to pay more.'"

Communion

Communion, as defined in the introduction to this volume, involves joint arrangements regulated by shared values and interests. Communion entails mutual dependence and prevents flexibility and the advantages of market mechanisms (Smith and Lipsky 1993). Gone is the government agency's ability to easily terminate contracts with inefficient or ineffective providers. Gone, too, is the independent voice of the third sector agency as a watchdog over government activity. In their place, government and third sector partners painstakingly develop program objectives and modes of operation which reflect careful compromises between the interests of the parties (Toulemonde et al. 1993). Both partners have vested interests in portraying the program as a success. Neither side has an interest in evaluation which is liable to rock the carefully balanced boat. This rings particularly true when individuals reap personal benefits from the collaborative effort. Where government collaborates with high prestige third sector organizations, there is even less incentive to evaluate.

A communion-type relationship between the Israeli Ministry of Education and a not-for-profit teachers college shows how personal benefits are likely to inhibit meaningful evaluation. The Ministry of Education's Technological Education Department and the Holon Center for Technological Education have a long-standing collaborative arrangement for determination and implementation of policy. Practically all endeavors in technological education are carried out by way of the Holon Center. The State Comptroller (1995), criticized this arrangement on three points:

1. The absence of a bidding process meant the loss of opportunity to maximize price and quality of service.

2. The dependence of the ministry on the Holon Center prevented the ministry from conducting effective surveillance of the work (the Comptroller observed, for example, that the director of the ministry's Technological Education Division sat on the Board of Directors of the Holon Center and in this capacity faced a conflict of interests between his duty to advance the needs of the Center and his duty to protect ministry interests).

3. Senior officials in the ministry benefited personally from the collaborative arrangement in that they received perks from the Holon Center including secretarial assistance, office space and office equipment.

Government representation on boards of directors is an accountability mechanism common in Israeli collaborative efforts. Active participation by government representatives on boards of directors of collaborating third sector organizations provides ample opportunities for: joint decisions regarding policy directions, oversight of implementation and assuring fiscal and program accountability. At the same time, government directors risk conflicts between their duties to look after the best interests of both the government and the third sector organization. Because government appointed directors often gain personal advantage in the form of prestige and perks, there is a good chance that they will prefer organization interests over government interests. In an attempt to avoid such situations, the Ministry of Finance issued a directive restricting government representatives from membership on boards of directors to cases in which the government controlled at least 50 percent of the seats. The next example shows that there is a certain "catch-22" in this situation.

In communion-type collaborations with some third sector organizations of high prestige, there may be an assumption that formal accountability is unnecessary. The Society for the Protection of Nature in Israel (SPNI) has done a good job of selling itself to the Israeli public and the government. It is by far the largest nature organization in the country. It runs 23 field schools and 14 community learning centers, provides nature hikes for pupils and adults, and operates several other programs of nature education and conservation. Policy and financial decisions concerning nature education and nature hikes are made collaboratively in joint Ministry-Society forums. An annual grant from the Ministry of Education, primarily for nature education directed at school groups, amounts to about 25 percent of the Society's budget. In 1997, however, the State Comptroller's evaluation of SPNI educational nature activities reported that SPNI work was largely ineffective and inefficient. Moreover, the Comptroller criticized the ministry for exercising little oversight over the use of its funds. In response, ministry officials explained that the society was a well-respected organization with support from powerful figures. In other words, the ministry shied away from any type of evaluation of SPNI activities for fear of up-setting prominent public figures who would rush to defend this do-good organization from ill-intentioned ministry officials. They also noted that cessation of ministry representation on the Board of Directors—in accordance with the above mentioned Ministry of Finance directive—made oversight more difficult (State Comptroller 1997).

The final example shows how communion-type collaboration can affect the nature of evaluation. Project Renewal is a collaborative program that has involved overseas donors, Israeli local authorities, Israeli central government officials, and the quasi-governmental Jewish Agency in a large-scale urban renewal effort. The project was accompanied by a series of evaluations commissioned by a committee with representatives of the various partners. The resulting evaluation reports proved to be "too polite," "poor olive oil," went "too far to please" (Dery 1990). Dery further notes that "In private (personal interviews with four key Renewal officials) the criticism was a bit harsher. The committee, they all agreed, produced only the kind of reports that were useful for fund raising and political rhetoric." Dery's respondents remarked that the committee was "too cautious," "very diplomatic"; "any politician could quote its findings to show how really great the project is." Lazin (1994) lends further support to Dery's suggestion that evaluation of this collaborative project was less than objective—revealing that two of the major evaluation studies were conducted by people and organizations who were dependent on Project Renewal for salaries and contracts.

It seems that the fragile relationships among the collaborating parties led them to avoid evaluation that might rock the boat too much. All of the collaboration partners were more interested in continuing the relationship than in delving into difficult issues which more cutting evaluation reports would undoubtedly have raised.

They preferred to use evaluation findings to support the public image of the collaborative activity rather than for (much needed) program improvement. While this type of political evaluation is common in non-collaborative programs as well, it seems that collaboration increases its likelihood.

Discussion

Collaboration with the third sector is presented by some as a way to promote healthy democratic culture. Supporters of this "third way" envision local communities of citizens participating actively in third sector organizations that collaborate closely with government bodies in setting policy and in delivering public programs. Imbued with the spirits of charity, volunteerism and communitarianism, these third sector organizations command a high degree of respect and trust from their government partners and from the wider citizen body. This scenario might be seen as largely precluding the need for formal accountability focused program evaluation as programs are subject to ongoing downward accountability to active citizen-volunteers.

This vision of government-third sector collaboration appears to be more a dream for the future than a portrayal of current reality. The literature paints a rather different picture of the nature of the third sector and its relationship with government. International data show that much of the third sector is made up of professional bureaucratized organizations dominated by hired staff (Salamon 1999). These organizations rely increasingly on government funding and compete with for-profits for government contracts. Promotion of healthy democratic culture may be one of the reasons that government collaborates with third sector organizations, but there are a number of rather less lofty reasons that include helping political cronies, supporting family members and furthering political goals. Historical accounts of government-third sector relations show us that government collaboration with third sector organizations is largely practical stemming from the need for supplementary or complementary provision of services that governments have been unable or unwilling to provide directly.

The place of evaluation in collaborations for the less lofty reasons is clearly nonexistent. When the main purpose of the collaboration is to promote parochial interests, neither the government representatives who initiate or facilitate the collaboration nor the third sector beneficiaries will be interested in evaluation. Attempts to impose external evaluation on these types of collaborations have been obfuscated due to political gaming—as demonstrated by the failure to implement Israeli government decisions in this direction.

It would seem that there would be a much more promising role for evaluation regarding collaborations in which third sector organizations provide services in a complimentary or supplementary fashion. Here, government partners ought to have a real interest in evaluating the effectiveness of programs that they support through grants or contracts. Government administrators may be even more prone to initiate evaluations of programs delivered by third parties than programs delivered directly by their own departments. The political problematic of self-evaluation in which an administrator does not wish to expose shortcomings to external review is potentially lessened. An administrator who orders evaluation of programs operated by third sector collaborators might be seen to be doing a good job of surveillance and monitoring. And he has little to lose from the possibility that the third sector provider might be replaced due to unflattering evaluation results.

Yet our analysis reveals a number of obstacles that detract from this optimistic view of the potential role of evaluation in collaboration stemming from the need for complementary or supplementary service provision. These include issues related to technical problems of measurement, surveillance capacity, multiple providers of funds, political sensitivities, dependence relations and the high prestige of many third sector organizations.

Technical problems of measurement are not unique to government-third sector collaboration. Difficulties in defining appropriate measures of success and obtaining reliable data are particularly salient to human service programs that account for the largest part of government-third sector collaboration. Measurement problems plague both evaluation and performance monitoring activities. A GAO review of American attempts at implementing performance reporting found, for example, that agencies had greatest difficulty with identification of appropriate outcome measures (GAO 1997). The short time frames of many collaborative efforts exacerbate measurement problems. Grants are generally made on a yearly basis and contracts rarely span more than three years. Short duration grants and contracts restrict opportunities to observe outcomes and may render in-depth evaluation unjustifiable in terms of cost and potential benefit.

Governments appear to be unwilling or unable to devote adequate resources to *surveillance capacity* of collaborative efforts. Devoting the kind of resources necessary for comprehensive surveillance defeats one purpose of collaboration—saving. The problem of surveillance—and hence evaluation—is particularly acute when a single government unit distributes funds to a large number of collaborators. Government administrators may also feel that they can trust these non-profit distributing agents. Government grants and contracts administrators may not have the expertise necessary to manage evaluations.

Third sector organizations often rely on *multiple providers of funds*. They may receive funding from charitable foundations, from several different government bodies and from local authorities. In such cases, the incentive of each "principal" to promote evaluative activity decreases. There may also be assumptions that "the other guy" is already doing it.

Whereas the organizational sensitivities of self-evaluation may decrease, collaboration comes with its own set of *political sensitivities*. As in any activity that involves two or more people, government-third sector collaboration is built on delicate compromises. Evaluation findings can threaten the very fabric of compromise by pointing at deficiencies in the work of one or another of the partners. Government administrators will be particularly reluctant to initiate evaluation in cases where they are *dependent* on third sector collaborators for service provision as for example when there are no reasonable alternative providers. The high *prestige* and public standing of some third sector organizations may also inhibit evaluation. Government officials may themselves hold a great deal of respect for such organizations. And they may be unwilling or unable to subject their political masters to evaluations that portray popular organizations in a bad light.

What happens to evaluation when government collaborates with the third sector? The picture presented here is not so pretty. Collaboration may decrease internal organizational politics of evaluation, but introduces a number of additional avenues for political influences on evaluation. The conceptual development of this chapter, supported by examples, suggests that collaboration with third sector organizations will decrease the propensity to conduct evaluation studies and increase the chance that evaluations conducted will be laden with political considerations. This is a preliminary suggestive finding that invites empirical investigation.

What is to be done? The politics of evaluating government-third sector collaboration is not something that can be cured by some sort of treatment. It is a reality to be reckoned with, not unlike the politics of evaluation of non-collaborative government programs. Awareness of the special politics surrounding government-third sector collaboration is a first step to finding appropriate evaluation functions and methodologies. One path taken in a number of countries regarding direct government programs is top-down requirements to periodically evaluate. While the results of such directives have been mixed in terms of the quality of evaluation, there is no doubt that they have helped put evaluation on the table. As governments rely more on collaborations with third sector organizations, they would do well to encourage greater central government, legislative and state audit attention to monitoring, evaluation and auditing. Left to themselves, individual government units have little incentive to engage in evaluation of collaborative programs.

There is a need to improve the surveillance capacity of government units involved in collaboration with third sector organizations. This might focus more on qualitative improvement rather than trying to hire enough staff so as to always being able to look over the shoulder of third sector providers. Specifically, there may be a need for training administrators of grants and contracts in evaluation management. They need to learn when and how to request and use different kinds of evaluative information about collaborative programs. For example, they must learn when to use performance monitoring as opposed to in-depth program evaluation and when to focus evaluative activity on process, output or outcome measures. These choices will be influenced by several variables including state of knowledge about particular program interventions, expected duration of the collaborative arrangement, developmental stage of the program and funding available for the evaluation function.

Evaluation management should also take into account the political sensitivities of government-third sector collaboration in choosing evaluation approaches. Participatory approaches may prove useful in situations of delicate compromises among partners. Participatory evaluators tuned in to such sensitive issues are most likely to produce evaluations that will strengthen programs without breaking down partnerships. Where there are serious doubts about whether particular collaborative programs are appropriate at all, evaluation managers should not hesitate to invite other types of evaluations.

There is a role for evaluation in government-third sector collaborations that is becoming more important as governments increasingly rely on them. Evaluation in general is a politically precarious exercise. Sensitivities peculiar to collaborations with third sector organizations heighten these risks, sharpening the need for skilled evaluation management and for greater attention on the part of central executive agencies, legislatures and supreme audit institutions.

References

Ashford, K., and J. Clarke. 1996. "Grant Monitoring by Charities: The Process of Grant-making and Evaluation." *Voluntas* 7(3): 279-299.

Auditor General of Canada. 1999. Collaborative Arrangements: Issues for the Federal Government. April 1999.

Bowsher, C. 1991. "General Management Reviews: Building Government's Capacity to Manage," in A. Friedberg, B. Geist, N. Mizrahi, and I. Sharkansky (eds.). *State Audit and Accountability.* Jerusalem: State Comptroller's Office, pp. 360-368.

Brett. E. A. 1993. "Voluntary Agencies as Development Organizations: Theorizing the Problem of Efficiency and Accountability." *Development and Change* 24: 269-303.

Central Bureau of Statistics. 1998. *Survey of Income and Expenditure of Non-profit Institututions 1980-1996.* Jerusalem: Central Bureau of Statistics.

Chelimsky, E. 1987. "The Politics of Program Evaluation." *Social Science and Modern Society* 25: 24-32.

Chelimsky, E. 1995. "Where We Stand Today in the Practice of Evaluation: Some Reflections." *Knowledge and Policy* 8: 8-19.

Crozier, M., S. Huntington, and J. Watanuki. 1975. *The Crisis of Democracy: Report on the Governability of Democracies to the Trilateral Commission.* New York: New York University Press.

Day, P., and R. Klein. 1987. *Accountabilities.* London: Tavistock.

DeHartog, A. 1998. "State Support of Public Institutions—the Blooming of Special Monies." *Mishpatim* 29:75-107.

Derlien, H-U. 1990. "Genesis and Structure of Evaluation Efforts in Comparative Perspective," in R. Rist (ed.), *Program Evaluation and the Management of Government.* New Brunswick, NJ: Transaction Publishers, pp. 147-175.

Dery, D. 1990. *Data and Policy Change: The Fragility of Data in the Policy Context.* Boston: Kluwer.

Friedberg, A 1985. "Public Audit in the Margins of the Public Administration System in Israel." Ph.D. diss., Jerusalem.

GAO (United States General Accounting Office). 1997. Managing for Results: Analytic Challenges in Measuring Performance. GAO/HEHS/GGD-97-138.

Gidron, B. 1992. "A Resurgent Third Sector and Its Relationship to Government in Israel," in B. Gidron, R. Kramer, and L. Salamon (eds.), *Government and the Third Sector: Emerging Relationships in Welfare States.* San Francisco: Jossey-Bass.

Gidron, B. 1997. "The Evolution of Israel's Third Sector: The Role of Predominant Ideology." *Voluntas* 8:11-38.

Gray, A., W. I. Jenkins, and R. V. Segsworth (eds.). 1993. *Budgeting, Auditing and Evaluation: Functions and Integration in Seven Governments.* New Brunswick, NJ: Transaction Publishers.

Grutch, R. 1990. *Partners or Agents?* London: NCVO.

Janowitz, M. 1976. *Social Control of the Welfare State.* New York: Elsevier.

Jenkins, W. I., and A. G. Gray. 1990. "Policy Evaluation in British Government: From Idealism to Realism," in R. Rist (ed.), *Program Evaluation and the Management of Government: Patterns and Prospects Across Eight Nations*. New Brunswick, NJ: Transaction Publishers.

Kettl, D. F. 1993. *Sharing Power: Public Governance and Private Markets*. Washington, DC: Brookings Institution.

Kramer, R. 1981. *Voluntary Agencies in the Welfare State*. Berkeley: University of California Press.

Kramer, R. 1993. "Reflections on the Voluntary Nonprofit Sector in Israel: An International Perspective," Arnulf M. Pins Memorial Lecture. The Hebrew University, Jerusalem, 21 February.

Lazin, F. (1994). *Politics and Policy Implementation: Project Renewal in Israel*. Albany: State University of New York Press.

Leeuw, F, R. Rist, and R. Sonnichsen (eds.). 1994. *Can Governments Learn? Comparative Perspectives on Evaluation and Organizational Learning*. New Brunswick, NJ: Transaction Publishers.

Lipsky, M., and R. Smith. 1989-90. "Nonprofit Organizations, Government, and the Welfare State." *Political Science Quarterly* 104(4): 625-648.

Normanton, E. L. 1966. *The Accountability and Audit of Governments: a Comparative Study*. Manchester: Manchester University Press.

Palumbo, Dennis J. (ed.). 1987. *The Politics of Program Evaluation*. Newbury Park: Sage.

Plantz, M. C., M.T. Greenway, and M. Hendricks. 1997. "Outcome Measurement: Showing Results in the Nonprofit Sector." *New Directions For Evaluation* (number 75, fall).

Razel, C. 1996. National Feedback for Achievements in Reading Comprehension and Math: The Experience of the 80s. Research Report 254. Jerusalem: Henrietta Szold Institute.

Reagan, M. 1975 "Accountability and Independence in Federal Grants-in-aid," in B. L. R. Smith (ed.), *The New Political Economy: The Public Use of the Private Sector*. London: Macmillan , pp. 181-211.

Rist, R. (ed.). 1990. *Program Evaluation and the Management of Government: Patterns and Prospects across Eight Nations*. New Brunswick, NJ: Transaction Publishers.

Rosen, B. 1986. *Holding Government Bureaucracies Accountable*. New York: Praeger.

Ross S., and S. P. Osborne. 1999. "Making a Reality of Community Governance: Structuring Government-Voluntary Sector Relationships at the Local Level." *Public Policy and Administration* 14 (2):49-61.

Salamon, L. M. 1995. *Partners in Public Service: Government-Non-Profit Relations in the Modern Welfare State*. Baltimore, MD: John Hopkins University Press.

Salamon, L. M. 1999. "The Nonprofit Sector at a Crossroads: The Case of America." *Voluntas* 10 (1): 5-23.

Salamon, L. M., and H. K. Anheier. 1992. "In Search of the Nonprofit Sector I: The Question of Definitions." *Voluntas* 3(2): 125-152.

Salamon, L. M., et al. 1998. *The Emerging Sector Revisited*. Baltimore, MD: Johns Hopkins University Institute for Policy Studies.

Schwartz, R. 1998. "The Politics of Evaluation Reconsidered: A Comparative Study of Israeli Programs." *Evaluation* 4 (3):294-309.

Schwartz, R., and I. Sharkansky. 2000. "Collaboration with the Third Sector—Issues of Accountability: Mapping Israeli versions of This problematic." *Public Policy and Administration* 15 (3): 92-106.

Sharkansky, I. 1979. *Wither the State? Politics and Public Enterprise in Three Countries*. Chatham, NJ: Chatham House.

Smith, B. 1971. "Accountability and Independence in the Contract State," in B. Smith and D.C. Hague (eds.), *The Dilemma of Accountability in Modern Government: Independence versus Control*. London: Macmillan, pp. 3-69.

Smith, R., and M. Lipsky. 1993. *NonProfits for Hire: The Welfare State in an Age of Contracting*. Cambridge: Harvard University Press.

State Comptroller. 1994. *Annual Report #44*. Jerusalem: State Comptroller.

State Comptroller. 1995. *Annual Report #45*. Jerusalem: State Comptroller.

State Comptroller. 1997. *Annual Report #47*. Jerusalem: State Comptroller.

State Comptroller. 1998. *Annual Report #48*. Jerusalem: State Comptroller.

Taylor, M. 1996. "Between Public and Private: Accountability and Voluntary Organizations." *Policy and Politics* 24:57-72.

Taylor, M. E., and R. D. Sumariwalla. 1993. "Evaluating Nonprofit Effectiveness: Overcoming the Barriers," in D. R. Young, R. M. Hollister, and V. A. Hodgkinson (eds.), *Governing, Leading, and Managing Nonprofit Organizations*. San Francisco: Jossey-Bass.

Toulemonde, J., C. Fontaine, E. Laudren, and P. Vincke. 1998. "Evaluation in Partnership." *Evaluation* 4 (2): 171-188.

Weiss, C. H. 1970. 'The Politicization of Evaluation Research.' *Journal of Social Issues* 26: 57-68.

Weiss, C. H. 1973. "Where Politics and Evaluation Research Meet." *Evaluation* 1: 37-45.

Weiss, C. H. 1988. "Evaluation for Decisions: Is Anybody There? Does Anybody Care?" *Evaluation Practice* 9: 5-19.

Wildavsky, A. 1972. "The Self-Evaluating Organization." *Public Administration Review* 32:509-520.

Yates, D. 1982. *Bureaucratic Democracy: The Search for Democracy and Efficiency in American Government*. Cambridge: Harvard University Press.

5

Collaborating for Public Service Quality: The Implications for Evaluation

John Mayne and Olaf Rieper

As this volume demonstrates, collaboration has become the norm in many parts of the public sector. Governments are engaging with partners in order to be able to deliver their programs and services to citizens more efficiently and effectively. In addition to any cost savings that collaboration may bring about, a key aim of governments remains to deliver quality services. In the UK, for example, service quality is a key element and objective of modernized and joined-up government (Prime Minister and the Minister for the Cabinet Office 1999). Collaborative delivery of services is increasingly being used to rationalize delivery between levels of government and to make best use of relevant private and voluntary sector expertise.

As we will see, however, increased collaboration in no way guarantees better quality services. Indeed, collaboration in important ways can complicate the quest for quality by introducing more players and more complexity into the service delivery regime. In this chapter, we will explore how collaboration affects the drive to provide quality service and, in turn, the implications for evaluation. We will see that evaluation needs to adapt to the realities of collaborative service delivery. Before discussing these collaborative issues, however, we need to provide some background on the main ideas behind public service quality as part of public service reforms.

Concepts and Context of Public Service Quality

Public service quality has become an important ingredient in the widespread efforts at reforming and revitalizing public service, including the increasing use of collaborative arrangements. Whatever elements are used to characterize these public sector reforms, service quality usually belongs to the list of reforms initiated (Pollitt 1995; Naschold 1995: 180). However, in comparison to other elements of the new public management movement, service quality issues seem to have received less attention and have been somewhat of a late comer.

The organizational transformations within the public sector (such as breaking bureaucratic organizations into separate agencies, decentralizing management authority, delivering service through collaborative partnerships with other levels of government or the private sector, and separating the provision of public services from the setting of policy) as well as changes in human resource management (such as consulting with staff on service improvements, requiring staff to work to performance targets, and shifting towards term contracts and performance-related pay) usually occurred earlier than the focus on quality. Certainly in the literature, these other elements of reform have received more attention than the seemingly more operational issue of service quality.

It is obvious, however, that improvement of the quality of the service provided to citizens should follow other organizational changes in the public sector. In fact, if the organizational changes are going to have any impact on the wider society who are the consumers of the public service, one important implementation mechanism will be through development of improved public service quality. Through customer surveys, the voices of the market are echoed and through client consultations, quality criteria are being built into the performance standards and the managing for results approach to public sector management. The use of a variety of collaborative arrangements to deliver service has complicated even further the question of quality and the consumer's voice. As we shall see, some forms of collaboration run counter to better service delivery.

One can distinguish between at least three approaches to public service quality (Naschold 1995: 181):

1. A scientific/expert approach, in which quality standards are set by experts, who ensure that the standards are made independently of the user/customer, albeit with a view to the "best interests" of the service user as determined by the expert. Various national and technical standards reflect this approach, such as standards for medical treatment and building codes. This approach has a long tradition within the more technical and professional public services.

2.   A managerial (excellence) approach in which the aim is "getting closer to the service users" to deliver what they value most. Tools and models such as customer satisfaction surveys, client and staff consultation and total quality management are being used by an increasing number of public sector organizations in many countries. This is a powerful approach within the new public management.

3.   A consumerist approach with the aim of empowering and engaging the users/customers through, for example, consumer rights (the UK Citizen Charter) and consumers' choice leading to competition among public service providers, but also through the development of a more active role for the user in service delivery.

This last approach has two tracks: one is minimalist, guaranteeing a minimum level of quality, while another is a directly empowering one, in which the participation of the user in the service design, production and evaluation becomes essential, for example, in the care for elderly and in the health sector in general, where the credo is that elderly patients/users should be "empowered" to become more and more self activating. In fact, the very use of the concepts "user," "customer," and "client" indicates a shift of roles between the citizen receiving services and public organizations as providers of those services.

The sources of learning in the public sector concerning quality service come mainly, if not solely, from the practice of the private sector over the last couple of decades. Extensive systems of standards for producing products that conform to clear standards of quality have been designed and put into practice, for example, the International Organization for Standardization (ISO) 9000 standards, and in the service sector, the title *In Search of Excellence* (Peters and Waterman 1992) still echoes.

Thus, public service quality is developed and implemented through a number of tools, in which evaluation plays or should play a significant role. However, before exploring this issue, we will first examine some general approaches to service quality; second, discuss some examples of collaborative service quality initiatives in Canada and Denmark; and third, look at the complexities resulting from the use of collaborative arrangements to deliver service.

Collaborative Service Quality Initiatives in Canada and Denmark

In our discussion of collaborative delivery mechanisms we will use examples from two countries, Canada and Denmark, both of which have had active service quality initiatives underway for some time.

Collaborative Public Service Quality Activities in Canada

Canada is a federal state with a division of powers between the national government and the provincial governments which have their own revenue raising and spending powers. For example, education, health care, social welfare and most surface transportation services are provided by the provinces. Since many of the more technical and professional services are provided at the provincial level, there has been less focus on the scientific/expert approach to service quality at the national level in Canada. To some extent the consumerist approach is evident through the establishment of service standards to allow service users to know what level of service they should be getting, but competition among service providers has not been actively pursued. The managerial (excellence) approach probably typifies the main service quality strategy used at the national level in Canada.

The focus on the users of public services as a key criterion in designing quality services has proven a powerful impetus for change in the public sector. In some jurisdictions where there are several levels of government, this perspective has resulted in collaborative initiatives which have pulled together and rationalized the service provided to users from several different levels of government, national, regional and local, which had previously been delivered in isolation from their counterparts. As a result, new forms of delivery arrangements have been developed.

One example of the collaborative delivery of services in Canada is the Canada Business Service Centers. Starting in 1992, the federal government set about establishing single window service centers in each province, aimed at providing business with one-stop shopping for all services provided by all levels of federal, provincial and municipal government. Extensive consultation with business illustrated that the difficulty of finding where exactly to get the specific service wanted was a major complaint of the business community, who faced up to nineteen federal departments and many provincial, municipal and private sector organizations.

Canada Business Service Centers provide a single window in many cases to all these services, where business clients can, with one contact, either find the information they want or get a specific reference to where they need to go for what they want. Some provide a 24-hour telephone service and many provide a faxback service giving instant access to information on government programs and services. All but one provide personal service. Establishing the centers often proved to be a challenge, bringing together levels of government and the private sector who have not traditionally worked together. The desire to provide convenient service to the business community was the unifying goal. The initiative was started with no new operating resources, but, later, federal funding was established for several years, despite restraint and general downsizing (Seidle 1995: 129).

The Auditor General of Canada reported:

> In a short period of time, Canada Business Service Centres (CBSC) have made progress in forming partnerships with federal departments, agencies and provinces. They have established a presence across the country through 10 centres and attracted a clientele for their services; CBSC statistics show that inquiries have increased significantly. (Auditor General of Canada 1995, para 14.109).

More recently, the federal government launched the Service Canada initiative to encourage the collaborative delivery of most federal services aimed at individuals. The purpose is to provide individual Canadians with one-stop access to a range of governement services in person, by telephone, or electronically through the Internet. It involves three types of services: (1) providing general information about federal programs and services and those of other levels of government, (2) offering multiple transactions through one-stop access points, and (3) providing referrals to sources of more detailed information. Service Canada is a collaboration of partners (Treasury Board of Canada Secretariat 1999).

The success of these single windows remains to be seen. One report on single window delivery at the provincial level has been critical, arguing, for example, that requiring the elderly to come to the same location to get service as those who are receiving social assistance is not quality service from the perspective of the elderly who may feel uncomfortable with the arrangement (Dubuisson 1999).

Public Service Quality Activites in Denmark

In Denmark, local governments, the counties and the municipalities have a strong position in terms of service delivery and political autonomy. About 60 percent of public consumption is absorbed by local governments. Thus, having the responsibility of delivering the major share of social, educational, and health services as well as major tasks within planning and environment, the local governments have a strong bargaining position with the national government and its agencies. The Danish case of developing public service quality in local government should be regarded in the context of the political administrative changes that have been going on in Denmark over the last decade, and with some variation in other Nordic welfare countries.

From the late 1980s, a number of internal reforms in local governments were implemented in management-oriented and service-oriented directions. The main ingredients have been desectoralization, strengthening of political and administrative leadership, management by objectives (MBO), framework budgeting, delegation of work, including some privatization and notions of customer service.

The idea behind these reforms and the incremental, locally initiated changes, inspired by the market (considered by liberal and conservative politicians to be the ideal steering mechanism), represents a shift in the basic values in the organization of Nordic welfare communes from community-oriented to individual-oriented, a shift from a political democracy to a consumer democracy without politics.

What does this shift in values, which seems to characterize the Nordic welfare states if not most European states, imply for the notion of service quality? In a political democracy with a highly developed welfare sector, the needs and demands of citizens are channeled through local party branches, local elections and local interest organizations, and service quality is governed by professional norms and standards. In a consumer democracy, in contrast, the assessment of service needs and assurance of quality of service is located in the direct encounter of the public organization with the consumer demand, the user. The hierarchy of authority as well as the professional norms and standards will be less important, and the influence of the direct demands of service users on the scope and quality of local authority service tends to increase (Albaek 1995: 252). It is no longer the service encounter governed by professional norms that is central for the service quality. There is a shift in focus towards the life situation of the citizen, and towards empowerment of the user in his or her own setting.

These changes imply that if the local politician and the administrative management in local government, as well as the street-level bureaucrat, are to develop new relations, not only towards the individual citizen but also towards voluntary associations, private service companies and consumer organizations, collaboration is called for. For example, the municipality, which has the main responsibility for disabled people, has to develop relations with various groups and special interest organizations of disabled people with specific handicaps.

It has been within the dynamics of this political and administrative context that specific initiatives to develop service quality have been taken by individual municipalities and counties in Denmark. In the late 1980s most of these efforts were from the frontline in local agencies such as schools, hospitals, and business centers, supported by administrative senior management that could see the operational and motivational value of the specific client orientation in the individual services. In the early 1990s, the quality activities of Danish local governments expanded rapidly. Sixty percent of Denmark's 275 municipalities had implemented service quality activities by 1995 and 73 percent had plans to start new quality activities. In 20 percent of municipalities quality requests had been integrated into contracts with agencies, and in 13 percent there were formalized agreements on autonomy with the agencies, based on notions of public service quality (FOKUS 1995a). Such a development indicates a change in the form of collaboration between the municipality and the institutions.

The two national associations of local governments in Denmark that provide consultant assistance to the service quality activities have supported public service quality activities by developing training seminars for officers in local government. The two national associations together with the Institute for Local Governments Studies (AKF) have set up a special initiative to initiate and fund evaluation and research and development in the field, as well as organizing for an exchange of experience and information on good practices in public service quality. This implies that a new collaborative structure has been set up and a meeting place created to stimulate exchange of experience on service quality across three levels of government (municipalities, counties and national government).

It was recognized early by the local government associations as well as by their central government counterpart that the trend towards public service quality could be used as a strategic instrument in setting quality standards and channeling the development of the content of public services (with implications for the costs). Therefore, the initiative by the national associations of local governments was complemented in its first year by an initiative from the Ministry of Finance to set up and support a small central agency for the developing of service quality to match the volume of local initiatives in the field. Also a Danish Quality prize for the public sector has been set up by the national government. Thus, the public service quality movement has initiated and assisted the development of new collaborative arrangements between the municipalities and the counties at the national level, while new arrangements have been set up on the initiative of national government.

Two trends can be distinguished. One is the locally based bottom-up approach to public service quality, another is the centrally steered development of standards and norms for service quality. For instance, the Ministry of Education wants all schools to obtain a minimum level of reading ability among the students. Test methods and quality standards are developed centrally for this purpose. The individual school might, however, within the general purpose of the School Law apply supplementary quality standards on pedagogies, student performance, etc., developed through a local political process. It is to be expected that evaluation has very different functions in these two approaches, and the two approaches represent different interests and concerns.

A bottom-up approach was used in a recent program for enhancing the quality of adult education centers in Copenhagen County. The county recruited a private consultant as well as a teacher of one of the centers as program manager. Through the program manager's contact with the individual centers initiatives were developed by center staff, and criteria for quality were set up by groups of teachers in each center. Meetings to exchange ideas and experience across all centers were organized by the program manager, but the quality concept and the activities were driven by the local centers. The overall idea of the program was to define space and stimulate involvement in the centers. Thus, a scheduled evaluation of the program will have to be driven by the centers. This implies a new, specific kind of cooperation between the county, which provides the finance, and the centers, which determine operational criteria (Lester 2000).

These various developments in service quality illustrate that in Denmark the previously mentioned three approaches to service quality exist in parallel. The national government is using a mix of the scientific/expert approach and consumerist approach by attempting to influence local governments indirectly not only through legislation and financing, but also by influencing norms and standards of service quality. The local agencies and institutions are using a managerial (excellence) approach and strive for maximum flexibility, as can be seen above.

The Unintended Consequences of Collaboration

Obtaining a specific service from government can be a daunting experience for an individual, especially if more than one organization is involved. From finding the right physical location or phone number, to using the right language to explain oneself, to filling out numerous yet similar forms, to endless waiting, all can pose significant challenges to the citizen. On the surface, providing a single window where all the citizen's service needs can be met or using private sector companies to deliver a service efficiently sounds like a good management approach to strive for. Getting the private sector to deliver a service more efficiently appears a good idea. Rationalizing service delivery among different levels of government should be a sensible approach to take.

These approaches can and have worked well in specific cases. But they are not panaceas for improving quality service and should be evaluated carefully to see if better quality is, in fact, forthcoming. Moreover, the collaboration they involve may create a variety of problems.

Difuse accountability. When a single government organization is delivering a service, it is reasonably clear to the service user where to complain when things go wrong and which elected official is on the line. The minister's office is a long-standing and often effective mechanism for redress. In a collaborative arrangement, either with another level of government or with the private sector, it is often no longer so clear who is in charge (Mulgan 1997; Auditor General of Canada, 1999a). The more partners involved, the more confusing things may become.

Unintended competition for the consumer. When there are several co-located partners involved in single window type delivery approaches, how quality is defined may become contentious, since each is still trying to deliver its service best, through the single window. Without considerable training, the staff who deal with the service user, will have some home-based loyalties and preferential knowledge. Their idea of what is quality service may differ from that of the organizations involved and from what the user actually wishes to receive. Single windows, by their design, will often be trying to deliver different services to the same clientele. The resulting competition may not result in improved quality for the user.

Clientele not wanting to be treated the same. In noncollaborative service delivery, the government organization can organize itself to best meet the needs of its particular clientele, and build an ongoing relationship. In single window situations, many different types of services users are involved. Veterans, for example, getting financial assistance, will likely not want to be associated with the underprivileged: veterans may feel they are receiving payment for past services rendered, not social assistance.

Private sector efficiency not always appreciated. Having the private sector deliver a government service does not necessarily produce quality service. The private sector is seeking a profit. The service user may be demanding due process and equal treatment, qualities which can be quite expensive to provide from the perspective of the private sector. This becomes a particularly important consideration when there are no or few alternatives to the government service. Partnering with the private sector brings together two quite different mind sets (Jacobs 1992), and the marriage might not produce public service quality.

Determining success more of a challenge. As this chapter will discuss later, the involvement of multiple partners in the the delivery of a service makes evaluating the success of the service that much more difficult. Problems range from obtaining a working agreement on what, how and when to evaluate, dealing with partners who are not meeting commitments, to ensuring data collection compatibility among various delivery elements when they are run by different partners.

We are not saying that collaboration cannot result in quality service. We are saying that quality service in collaborative arrangements is not guaranteed. More empirical evidence is needed to understand what works and what does not. Evaluation should be built into new collaborative arrangements, as it should for all public sector reforms. The issues raised above point to the kinds of questions that evaluation of collaborative service delivery should seek to address.

Users of Evaluation on Public Service Quality

Before we turn to the role of evaluation in relation to public service quality initiatives, including collaborative ones, we will discuss briefly the major orientations and interest of the users of evaluation in public service quality. It is widely recognized that there are usually a variety of users of evaluations and that their interests will differ considerably (Mayne and Hudson 1992; Mayne, Divorski, and Lemaire 1999). The main stakeholders in public service quality are politicians, managers, frontline staff and professionals, service users, taxpayers and the general public. The orientation (defensive or supportive) of evaluation users toward public service quality will influence the use of and the kinds of evaluation undertaken.

Politicians

The support and initiatives of politicians to improve public service quality have been different across countries. In some countries, the politicians have regarded public service quality as a tool to mobilize human resources in public agencies towards the needs of the electorate, and national initiatives have been launched such as in the United Kingdom and the United States. In other countries, the politicians have been less interested, letting the civil servants take the lead.

In local governments in Denmark, the politicians have been only modestly active in initiating public service quality activities. The administrative managers have been the initiators in almost all of the municipalities who have implemented public service quality activities, and in half of those, the managers have cooperated with the politicians. Similarly, in Canada, most service quality initiatives have been proposed and pushed by public servants, with occasional interest and support from politicians.

In the countries where the politicians take a more active role in public service quality, one might expect an interest in getting evaluations of overall service quality strategy launched and used. To some extent this has occurred in the United Kingdom and Australia which have undertaken evaluations of their public service reform efforts (Efficiency Unit 1991; Trosa 1994; Management Advisory Board and Management Improvement Advisory Committee 1993).

However, evaluating public sector reform efforts is often not a high priority in many countries. This is perhaps understandable, since rhetoric has a positive function by acting as a mobilizing and motivating force offering clear principles and models that provide a starting point to cope with the complex realities. In this light, evaluation can have a unveiling role in showing how and to what extent the service quality initiatives work in reality. This might not always be appreciated at the political level.

Managers: Purchasers, Providers and Regulators

In some countries, the managerial levels in public organizations have been the key initiators of public service quality activities. The explanation might be that public service quality has been regarded by the managers as a tool for steering semi-autonomous agencies, as well as an instrument for motivating the staff. Front line staff might welcome service quality. However, even though there might be a real commitment to service quality, there could be a reluctance from senior management towards implementing this since service quality demands a different style of leadership, moving away from a bureaucratic one towards a more team- and process-based one (Gilbert 1991).

However, managers in the new public organizations which separate the purchaser and the provider of public services have different information needs. One might expect evaluation to perform different functions for these different categories of managers. For example, the new collaborative arrangements involving service users in boards or committees might give the users the opportunity to influence the evaluation criteria from their point of view as well as to influence the way the evaluation results are used in practice.

Consider the following example. A municipality has contracted out home service for elderly. The director of the department for social services has specified the quality standards to be followed in agreement with the politicians. The director (as service purchaser) wants evaluation to determine if the provider of the home service has fulfilled the contract. Evaluation can be used to decide whether to prolong the provider's contract or not, and whether to adjust the requirements of the new contract. The provider might be interested in evaluation in order to know where to improve or adjust the service in order to respond to the needs of the elderly in the most efficient way.

A different type of public manager might also be involved. The role of this principal or regulator (see Arvidsson, Ch. 6) is to set general quality standards and determine what part of the public services local governments are allowed to outsource. The role of such regulatory and supervisory bodies will be to define the general context for service quality activities. In the case of home service, the principal would be the minister for social affairs, but part of the general functions could also be performed by a national association of local governments. Such supervisory bodies will be interested in using evaluation information to identify negative and unintended outcomes of the outsourcing of services, for example, failures of quasi-markets leading to cherry picking rather than providing service to all those eligible.

Yet collaborative arrangements cause other concerns. Before getting into the arrangements managers are likely to want to know if the partners they are involved with are likely to be able to deliver their part. For example, in Canada, the Commissioner of the Environment and Sustainable Development (1999) has been critical of the federal government for not assessing adequately the capacities of the provincial governments to manage federal environmental regulation as part of joint federal/provincial agreements. In addition, as in the case of a contracted service, they will want to know if each partner has delivered as expected. Consequently, it is clear that managers in different roles will have a variety of perspectives and, hence, different interests in evaluation.

Service Deliverers: Professionals and Other Staff

The frontline service deliverers in direct contact with the service user are directly affected by service quality changes and therefore face a number of sometimes conflicting incentives. On the one hand, they would normally welcome efforts to improve the delivery of service to their clientele and to enhance their skills. On the other hand, these changes might be viewed as being imposed and might be seen, as has often been the case, as efforts to downsize their jobs through increased productivity.

A further element is introduced when the service deliverers are accredited professionalized groups, for example, school teachers, auditors, nurses, and doctors, with self-regulating standards of practice. These professional groups have a strategic role in public service quality activities because they have a high degree of control over the service delivered. Public service quality is facilitated by these groups to the extent that quality development is seen as consistent with their professional standards and values, and strengthens their autonomy, or at least does not threaten it. In these cases, service quality innovations will be welcomed and supported as ways of improving service to their clients (Sehested et al. 1992).

However, if service quality activities are perceived as threatening to their values, standards or their autonomy, these professionalized groups may react defensively (Kirkpatrick and Lucio 1995: 272). The health sector, for example, has traditionally been steered by norms of highly professionalized groups of doctors and nurses. A strong user orientation might be considered threatening to the professional norms of the doctors, because then the effects of treatments are not only judged by the medical profession on the basis of technical norms, but by the patients themselves based on their daily life context and their involvement in the healing process (Launsø 1997).

A supporting strategy from the professional groups would be to influence public service quality by getting involved in its implementation and to shape the design of the evaluations of the impact of these efforts. In Denmark, for example, the trade unions support public service quality activities involving teachers in homes for handicapped young people. A focus on service quality requires more use of teacher's qualifications and skills in the treatment they provide, resulting in semi-autonomous working groups and job enrichment. In addition, quality service implies longer term involvement with their clients. Thus, professionals' interest and that of management are perceived to converge (FOKUS 1995b).

In the case of service deliverers who are not part of professional groups, an interest and support of public service quality activities and their evaluation will similarly depend on the extent to which the deliverers see the initiatives as truly improving services, giving them more empowerment, more control of their work environment, and sustaining job security.

Service Users

Because the whole raison d'être of public service quality is the user, one would expect that users would perceive the quality movement very positively. However, several factors can work against this expectation. First, even if the encounter between the provider and user is improved, the long term effect (for example, of education or health care) might not occur or might not be seen, negating the quality service encounter. Second, in some instances, as in Canada, cutbacks of levels of service took place at the same time as the launch of public service quality initiatives. Third, there is often a long delay between users responses to client satisfaction questionnaires and action to improve the service. Efforts at involving users in improving quality can create overly optimistic expectations on the part of the user. However, in the many cases where the user is personally involved in the service design and has had a quality service encounter, one should expect support for service quality activities.

The main interest on the part of the user in evaluation of public service quality should be to make informed choices on which services to use where such choices are assisted by information on actual levels of service provided, and if user fees are involved, to know if the service provides value for money. Another more direct strategy on the part of the service users is to influence service quality through organized efforts by consumer associations and social movements. These associations and movements often have a strong interest in the design of evaluations and the use of evaluation findings to reshape the concept of service quality (Kirkpatrick and Lucio 1995). This offers new possibilities for evaluations in shaping as well as testing out the ideas of consumer associations and movements in controversial fields of services (for example, unconventional health treatments, Launsø 1997).

Taxpayers and Citizens

There are groups of stakeholders who are not interested in the service encounter per se but rather in the cost of service being provided and whether or not the public objective behind the service has been met. They have an interest in the evaluation of service quality to know if they and the country are getting value for their tax money. In addition, they also may want evaluative information in order to be able to hold public servants and politicians to account for their actions and decisions on service levels and delivery. This may be particularly the case where services are delivered through a collaborative arrangement involving several levels of government and where accountability for the resulting service may not be as clear as it was when the services were delivered by a single government. Transparency is important here.

Table 5.1 summarizes this discussion on the orientation and potential use made by the various stakeholders in service quality initiatives. Clearly, evaluation can play a wide variety of roles in service quality. It is important to know what role is expected from evaluation before embarking on an evaluation.

Evaluation Roles in Public Service Quality

The extensive attention being paid to public service quality in many countries is not generally reflected in the evaluation literature. There are a few exceptions (Mark and Pines 1995; Wargo 1994), but a review of the recent evaluation literature hardly leads to the knowledge that public sectors are being significantly reformed and that consultation and dialogue with service users (through surveys, focus groups, measurement and interviews and in user committees) are key features of this process. Conversely, the public service quality literature does not often make explicit reference to evaluation practices, even though it discusses many "evaluation" topics without referring specifically to evaluation, for example with regard to the general area of measurement, measuring client satisfaction, con-

Table 5.1
Service Quality Stakeholder Perspectives on Using Evaluation

Stakeholders	*Potential Use of Evaluation*
Politicians	• to reconsider the overall public service quality strategy
Managers Purchasers	• to decide renewal of contract • to adjust requirements in new contract
Providers	• to make the service more effective and efficient • to document what has be delivered • to assess potential partners and the achieved performance of partners in collaborative arrangements
Supervisory bodies	• to adjust the general context for quality service activities
Service Deliverers	• to improve service to clients • to improve/defend professional autonomy and values; • to gain control over job activities
Service Users	• to make an informed choice of service providers • to suggest improvements in service delivery
Taxpayers and the Public	• to assess value for money and to hold to account

tinuous learning, the use of pilot projects to assess new innovations, and a variety of survey work.

Yet a little thought leads one to identify a number of ways in which evaluation practice and public service quality could complement each other. Efforts at improving public service quality ought to benefit from the experience and lessons learned from evaluation, and should use the skills of evaluators. In an organization involved with both public service quality and having an evaluation capacity, one should see a close link between these two areas. However, a review of the literature suggests that this link is not very strong. More frequently, evaluators and quality service groups in organizations and the professions have remained isolated from each other. This reflects two things. First, the traditional vertical differentiation in organizations often means that different functions tend to operate in isolation. Second, service quality initiatives have tended not to emphasize the key role of measurement, often focusing on "softer" aspects of quality service efforts. Hence, the link to evaluation may not be immediately evident.

Using new and essentially untried collaborative approaches to deliver services ought to call for extensive evaluation to determine how the new arrangement is working as a whole and for each partner to assess its own performance. There is some evidence of this in Canada where many of the new collaborative arrangements being set up indeed include evaluation provisions (Auditor General of Canada 1999b). Nonetheless, evaluation is not always a key element of these new approaches. However, we suggest at least three roles for evaluation in public service quality:

- assisting in the implementation of public service quality,
- assessing the success of public service quality, and
- assessing the success of programs or institutions which include collaborative service quality arrangements.

We will discuss each of these below. Each role demonstrates a rather different purpose for the evaluation work undertaken, reflecting different stakeholders' perspectives on public service quality reform efforts as well as different intended users of the evaluation information.

The involvement of various stakeholders in cooperative efforts of service quality activities is expected to have implications for evaluation similar to the evaluation of intergovernmental programs. Even if each stakeholder does not represent a level of government, the different roles and perspectives of the actors, as mentioned above, might be significant for the evaluation. As noted by Rieper and Toulemonde (1997: 151-166) the various stakeholders' levels of government might evaluate (1) together in partnership, (2) together, but with one in command, (3) one evaluating on behalf of the others. In many instances, the conflicting issues among the stakeholders tend to be neglected or diminished in order to run the evaluation smoothly. However, the examples mentioned by Rieper and Toulemonde demonstrated that the more useful evaluations were done by multiple stakeholders involved together in all phases of the evaluation process.

Evaluation in Implementing Public Service Quality

Implementing quality service initiatives is a challenge since it involves organizational change and the need to adopt a learning culture. We have argued earlier that measurement is an essential feature of public service quality and related Total Quality Management (TQM) types of reforms, whereby empirical evidence is used to help guide service delivery operations. This is perhaps more the case where collaborative arrangements are being used. The focus of the measurement is often on the service user or deliverer, involving one or more of a number of issues:

1.   trying to understand better the user's service needs and expectations,

2.   getting feedback from the staff who are delivering the service,

3.   engaging the user in a dialogue on how service can best be improved, usually within a tight budget restriction,

4.   using complaints as a valuable information source, and/or assessing the degree of satisfaction the user has with the service received.

These issues can be addressed through a variety of standard evaluation techniques: customer surveys, focus groups or exit interviews. Involvement of service users (stakeholders) has long been a principle of good evaluation practice. The change in role relations whereby users are empowered and involved might affect evaluation design and methodology by encouraging evaluations of the participative or collaborative type in which the user of the evaluation overlaps with the service user who expects a more active role in the evaluation than simply being provider of information. For example, users might be involved in framing the evaluation questions by the use of focus group interviews with service users, or user representatives from consumer organizations might be involved in designing the evaluation. Indeed, participatory evaluation (Krogstrup 1997) involves just those activities public service quality is attempting to achieve.

Given that the underlying aim of quality service is to provide users with the kind of service they feel is most beneficial to them, providers must be able to consult with potential users and assess their satisfaction with the service received. There is thus a need for market-like mechanisms to evaluate the citizen's response to services, especially in cases where the user has little or no alternative, particularly since in these situations appealing to professional norms to define good service is no longer relevant.

Measurement can also be seen as an essential aspect of managing public service quality efforts, where a premium is placed on creating learning organizations and empowered employees are encouraged to learn from their experience. To this end, evaluation can assist public service quality efforts in measuring the actual level of service being delivered, and in identifying best and worst practices.

Each of the issues identified in this section is important, if not critical, to the success of public service quality initiatives. To fail to take advantage of evaluation expertise in these endeavors is an inefficient use of professional resources. The main users of evaluation in respect to implementing quality service activities are the management of the service provider or providers as well as the front line professionals. They will typically use the evaluation to adjust the content and level of quality or to deliver the service in a more efficient way.

Evaluation in Assessing the Success of Public Service Quality

As we have seen, public service quality promises much. However, as with other elements of the new public management, much of the vigor with which it is being pursued is based more on faith than on evidence of success (Pollitt 1995). This is equally true for new collaborative arrangements. The questions in need of answers remain the same: have services to the public been improved; if so, at what cost; are there most efficient ways of delivering the services; is any success achieved seen likely to continue as other elements of public sector reform continue and develop? As noted above this leads to a number of evaluation issues that may arise specifically in collaborative arrangements.

Evaluation might start, for example, with a number of modest endeavors. The assumptions behind many public service quality efforts need to be aired and made more explicit. The planning and model building that is part of the front end evaluation assessment (Office of the Comptroller General 1981) or evaluability assessment (Wholey 1983) would be useful to sorting out the untested assumption of public service quality. A logic chart logframe of the implied casual linkages among activities and expected outcomes would help in exploring why certain elements succeeded or not.

Evaluation can also play a useful role in identifying which public service quality activities have worked best and why? In the rush to embrace public service quality, evaluation can also look to see if there have been any significant unintended problems or outcomes. Hence, in the discussion above, we identified a number of unintended outcomes that might arise from collaborative service delivery.

Finally, evaluation is needed to determine if service quality has improved. This is not a straightforward task, as several authors have pointed out (Bouckaert 1995; Shand 1995). Quality tends to be in the eye of the beholder and classical evaluation questions about evaluating from whose perspective and against what criteria need to be addressed. Nevertheless, evaluating the success of service quality initiatives ought to be relatively straightforward. Performance indicators can be used to measure and track actual levels of service provided and such approaches as "mystery shopping" can be used where researchers test services by pretending to be clients. As we said earlier, satisfaction of service users can be assessed. Indeed, external evaluation and review by inspectorate organizations occurs in some jurisdictions, while in a few countries independent audit of reported performance information including public service quality performance is required (e.g., Finland, Sweden, and UK local government).

Of course, good evaluation practice makes sure that evaluation is an essential component of public service quality activities while they are being planned and implemented. To see if quality service is working, a benchmark is needed to establish some basis for comparison. However, with many elements of public service reform operating at the same time, a well thought out design will be needed to determine whether a specific public service quality initiative has been successful. Nevertheless, since considerable time and resources have been spent on public service quality activities in many countries much more effort ought to be spent in trying to evaluate what is working and what is not.

Evaluating the Programs Involving Collaborative Service Quality Arrangements

Public service quality focuses on the service being provided to customers and clients. This attention to service is thought by many to be long overdue. However, we must not lose sight of the fact that we are talking about the public sector where there are by definition broader public objectives behind the program or service in question (Beck Jørgensen 1996). Thus, national theaters and museums have audiences and visitors to attract, but they also have the public responsibility of preserving the national heritage for coming generations. Public service quality by its very nature focuses on outputs and intermediate outcomes, but the real purposes of public funding is often at a higher level of impact, namely on the general public.

These higher level impacts and effects are the bread and butter of evaluation efforts. A focus on more immediate outcomes such as customer satisfaction and turnaround times is not enough. The "public" nature of the activity may tend to get lost. We need to know if the public objectives in question are being met. In all the attention paid to improving service quality, evaluators should be among those who continue to ask if the program in question is effective, that is, is it meeting its public sector objectives? Mark and Pines (1995: 137) make this point when they say that "Society can ill afford to improve the 'quality' of ineffective social...programs."

This issue of losing sight of the public objectives is perhaps more likely to occur with collaborative arrangements (Auditor General of Canada 1999b). Different levels of government may have different objectives, efficiency might be the overriding aim or private sector partners may not relate well to the public objectives sought. Once again, the complexity of managing the arrangement can push the public interest aside.

Consequently, there are some who now question if quality service initiatives are distorting public sector activities (Kirkpatrick and Lucio 1995) while (Aucoin 1995: 194) comments that "some worry that the British approach [to service quality] has not adequately addressed the classic dilemma in public management of doing the wrong things well. ...better policy may well become tantamount to cheaper public services." Kikert and Beck Jørgensen (1995: 586) also make the point that the managerialism, client and market orientation constitute an ideological alternative to the social welfare state in which traditional public values such as legality, social justice and equality no longer play a predominant role. The individual customer is primarily interested in the quality and price of public goods and services. Better evaluations in this area might illuminate the real trade-offs being made in the name of the new public management.

At this level of evaluation the users should be governmental and parliamentary committees and other political bodies who have the responsibility of deciding upon institution and program building in the public sector. Here the political ideology, the values of the politicians, and the opinion of the electorate have the predominant influence. But credible evaluation information will help in clarifying long-term consequences of service quality for public objectives and basic structures.

The Future of Public Service Quality and Evaluation

In conclusion, we offer a number of observations relating the challenges of linking collaborative arrangements and public service quality to effective evaluative systems. First, the changes in the relations between citizens, the public authority and service delivery system are reflected in a more active and demanding role for citizens in service planning, delivery and assessment. The citizens are "users" and "consumers" and not clients or patients. There are a wide variety of collaborative arrangements being used to deliver services, ranging from loose networks to formal contracts. These include:

1. *Single window delivery.* Several government organizations working together provide access to their services at a single location for the citizen.

2. *Contracting out.* Government formally contracts out the delivery of a service to a nongovernmental organization which then delivers the service to the specifications set out in the contract.

3. *Cooperation with the volunteer sector and/or interst groups.* Government engages interested outside parties including voluntary organizations and special interest groups to participate in the delivery of a service. Delegating more autonomy to delivery agencies and institutions from a central authority to obtain services that are more responsive towards the users requires new ways of collaboration by agreement or contract.

4. *Cooperation with other governments.* Across levels of government, collaboration structures have been developed to stimulate service quality activities between national, regional and local government.

5.   *Collaboration with service users.* Government work with the service
     users to deliver better services to the users. Collaborative arrangements
     have been established to stimulate the development of public service
     quality and the involvement of citizens through joint arrangements and
     setting up of users' committees, either voluntary or by statute.

We see that the drive for public service quality has stimulated a mix
of new forms of collaborative delivery both vertically and horizontally
among levels of government, and between government and citizens.

Second, we have argued that many basic, well-known evaluation
methodologies can be used to assess the impact of service quality
activities. However, an added complexity is the collaborative nature of the evaluation effort required. Thus, in many instances, in-
tergovernmental-type evaluations are needed, bringing with them a
distinctive set of problems (Rieper and Toulemonde 1997). The evaluation of service quality activities also raises other challenges such as
the involvement of the service or end users in the evaluation process. If
the users are involved in the development of the services, they might
also expect to be part of the evaluation process beyond a contribution
to user surveys. This demands a bottom-up approach such as found
in various forms of participatory evaluation. Another challenge may
be the pressure on evaluators to assess only the level of quality achieved.
While important, happy clients are rarely an objective of public sector
programs. There is a need to look beyond service quality.

Third, a number of writers have observed that the move towards
improving service quality in the public sector is not a minor administrative change. These reforms put at question a number of basic
structures, particularly in Westminster type governments (Stone 1995;
Holmes and Shand 1995; Pollitt 1995). For example:

• Ministerial accountability appears to be changing in Westminster-
  style systems as public servants build accountability relationships
  with their direct clients through engaging citizens via increased consultation, user/client involvement, user boards and service standards.

• Parliamentary control and oversight are being challenged with empowered public servants being encouraged to take risks with taxpayer's
  money and be more entrepreneurial.

• Governments are entering increasingly into collaborative arrangements
  with other levels of government and/or the private sector to deliver
  services previously directly provided by a single government organization, often confusing who is responsible for what, and leaving Parliaments out of the picture.

- The role of Parliament or elected counsellors in local government is being completely bypassed in some forms of market-driven delivery of public services; accountability is through the public market not Parliament: vertical accountability is being replaced or substituted for a more direct, horizontal accountability.

These and related trends are not the direct subject of this chapter. Rather, we suggest that we not lose sight of the fact that the services we are considering remain in the public sector and serve the public good, no matter how they are being delivered. The goal is not simply to please service users or be efficient since public services are not subject to normal market forces. Citizens and taxpayers who pay for these services want to know they are getting value for money and that those responsible are accountable. Yet in most cases the market cannot adequately provide for these concerns in particular since there are at best only quasi-markets operating. More than periodic elections are required and whatever accountability becomes, some form of evaluation is essential to allow for consideration of a "bottom line" in the public sector. We suggest that those considering the role of evaluation should be aware of the larger changes occurring in public management and the contribution that evaluation can or should make to those ends.

These issues become more complex with the emergence of collaborative-type arrangements to deliver services. Evaluation in these situations faces not only the issues discussed here but adds the challenge of undertaking in many cases joint collaborative evaluations leading to different and distinctive problems (Rieper and Toulemonde 1997; Toulemonde 1998). The greater focus on service users, for example, seems strong and lasting and the approach of looking at redesigning government services from the perspective of the citizen is also proving quite powerful. Yet frequently this trend is associated with the creation of a quasi-market for public services. One might then ask, is there a need for evaluation since poor quality services will be abandoned by users who in so doing, "evaluate" the services in a manner far more effective than an evaluation study?

We have argued that there indeed remains a number of important roles for evaluation in relation to quality service initiatives: in helping to design quality service, in measuring quality service, and in evaluating public programs that have a service component. Even in cases where "markets" are created to "evaluate" public services, service organizations will need to know and understand customer reaction to their service. In all these instances evaluation-type information is needed for effective accountability in the public sector. The growing use of collaborative approaches increases the need for effective evaluation so that learning can indeed occur. In the private sector, evaluation is called market research and is thriving. Evaluation should do similarly in a public sector with a strong focus on service quality. Reforms to improve a quality public service, including those of collaborative government, should be evidence based.

References

Albaek, E. 1995. "Reforming the Nordic Welfare Communes." *International Review of Administrative Sciences*, 61: 241-264.

Aucoin, P. 1995. *The New Public Management: Canada a Comparative Perspective.* Montreal: Institute for Research on Public Policy.

Auditor General of Canada. 1995. *Business Assistance Programs in Transition. Report to the House of Commons.* Chapter 14. Ottawa.

Auditor General of Canada. 1999a. *Collaborative Arrangements: Issues for the Federal Government. Report to the House of Commons.* Chapter 5. Ottawa.

Auditor General of Canada. 1999b. *Involving Others in Governing: Accountability at Risk. Report to the House of Commons.* Chapter 23. Ottawa.

Beck Jørgensen, T. 1996. "Rescuing Public Services: On the tasks of public organisations," in H. Hill, H. Klages, and E. Löffler (eds), *Quality, Innovation and Measurement in the Public Sector.* Peter Lang, 161-182.

Bouckaert, G. 1995. "Measuring Quality," in C. Pollitt and G. Bouckaert (ed.). *Quality Improvement in European Public Services: Concepts, Cases and Commentary.* London: Sage.

Commissioner of the Environment and Sustainable Development. 1999. *Streamlining Environmental Protection Through Federal-Provincial Agreements: Are They Working?* Report to the House of Commons. Chapter 5. Ottawa.

Dubuisson, P. 1999. Cafouillage à la maindòeuvre. *La Presse.* Éditorial. Montréal. Avril 9.

Fraser Report. 1991. *The Management of Ministers' Departments and Their Executive Agencies.* A Report to the Prime Minister. London: HMSO.

Efficiency Unit. 1991. *Making the Most of Next Steps: The Management of Ministers' Departments and Their Executive Agencies.* Report to the Prime Minister. London: HMSO.

FOKUS. 1995a.. *Kvalitetsudvikling—en genvej til det udviklende arbejde.* Forlagte Kommuneinformation, København.

FOKUS. 1995b. *Kvalitetsudvikling amter og kommuner.* Kommunernes Landsforening, København.

Gilbert, R. G. 1991. "Human Resource Management Practices to Improve Quality: A Case Example of Human Resource Management in Government." *Human Resource Management,* 30 (2): 183-198.

Holmes, M., and D. Shand. 1995. "Management Reform: Some Practitioner Perspectives on the Past Ten Years." *Governance*, 84: 551-578.

Jacobs, J. 1992. *Systems of Survival.* New York: Random House.

Kikert, W. J. M., and T. B. Jørgensen. 1995. "Conclusion and Discussion: Management, Policy, Politics and Public Values," *International Review of Administrative Sciences*, 61: 577-586.

Kirkpatrick, I., and M. Martinez Lucio (eds.). 1995. *The Politics of Quality in the Public sector*. London and New York: Routledge.

Krogstrup, H. K. 1997. "User Participation in Quality Assessment." *Evaluation*, 32: 205-224.

Launsø, L. 1997. "The Connection between Scope of Diagnosis and the User's Scope of Action Empirical Findings and Theoretical Perspectives," in Søren Gosvig Olsen, and Erling Høg (eds.), *Studies in Alternative Therapy 4. Lifestyle and Paradigms*. Denmark: Odense University Press, 136-149.

Lester, C. 2000. *Kvalitetsudvikling på VUC. Hvorfor, hvordan?* In KRAKA, Kulturelforvaltning, Københavns Amt.

Management Advisory Board and Management Improvement Advisory Committee. 1993. *Building a Better Public Service*. Australian Government Publishing Service, Canberra.

Management Advisory Board. 1994. *Ongoing Reform in Australian Public Service*. Occasional Report no. 15, Canberra, MAB.

Mark, M. M., and E. Pines. 1995. "Implications of Continuous Quality Improvements for Program Evaluation and Evaluators," *Evaluation Practice*, 162: 131-139.

Mayne, J., and J. Hudson. 1992. "Program Evaluation: An Overview," in J. Hudson, J. Mayne, and R. Thomlison (eds.), *Action Oriented Evaluation in Organizations: Canadian Practices*. Toronto: Wall and Emerson, Chapter 1: 1-19.

Mayne, J., S. Divorski, and D. Lemaire. 1999. "Locating Evaluation in the Legislative, Executive or Both," in R. Boyle and D. Lemaire (eds.), *Building Evaluation Capacity*. New Brunswick, NJ: Transaction Publishers, Chapter 1: 1-19.

Mulgan, R. 1997. "Contracting Out and Accountability." *Australian Journal of Public Administration,* 564: 106-116.

Naschold, F. 1995. *The Modernisation of the Public Sector in Europe. A Comparative Perspective on the Scandinavian Experience*. Helsinki: Ministry of Labour.

Office of the Comptroller General. 1981. *Guide on the Program Evaluation Function in Federal Departments and Agencies*. Supply and Services Canada. Ottawa.

Peters, J., and R. H. Waterman. 1992. *In Search of Excellence: Lessons from America's Best Run Companies* . New York: Harper and Row.

Pollitt, C. 1995. "Justification by Works or by Faith? Evaluating the New Public Management." *Evaluation*, 12: 133-154.

Prime Minister and the Minister for the Cabinet Office. 1999. *Modernising Government*. Cm 4310. London: Stationery Office.

Rieper, O., and J. Toulemonde (eds.). 1997. *Politics and Practices of Intergovernmental Evaluation*. New Brunswick, NJ: Transaction Publishers.

Shand, D. 1995. *Evaluating Service Quality*. Sydney: Australian Evaluation Society.

Sehested, Karina et al. 1992: *Effekter af strukturaendringer i kommuner*. AKF Forlaget, Koebenhavn, Effects of Structural Change within Municipalities (with an English summary).

Seidle, F. L. 1995. *Rethinking the Delivery of Public Services to Citizens*. Montreal: Institute for Research on Public Policy.

Stone, B. 1995. "Administrative Accountability in the 'Westminster' Democracies: Towards a New Conceptual Framework." *Governance*, 84, 505-526.

Toulemonde, J. 1998. "Evaluation in Partnership: Practical Suggestions for Improving Their Quality." *Evaluation*, 42, 171-188.

Treasury Board of Canada Secretariat. 1999. Service Canada Strategic Business Plan. Ottawa. *http://servicecanada.gc.ca/.*

Trosa, Sylvie. 1994. *Next Steps: Moving On*. London. Next Steps Team, Cabinet Office.

Wargo, M. J. 1994. "The Impact of the President's Reinvention Plan on Evaluation." *Evaluation Practice*, 151: 63-72.

Wholey, J. 1983. *Evaluation and Effective Public Management*. Boston: Little, Brown and Co.

6

Collaboration by Contract and Pooling Resources: The Implications for Evaluation

Göran Arvidsson

This chapter is intended to explore the functions and evaluands of evaluation in two typical, institutionally different types of collaborative arrangements between public and private partners: *contracting out* (with triangular arrangements with a third-party payer as a special case) and the *pooling* of efforts and resources. In the first case, a public body typically has the role of a principal and funder, while provision is contracted out to other agents. In the second case, the relationship is basically lateral. The parties participate on more or less equal terms.

The basic issue here is to gain a better understanding of the conditions for, and characteristics of, evaluation in these types of organizational collaboration and to establish how they differ from the situation in a traditional comprehensive, hierarchical public agency. The discussion is based on a selective literature survey and a collection of examples of current practice. The examples are collected from different policy areas and mainly from Sweden, where government collaboration with the private sector is nothing new, but where collaboration has taken new forms as public sector reforms have included privatization, outsourcing, customer choice, competition among providers of services, and formation of consortia.

From Integrated Hierarchies to Lateral, Contractual Arrangements

In many welfare states, with the Nordic countries being the most obvious examples, collaboration in the delivery of public services is nothing new. On the contrary, a strong spirit of cooperation between different stakeholders is considered a specific characteristic of these countries. A well-known example is the Swedish labor market where the state and the labor market organizations have worked closely together since the 1930s, with the aim to find stable institutions and reduce the risk of open conflict. But there are many other cases of close relations that may be of a more or less formal character. An earlier corporatist model with, for example, government representatives on the boards of directors of private banks and insurance companies, and industry (and labor union) representatives on the boards of selected government agencies, has been replaced by collaboration in other forms such as informal advisory boards, task forces, and joint projects.

Collaboration can also be hidden, or at least not formally sanctioned. A Norwegian study of power and democracy identified in the 1970s informal "iron triangles" of leading representatives of ministries, industry and unions, who, in fact, governed many policy areas (Hernes 1975). Variants of iron triangles can probably be found in many other countries as well. The post-war American "military-industrial complex" and the Japanese economy (Pempel 1998) are two well-known cases of an informal, yet powerful collaborative arrangement.

Even if the collaborative government is not a new phenomenon in these respects,[1] there are indeed new types of collaboration that have evolved specifically in recent times. As was pointed out in the introductory chapter, competitive strategies in public service delivery—one of the major ingredients in the New Public Management movement (NPM)—are tending to be replaced by collaborative arrangements. In Sweden, for example, competition between providers of publicly financed services is promoted at the same time as collaboration is encouraged. This seeming contradiction is to a large extent explained by the different phases in the contracting processes. Competition for contracts may well be combined with collaboration in the delivery. But there are also different policies for different areas; in some competition is the main concept, in others collaboration and partnering.

In a search for interesting examples of policy changes with clear consequences for the roles, forms and methods of evaluation, it is therefore reasonable to look at the delivery of public services in mature welfare states. Many of these systems seem to follow a common trend, albeit at different speeds and with different scopes: moving from (a) comprehensive, integrated, public service delivery systems, over (b) a period of "marketization" of the public sector, "corporatization" of public agencies and competitive bidding for contracts, towards (c) the application of a new concept: partnerships, lateral collaboration by agreements, and pooling of resources and efforts.

In short, the history may be described as follows. Public administration traditionally relied on vertical information and command chains in hierarchical organizations. This type of organization was intended for—and might be adequate for—executing the powers of government, but it was also the typical organizational form for the growing public service "industry." Such organizational arrangements have, however, a number of drawbacks, especially evident in very large organizations: inflexibility, lack of responsiveness to external demands, lack of incentives for higher efficiency, over-concern with procedures rather than performance and information overload of central units. One of the remedies included in the NPM prescription is to make multilevel, vertically integrated public organizations more flat, reorganize their activities into responsibility centers and introduce market-like relations between these bodies. Other parts of the cure are to help employees to establish themselves as private entrepreneurs, contracting out specific services to private companies, and allowing user choice between public and/or private providers with financial support in the form of service checks/vouchers (Bös 1993; Walsh 1995).

Over-reliance on the benefits of markets and over-use of market analogies and mechanisms has gradually led to reactions. Often, these have implied that collaboration is the ideal form for interplay of public sector agencies internally and externally, not competition. The attractive concept replacing NPM is collaborative government.

The Changing Functions of Evaluation in Public Management

We may now summarize and expand on the previous discussion. Three "waves," or stages, of modernization of public management (in a comprehensive welfare state) may be distinguished, with important implications for the functions of evaluation. In the collectively financed public sector, producers have typically no paying customers to lose and seldom competitors to be compared with and, potentially, be defeated by. In the absence of the self-regulating mechanisms of a market, where the interplay of buyers' demand and sellers' supply decides what transactions will take place, and to which price, other control mechanisms are necessary. One is, obviously, political control, since we are concerned with public sector activities. Another is judicial control, since public sector activities are governed by law. For reasons of efficiency, it is, however, necessary to complement political—or democratic—control and legal supervision with management (economic/administrative) control. The larger, more comprehensive and expensive the public sector, the more evident is this.

Great efforts have been made to establish planning, budgeting, follow-up and auditing as standard tools in modern public administration. Evaluation has followed suit, initially, in the first wave, as an integral—but lagging—part of the internal planning and budgeting processes, and later, in the second wave of reform, as a method for learning how to handle external relations, for example, contractual arrangements.

The First Wave: Management by Results and Evaluation

Previous managerial emphasis on planning, budgeting and monitoring of operations gradually shifted towards evaluation in the 1980s. This was the logical consequence of decentralization, management by objectives (MbO), formation of responsibility centers, and new incentive schemes. To retain control without constantly interfering in local activities, it was considered necessary to organize assessments of the efficiency of operations, quality of products, benefits compared to costs, etc. In commercial companies, research projects and marketing campaigns may be—and are indeed—evaluated, but the real test of the products and the overall performance of the company is in the market's reactions. In the public sector, the concern for output, performance and effectiveness needed other manifestations. Internal and external evaluation were the answer.

The first wave of managerial reform, initiated in the sixties and not yet leveled out in many stratas of public administration, therefore included a crucial role for evaluation. This is easily seen in many governments: evaluation units were formed, management by results was introduced (seen as more relevant and less abstract than MbO), and performance monitoring systems became more important than input control (Gray et al. 1993; Rist 1990).

The Second Wave: Market-Like Solutions and Corporatization of Public Agencies

The second stage, the introduction of market-like arrangements in the eighties could, by analogy, be expected to be accompanied with a reduced demand for evaluation. Feed-back would be provided via market reactions, thus reducing the need for information via evaluation. How, then, to explain why adoption of market mechanisms are often accompanied by explicit demand for more, and more thorough evaluation? As a matter of fact, the whole NPM movement is surrounded by evaluations (for an overview, see Pollitt 1995). For example, the reforms of the UK National Health Service (NHS) in the 1990s relied heavily on the concept of a purchaser-provider split and internal markets. This reform process and its effects are well documented in the evaluation literature (e.g., Robinson and Le Grand 1995).

Two similar reforms have been made in Stockholm. One concerns a major change in 1991 of the Greater-Stockholm health care system, including an internal market where six (initially nine) health-care districts purchase medical care for their inhabitants from a separate producing division, containing hospitals, special clinics and primary health care centers, and also from private hospitals and clinics.[2] In the City of Stockholm, a similar change was made concerning care for elderly people in their private homes or in special homes for the elderly. Competitive bidding for contracts by internal and private providers was introduced successively from 1993. Both reforms have been studied in fairly large evaluation projects by external, academic evaluators as well as by internal evaluators. Never before has such comprehensive and informative descriptions and analyses been made available concerning the outcomes, costs and efficiency.

At first, it may seem paradoxical that introducing market mechanisms does not decrease but seemingly tends to increase the demand for as well as the supply of evaluation. On second thought, however, there is no paradox. The two main purposes of the external evaluations of the reforms of health and elderly care in Stockholm were to assess the effects on quality, productivity and costs and to submit information for subsequent adjustments of the models. What we can see here, and in many other places, is a new *type* of evaluation, one of the functioning and design of new organizational models. With previous internal relations replaced by external relations, and old information routines and command chains that admitted ad hoc sequential adjustments of operations no longer viable, control had to be executed in forms compatible with the contracts. The system itself became an important evaluand. In order to evaluate at the system level, however, it is necessary to evaluate also at the micro level, that is, with respect to the outcomes and costs of individual programs and outputs.

These and many similar examples in other policy areas illustrate that NPM created a new, and more important, role for evaluation as an information tool in change processes and afterwards. To go beyond this general observation, it is necessary to focus on the parties involved. New stakeholders have entered the arena and each of them have their specific needs and use for the type of information that evaluation may provide. Therefore, it should be no surprise that evaluations used as regular information and control instruments by NPM-type of authorities are of a different kind than those used by "traditional" public agencies, and also that their scope and functions differ between policymakers, purchasers and providers, respectively.

The Third Wave: Collaborative Arrangements

What is now happening could perhaps be described as "reinventing collaborative government"—but with new driving-forces and other institutional arrangements. After a long period of expanding the comprehensive welfare state, the overriding efforts now concern retrenchment—not only to lessen tax burdens but also to open up for diversity, flexibility, innovation and citizen involvement. Government strategies to introduce and strengthen collaborative arrangements with private producers and private investors—as well as encouraging voluntary organizations to take on greater responsibilities—should be viewed in this light. But, and this seems important, this is taking place after a period more or less dominated by NPM values and concepts. This heritage makes itself visible in several ways, for example, in the emphasis on explicit agreements (legally binding contracts plus morally binding letter of intents) and accountability.

Giving room for more private initiatives and activities in service delivery does not necessarily lead to a situation of a rather passive government. Nor is it self-evident that the development of new forms of co-financing, co-working, partnering and collaboration means the emergence of a new model to replace New Public Management. There is much rhetoric about networking, partnerships and virtual organizations. A government stepping back from operational and financial responsibilities, however, does not have to accept that its role should be reduced to that of one player among others. A reasonable hypothesis is that government in general wants—and tends to use strategies to—stay in control, keeping its formal and real role as the "principal," while allowing new "agents" into the arena. To achieve this, government needs instruments for feedback and control. Evaluation offers a legitimate, cheap and comprehensive instrument.

This explains, at least partly, why increased reliance on market mechanisms as well as other forms of linkages with external partners seems to increase rather than decrease government concern with evaluation. It has, in turn, consequences for the roles and objects of evaluation. Contractual partners need to know what comes out of a deal, and they need to learn how to improve their roles as partners. This could give evaluation a more managerial and (perhaps) less scientific relevance and image. There is growing evidence that this is the case in health care, education, industrial and R&D policy, transport infrastructure and telecommunications—to mention some important policy areas.

Chapter 1 of this volume identifies five possible functions of evaluation in collaborative government: (a) to check whether the intrinsic mechanisms are working (and cost-effective), (b) to bring order to the potential complexity, (c) to assess the collaborative relationship itself, (d) to facilitate knowledge building, and (e) to inform debates and choices about collaborative alternatives. With a stakeholder perspective all of them seem relevant to any accountable public agency entering a collaborative agreement. For private stakeholders, items (b) and (c) could be expected to be most relevant. Basically, however, more operationally oriented evaluations would probably be considered most useful. It is easy to find practical examples of this. If this is so, one could hypothesize that new collaborative arrangements imply greater changes of the functions of evaluation for the public partner than for the private ones. To find valid relationships between institutional arrangements, stakeholders and evaluation functions, however, would require a major research effort. The ambition here is more modest: to identify some alternative functions of evaluation and search for evidence of whether and how these have been effected in specific instances of "new" forms of collaboration.

The following three functions of evaluation will be distinguished:

1. *Control*, in the sense of finding out whether what was decided/ordered/agreed was actually carried out in accordance with specifications/expectations.

2.   *Validation*, that is, finding out if anticipated cause-effect relationships exist, if programs have the intended effects.

3.   *Innovation*, where evaluation is a tool for collective learning, knowledge-based organizational change, improving intellectual capital.

The evaluators' roles are closely linked to the types and functions of evaluation (Arvidsson 1992: 259). With a control perspective, it is logical that an evaluator's role resembles that of an auditor or controller. If validation is the overriding function, it seems reasonable that the evaluator's professional identity and approach is that of a researcher. If evaluation is used to support innovation by (action) learning, the adequate evaluator role would be that of a consultant: a tutor, guide, "enlightener" or change agent. With this background, the following discussion will focus on two principally different forms of collaboration, and the roles of evaluation and evaluators in each case: Contracting out (with outsourcing and the purchaser-provider split model as two special cases) and pooling (of public and private resources and efforts).

Contracting out

In both government and commercial firms, it is a tendency since at least the 1980s to concentrate on core business. What is not strategically important to do in-house by employed staff, is contracted out to external providers. Typically, such providers have no ownership links with the purchaser. The relationship is contractual, for longer or shorter periods of time. The forms of the contractual arrangements can, however, differ widely, with important consequences for the evaluation function. Outsourcing and the purchaser-provider split offer two interesting cases.

Outsourcing

Outsourcing of certain functions, especially support functions, is a frequent managerial strategy. There often exist external suppliers specialized in the goods and services demanded. By contracting out, the purchaser can benefit from the supplier's competitive advantage and at the same time decrease its own managerial burden.

In the case of standard products, offered by several external suppliers, the situation is—or is close to—a regular market relationship. The more specific the needs of the purchaser, and the fewer the alternative contracting partners on both sides, the higher the degree of dependence between the parties and the more appropriate the first element in the term "quasi market." In industry, specialization may mean that brand owners subcontract even core components, for instance engines in motor cars, or core services, such as running the firm's computer department. In such cases, there are often long-term relations of a partnership character. Cooperation for higher joint profits to be split in a fair manner, rather than suboptimization by each of the parties, is the common objective. Efficient division of labor is the guiding principle.

Strategies to focus on core competencies have meant a similar interest for outsourcing in the public sector. Reducing costs is probably the main motive. Cutting costs is probably important to a private buyer as well, but the opportunity to increase revenues by better product quality may turn the relationship from a zero-sum game to a plus-sum game. For a tax financed public institution, outsourcing is probably either a means to improve operations given the cost level or a method for reducing costs for a given production. Numerous examples exist from areas such as real estate maintenance, cleaning, computer services and call centers.

What is the role of evaluation in this situation? The main conclusion from discussions with public officials in Swedish central and local government is that the role of evaluation is not basically affected by outsourcing of internal functions. Controlling and evaluating external sub-contractors supplying intermediary products is, in many respects, not so different from controlling and evaluating internal providers. In both cases the products are delivered to the buyer to meet the buyer's own needs and specifications. Indeed, a contractual relationship offers other types of information disclosure, supervision and sanctions than a hierarchical one, but in both cases the buyer is also the recipient. There is (or should be) no fundamental change in the ability and the incentive to control quality and cost of products delivered. The principal consequences for evaluation do not concern the products but the relationship as such: How does it work? What are the risks? Is it a good relationship worth continuing?

From the perspective of the buyer, the advantages of outsourcing could be off-set by new transaction costs, including costs for the contracting process, monitoring of deliveries and protecting the contractual rights. These aspects seemingly belong to follow-up processes and to the control functions of evaluation. Informal interviews with procurement officers in some business firms and in local government support this supposition by indicating that evaluation, when it exists, is mainly of a control type. Evaluation questions then tend to concern aspects not covered in the regular monitoring and follow-up systems and are typically raised when preparing for a new contracting process.

There are, however, other uses of evaluation. One is to assess the contracting model as such (compared with its alternatives), which means a validation function. Another is to involve an evaluation team in the building of the new relationship with the task to produce feed-back information and support change. The function of evaluation would be advisory and formative.

The main normative conclusion would be that outsourcing of previously internal functions does not require radical changes in evaluation policies. Basically, it is a question of combining what was needed with respect to the previous internal suppliers with what is generally demanded working with external suppliers.

Purchaser-provider Split

The case of a purchaser-provider split is of a different character. One public authority acts as the buyer and other agencies—or independent bodies—produce and deliver to someone other than the buyer. There exists a number of variants ranging from a situation of only public providers, through a mixture of public and private providers to a situation where government has entrusted the delivery function completely to one or several independent bodies, for example, private companies or nonprofit organizations.

Some familiar examples of arrangements where a government body has contracted out traditionally core public services to independent suppliers are medical treatment provided to a specified population according to a contract with a public health authority, school education by contract with a public school authority, and elderly care by contract with a municipality. Contracts may be signed after a process of competitive bidding for a certain market or take the form of a license to operate in the market. Both models are frequent in health care, education and elderly care in, for example, Sweden. The public agency typically keeps the responsibility for admittance decisions, that is, who should benefit from the services, and financing (directly or via vouchers), while the provider delivers according to the existing regulations (Arvidsson 1995).

A government purchaser of services to the public can adopt either a partnership or a strictly business-like strategy vis-à-vis potential and existing private providers. Evidently, the choice would have implications for the functions of evaluation and for the roles of the evaluators as will be seen from the following cases.

Case 1: Contracting out in Danish National Government. Contracting out has been a major strategy in recent years' reforms in Denmark aimed at making public activities more autonomous and decentralized. The official policy of the Danish National Government states that the purpose of contracting out is to make sure that higher effectiveness in the public sector is achieved, and through this also the best possible use of public resources.

The use of external suppliers increased in the period 1992-95 but since then has stagnated. This seems to have worried the authorities. In 1999, *Udliciteringsrådet* (The National Outsourcing Council) initiated an investigation to find out how ministry departments and other state agencies implement the national directives and use tenders and outsourcing. Another purpose was to reveal obstacles for a wider implementation (Andersen 2000: 341).

In his abstract (in January 2000) of a keynote speech to be delivered at the annual meeting of the Nordic Administrative Association in August 2000, Andersen, chairman of the Outsourcing Council, pointed out a number issues of present concern: "How many tasks can the public sector transfer to private institutions? How should the public sector be organized to make the contracting processes run more smoothly? How are the increasing demands of citizens, users and customers being met? Can politicians steer the development in the public sector in the future?"[3]

These are typical evaluation questions, and they are all genuinely related to the new public-private interplay. The three basic functions of evaluation identified above (control, validation, and innovation) are all relevant here. The first and the fourth of Andersen's questions concern validation: "Is this a good idea?" and "How far should we go?" The second question concerns learning and improvement: "How can we (learn to) do better given the contracting model?" The third question is about control: "Do the beneficiaries get what they should get?"

It is not surprising that questions like these occupy the thoughts of a government official in charge of advancing subcontracting to private producers. But how should he get the answers except by professional evaluation? There is definitely a place for evaluation here.[4]

Case 2: Healthcare in Stockholm. Over the past decade, the Stockholm County Council, which is in charge of healthcare in the Greater Stockholm Area, has implemented a clear purchaser-provider split. Under the directly elected county council there are now two separate organizations: One organization (headed by the Healthcare Board and organized in six health care districts, each with a board of politicians) acts as buyers of care, and another organization (headed by the Healthcare Production Board) is in charge of the (dominant) part of care provided by the county itself. The supply side consists of two university hospitals, two very large acute hospitals, a handful of medium-sized general or specialized acute hospitals (one is privately owned and operated), fourteen other hospitals (a majority of them privately owned and operated), and several hundred primary care centers and specialist clinics. In the last category there are public health care centers, private groups or individual practices, psychiatric clinics, geriatric clinics and rehabilitation centers.

The most spectacular change in the public-private mix in recent years is the sale in December 1999 of one the acute hospitals, *St. Görans sjukhus AB*, to *Bure Hälsa och Sjukvård AB*, a subsidiary of *Investment AB Bure*, which is a private corporation listed on the Stockholm Stock Exchange.[5] This is the only commercially operated major acute hospital in Sweden. (Other private hospitals are small and specialized, and most are run by not-for-profit organizations or producer cooperatives.) The hospital is now operated under a three-year contract. Everything except the buildings, which were and still are owned by the County Council's real estate company and leased to St. Göran's on a ten-year contract, was transferred to the new owners. Almost all staff were positive and assumed positions in the new organization.

St. Göran's hospital was transformed from a budgetary unit to a separate legal entity (subsidiary company wholly owned by the county) several years ago. The autonomy created by this change was considered overwhelmingly positive in most identifiable respects: cost-effectiveness, patient satisfaction, employee satisfaction, and cost control. According to both the chairman of the county's healthcare board and the hospital manager, who was "included in the deal," the main additional advantage of the sale—except securing diversity—is that it further strengthens the need to identify each party's roles and responsibilities. Transparency is, for them, a key issue. The contracts with St. Göran's could be a bench-mark for other relations.

Before, during and after the contracting-out process, there has been an intensive political debate on the wisdom of this sale. It was decided and executed by the non-socialist county council majority that took power after the autumn 1998 elections. The Social Democratic National Government, as well as their party colleagues in the Stockholm County Council, strongly opposed the move and feared more to come in Stockholm and in the other two urban regions (Skåne and Västra Götaland), now run by non-socialist coalition governments. In the autumn of 2000, Parliament passed a new, temporary law forbidding further transfers of acute hospitals to private, for-profit owners. At the same time, government has taken steps to increase ownership diversity among primary health care providers. The Swedish Employers' Federation was upset and viewed the law as a threat against the freedom of trade, while the political opposition saw it as a centralist attack on local government autonomy and self-governance. The whole issue is still the object of political controversy.

The stepwise reorganization of the healthcare system in Stockholm has been accompanied by a number of academic as well as consultancy evaluations. It is likely that the St. Göran's case will be equally—and probably more—scrutinized from both inside and outside. The hospital itself advertises both favorable results from customer satisfaction surveys and data showing that it operates at approximately 10 percent lower costs than other hospitals in the region. From the perspective of the principal, the County Council, there are at least two dimensions that warrant observation and where evaluation could be an adequate, but not the only, instrument.

The first concerns how the contractor fulfills its obligations, including being a source of inspiration for other providers. Aspects of evaluation (evaluands) include medical quality, service quality, cost-effectiveness, customer and employee satisfaction, innovative behavior, and collaboration with other care providers. None of these aspects is principally different from what could, and should, be asked concerning any provider, public or private. There are stable experiences on which to form such evaluations, but most attempts have been on ad hoc bases. The interest in systematic benchmarking has increased notably in recent years.

The second dimension is new. It concerns the specific character-istics of a quasi-market relationship compared with a hierarchy. The term *quasi-market* (and more or less close synonyms such as *pseudo-market*, *planned market* and *administered market*) is commonly used to represent certain types of arrangements which, although using market mechanisms, are different from a "normal" market relation between several independent buyers and sellers. In the case of a purchaser-provider split within one organization, the two parties have a common superior that has the authority to limit the autonomy of the subordinate units in several ways. In the case of contracting out, for example, to private business firms there is, of course, no com-mon superior. However, if a public authority is the only buyer (i.e., is a monopsonist) and, in addition, controls the market conditions, this market has also a quasi character.

The creation of internal markets, as well as contracting out, thus splits the integrated public service organization into two distinct functions: purchaser and provider. The effects are sometimes dra-matic. Productivity gains of 10-20 percent are not uncommon. Qual-ity awareness is often strengthened. In general, very positive effects have been reported, at least initially. This is evident from a growing number of evaluations showing how a purchaser-provider split has affected cost containment, productivity, quality of services, etc. in areas so diverse as health care, elderly care, refuse collection, and road maintenance (Bailey and Davidson 1997, 1999).

On the other hand, when the first profits have been reaped, nega-tive consequences as higher transaction costs for the creation and surveillance of contracts, decreased purchaser influence, and com-plaints concerning less equal treatment of similar cases tend to dampen the enthusiasm. This is evident in Swedish healthcare and care for the elderly. "Marketization" strategies are sometimes based more on ideology than on solid theory and empirical evidence—but the same is often true of criticisms of these strategies. Neo-insti-tutional economic analyses show that contractual arrangements are not per se superior to hierarchical relationships (Klages and Löffler 1998: 43). The reverse is also true. It is a matter of preconditions, adaptation and implementation.[6]

An additional aspect is the specific type of problems linked to so-called market triangles where a buyer buys services from separate providers on behalf of group of beneficiaries. Typical examples exist in both the public and the private sector: a health care district buys medical care for its population; an insurance company buys repairs of damaged cars owned by its car insurance policy holders. Collusion of the provider and the beneficiary for excess services at the expense of the payer is a clear risk in such circumstances and an obvious candidate for evaluation.

Returning to the case of St. Göran's hospital, discussed above, one can ask: What are the implications for the evaluation of a for-profit hospital closely integrated in a regional healthcare system dominated by a public, tax-financed, single payer? Evidently, it is not enough to focus on effectiveness and productivity issues at the hospital level "and below." The hospital's contribution to the overall performance of the whole system is of overriding importance. This raises questions concerning macro-evaluation, an issue quite different from shop-floor assessments. Neither is it relevant for the healthcare principal and payer to use shareholder value as a proxy for effectiveness. Indeed, a private, for-profit hospital once accepted into the system must have the opportunity to make money. An inherent incentive in commercial organizations to make profits not only by out-performing competitors by better products but also by cutting costs, however, implies a risk of impaired quality over time and at its worst "hit, grab and run-strategies." If a fee for service payment system is used, there is also a risk of over-production in relation to what is medically feasible and cost-effective.

Even though formal monitoring of service delivery, site inspections and quality assurance schemes has its role, more information is needed in the case of such a complex enterprise as a hospital. Economic and legal means are not enough. Building and maintaining trust seems essential. This, if true, may give evaluation a completely new role, that of trust-building and promoting shared images of reality. What evaluation could supply is information of common interest (although not necessarily of *shared* interest) and arenas for processing the information, together as well as separately by each party.

Returning to the three evaluation functions identified earlier in this chapter—control, validation, and innovation—it should be obvious that they are all relevant in a case like St. Göran's and for both the principal and the provider. The five functions mentioned in chapter 1 and repeated above are of a "higher" level and more relevant to the purchaser, which is also the principal and accountable for the system's overall effectiveness.

Pooling Resources

Combining efforts and resources to attain better results is the idea behind all organized activity, in business and elsewhere: joining forces in wars, shaping coalitions in politics, etc. What is of interest here is the specific type of pooling where public and private organizations enter into a formal partnership characterized by the ambition to create a win-win game. Opposing goals are acknowledged and respected but played down in contrast with regular market situations where buyers and sellers exchange products for money and are occupied with optimizing or satisficing their own goal functions.

Typically, the partners have basically different motives for engaging in a partnership as well as different types of resources to offer. For a public agency the motive may be to fulfill a public responsibility in a more cost-effective way, for a business company, to achieve higher return on investment. The public agency may supply legitimacy, authority, expertise and source of future income streams, the company, financial and human capital, technology and production capacity.

Various types of such collaboration were identified in the introductory chapter. Here we shall look in more detail at two Swedish examples: cooperation between schools and industry concerning workplace-located vocational education of high-school students (*arbetsplatsförlagd utbildning, APU*) and regional growth agreements (*regionala tillväxtavtal*) between regional bodies of government and industry/business.

Case 3: Workplace education, APU.[7] Since 1991, vocational training by APU is an integral and mandatory part of the non-theoretical programs at *gymnasium* (high school) level. These programs are three years long, the same as the theoretical programs. APU should be at least 15 percent of total student time and is located in regular workplaces. There are several interests involved: pupils and parents, schools and school authorities, local communities, individual firms and their organizations. All parties seem to agree that the APU is necessary to meet the objectives of the vocational programs: to prepare students for work life and to meet the demands for technically and socially skilled labor.

APU is viewed as and designed as education, not just work to get practical experience. National guidelines set the framework. The

municipalities are responsible for setting goals, planning, administration and follow-up while the companies involved assume an educational role and are supposed to supply specially trained instructors. Both in the preparations for the APU system and later, it has
been stressed that a successful implementation requires a well-de-
veloped dialogue between schools and business firms. Various joint
teams and networks exist as linking organizations.

In 1998, the Swedish National School Board published an evaluation, *Samverkan Skola-Arbetsliv* (Collaboration School-Work-Life).
The report was distributed to all high schools with vocational programs. Before this, conferences were organized at nine locations
around the country. The evaluation was based on the national goals
and its purpose was to show how APU functions with respect to
these goals. Other evaluations concern, for example, the training of
instructors, and the students' benefits of APU.

The purpose of the evaluation was specified in five questions:

1.   To what extent is APU implemented with the prescribed scope?

2.   What are the economic conditions governing APU?

3.   What are the organizational and pedagogical conditions for APU?

4.   What is the estimated importance of APU for attaining the educational
      goals of the program?

5.   How do students perceive and value their workplace located educa-
      tion?

The method of evaluation was a combination of a mail survey to
2,620 individuals belonging to three target groups—program managers (vocational teachers or school managers), students, and instructors—and personal interviews with 110 individuals in these
groups. The report contains detailed answers to each of the five questions. The summary includes a list of success criteria. Collaboration
between schools and workplaces is seen as a basic condition. It has
many facets and needs at all levels: managerial and daily work. Cultural factors and ways of thinking are important. The vocational teachers and the company instructors not only need to work together, they
need to understand and cope with the other organization.

As can be seen from the five questions, this evaluation had a
clear control and validation function, which indicates that it was
intended to meet primarily the needs of the supervising authorities.

There were two main users of the results: a parliamentary commission for the evaluation of "the new *gymnasieskolan*," and a working group formed by government to study the collaboration between schools and work-life. Representatives of these committees were interviewed by Englund (1999).

The parliamentary commission explicitly referred to the results of the APU evaluation in its report. It is concluded that APU works well, but that certain changes are needed: better interplay of theory and practice, more emphasis on theory to meet employers' requirements, increased share of the education in the form of APU (with very positive student opinions being one of the motivations), training of instructors in all programs where this was not completed, concentrating APU into fewer but longer periods. The evaluation was considered to give a good basis for decisions by organizations concerned with or affected by APU.

The governmental working group was formed by the Ministry of Education in March 1999 and included representatives of the ministry and the National School Board and of four central labor market organizations (*SAF, Kommunförbundet, LO* and *TCO*). Its task was to prepare a proposal concerning the future development of APU, including its scope, goals, adaptation to labor market needs, and collaborative arrangements. The evaluation was considered to provide vital information concerning differences between programs concerning both the content of APU and educational quality, deficiencies in the training of instructors, and mismatch between programs offered and the local industry structure, to mention a few key issues. Government wanted to increase the pressure on those municipalities that did not offer APU to the required extent, and at the same time find means to stimulate business to participate. According to the group's chairperson, no additional information was needed to do this besides what was provided by the evaluation. The predefined control and validation needs were satisfied, while innovation ideas were an extra bonus.

Case 4: Regional growth agreements.[8] Today's industrial policy in Sweden has three characteristics: (a) the view that the main function of the state is to provide a good business climate: efficient markets, stable institutions, incentives to make investments, etc., (b) a focus on regional and local conditions for business entrepreneurship: supply of competencies, a functioning infrastructure, etc., and (c) various kinds of support to industry and business. This industrial policy builds on modern growth theory emphasizing the importance of institutions, that is, social and legal norms, incentives, regulations, and so on. Other key concepts are clusters, networks, regionalization, and collaboration of government and industry.

In May 1998, the government asked its regional authorities to initiate and coordinate the process of forming regional growth agreements with the local business communities. The purpose was to improve the conditions for growth and employment. A basic idea was that growth takes place in the firms. To improve business conditions was—and is—therefore the overriding purpose. A requisite was that each agreement should show clearly how business representatives were involved in formulating the agreement and how they should participate in its implementation.

Regional partnership is a key concept, borrowed from the policies concerning structural funds of the EU. A partnership is formed for certain purposes and should involve broad participation of both public and private partners. Partnerships should be constellations built on mutual trust. State authorities and agencies within the policy area are expected to participate. Municipalities and counties are supposed to take on key roles. Beside this, there are no central directives as to participation. Different kinds of organizations may participate: universities, foundations, and various types of business organizations.

The agreements should have the character of contracts. It should be clear who are the contracting partners. It should also be clearly stated what is agreed upon, and who is financing what. A growth agreement is not legally binding. There are no formal sanctions for a party that does not fulfill its commitments. It is, however, morally binding. Each agreement should contain an analysis of the strengths and weaknesses of the region. It should identify opportunities and problems. It should include a program ranging from goals and priorities to concrete activities. The partners should be able to discuss and participate in its implementation. Many sources of government money—previously used for regional development, small business support, fighting unemployment—are redirected to these programs. Parts of the EU structural funds are also included. For the fiscal year 2000 the funds at disposal were SEK 19 billion (c. EUR 2.2 billion). The draft agreements submitted by April 1999 were assessed by two *ex ante*-evaluations: one made by Nordregio, a Nordic research institute, the other by a consultancy firm. Nordregio focused on program content and implementability and on the regional processes. The explicit purpose was that "the study should be useful for the ministries in their contacts with the regions, and a support for the regions in their continued work to develop the agreements and their contents" (Nordregio 1999: 7; author's translation). The other evaluation was an assessment of how the proposals were linked to the analyses of growth conditions in the region. The explicit purpose was to "identify growth agreements which seem more or less well thought-out with respect to analysis, goals, and activities proposed" (Ledningskonsulterna 1999: 2; author's translation).

Both studies were of a high professional standard. They put forward a number of short-term recommendations (such as strengthening the character of a contract, basing it on a clear vision, focusing on certain branches and clusters, and concentrating on activities with a direct bearing on local business) and they raised a number of issues to be dealt with in the longer run (for example the geographic delimitations of the regions defined in the agreements, relations with other government policies and programs for growth and development, involvement of other partners than the traditional ones). At the national level, the evaluations were used for revising the regulatory framework concerning the use of government funds within this and adjacent areas. In the regions, the evaluations were used as feed-back by the partnerships.

In the autumn of 2000, all 24 regions of Sweden participated with a three-year regional development program for 2000-2002. In May, an interdepartmental working group in the government offices finalized a plan for follow-up and evaluation (Statskontoret 2000). Evaluations are to be conducted at both regional and national levels and reported in spring 2001 and autumn 2003. A number of components and procedures are proposed. Of special interest here are the five issues mentioned as focal points for national evaluation:

1. The links in the cause-effect model on which the program is based and which consists of 12 steps from the regional growth agreements over improved cooperation, greater trust, improved business climate, more investments, new entrepreneurs, increased employment, structural change, etc. to the final impact of growth (i.e., *validation*).

2. Counties which develop in a particularly positive manner (*innovation*).

3. Case studies and other in-depth studies to provide deeper insight than the follow-up can provide (possibly for both *validation* and *innovation*).

4.   The allocation and utilization of public funds; this information may be used for future reallocation of funds (evaluation's *control* function).

5.   Variety between regions to find "best practice" (an *innovation* perspective).

Even if there are few explicit references to a focus on the various arrangements in the 24 regions, this evaluation has the benefit of concerning a "natural experiment" of public-private collaboration. Future studies will show what was learned by this experiment.

What, then, can be concluded from Cases 3 and 4 concerning the functions and evaluands of evaluation? In the APU evaluation (Case 3), there was no cost-effectiveness analysis and no attempt to bring order in relations (which were clear enough). An obvious function, however, was to check structures and processes for the collaboration, and comparing local experience with what was assumed by the central school authorities to be conditions for a successful APU. The informative functions contained benchmarking information to the parties involved, dispersed new ideas to schools wishing to develop their vocational programs, and—to some extent—information to the general public on the large differences between programs concerning scope and benefits. On the whole, however, this evaluation was mainly focused on the needs of the regulatory and supervisory authorities in National government and School administration. In terms of the categorization of functions set out earlier in this chapter, there were elements of each, of control, validation and innovation, with an emphasis on the first two.

As was mentioned above, the APU evaluation has been used by both government and Parliament. Interviews with officials there showed that they were satisfied with the evaluation. They had obtained relevant information and useful insights into the functioning of the system and the interplay between local partners. This information will be used in further reform work. It is probable that the report has been read and used by local school representatives, but very unlikely that is has reached the businesses directly. They tend to seek information from and act through their organizations and these are considered well informed.

The assessments of the regional growth agreements (Case 4) demonstrated most of the functions mentioned in chapter 1. Providing feed-back to government *and* the regional partnerships was a main function, which may seem logical of an *ex ante*-evaluation. The two studies provided descriptions and analyses of what had been done and what was under way, and submitted comments and recommendations. They did not, however, assess costs and benefits, and they had no function to inform the general public. As a matter of fact, these agreements—in spite of the effort and money that have been put in—are so far largely unknown outside the circles directly involved.

According to interviews with representatives of both the relevant ministry and one of the regions, there is an overall satisfaction with the two studies. Since this is an activity in process, it is interesting to note that the interviewees stress factors strengthening their own positions and ambitions. Tactical use of these evaluations is likely, which may not be an evil, after all. Stakeholder use of evaluation information should be expected to be tactical. Balancing interests and disclosure of evaluation results would diminish the risks of exploitation and abuse of information superiority.

Conclusion

A general conclusion from an analysis of the cases presented is that they do not support hypotheses that evaluation is not necessary in a collaborative environment. It also seems evident that the traditional methods and functions of evaluation are still valid, but need to be complemented. Traditional methods may be combined in new ways. Insights from behavioral sciences such as social psychology could complement economic and sociological frames of reference. More emphasis should be placed on identifying the dynamics of the relationships over and above what is usual in internal organizational evaluation. Stakeholder involvement in evaluations seems both more crucial and more complex than in traditional settings with clear distributions of roles and powers between the parties.

Little has been said in this chapter about evaluation quality. Generally, there is no direct relation between the "inner" quality of an evaluation and its use. The use is to a large extent dependent on the situational context. A low quality, quick-and-dirty study may have much more impact than a well-designed and professionally carried out evaluation. But it is, of course, desirable that what is being used for decisions is as good as possible for that purpose.

Judging from the rapidly increasing interest internationally to forming various kinds of collaborative relations between government and private entities, much remains to be done in order to understand and develop the functions and methodologies of evaluation in these new environments.

Notes

1. Actually, the tendency (very obvious in Sweden since the 1980s) seems to be a movement away from blurred mixed economy arrangements and elements of a corporatist state and towards more distinct roles of government and private institutions.
2. The present non-socialist majority is at the time of this writing planning for all hospital care to be open to tender in a few years.
3. This author's translation.
4. At the time of the conference, Mr. Andersen had assumed an executive position in private business and also left the Outsourcing Council. His speech did not address the issues raised in the abstract but the reasons why so little had happened despite the advantages of contracting out and the official policies (Andersen 2000). He remarked, however, that—paradoxically enough—systematic control often starts only when public welfare services are to be delivered by private providers. Only then government focuses seriously on what is best for the citizens (op cit, p. 339).
5. In 2000, *Bure Hälsa och Sjukvård* was organized as a separate public corporation, *Capio AB*.
6. For a discussion of the economic problems of quasi-markets, see Le Grand and Bartlett 1993:19-34.
7. This case draws on a study (Englund 1999) which was carried out to provide case material for the present chapter.
8. See note 7, op cit.

References

Andersen, A. 2000. "Fristilling af offentlig virksomhet: Udbud og udlicitering i Danmark." *Nordisk Administrativt Tidsskrift* 4/2000, pp. 337-346.

Arvidsson, G. 1992. "Increasing the Utilization of Evaluation by Matching the Interests of the Principal and the Evaluator," in J. Mayne, M. L. Bemelmans-Videc, J. Hudson, and R. Conner (eds.), *Advancing Public Policy Evaluation*. Amsterdam: North-Holland, pp 255-260.

Arvidsson, G. 1995. "Regulation of Planned Markets in Health Care," in R. B. Saltman and C. von Otter (eds.), *Implementing Planned Markets in Health Care: Balancing Social and Economic Responsibility*. Buckingham and Philadelphia: Open University Press, pp. 56-85.

Bailey, S. J., and C. Davidson. 1997. "Did quality really increase under Local Government CCT?," in L. Montainhero et al. (eds.), *Public and Private Partnerships: Learning for Growth*. Sheffield: SHU Press.

Bailey, S. J., and C. Davidson. 1999. "The Purchaser-Provider Split: Theory and UK Evidence." *Environment and Planning*, Vol. 17, pp. 161-175.

Bös D. 1993. *Privatization in Europe: A Comparison of Approaches*. Oxford Review of Economic Policy, Vol. 9, 1:95-111.

Englund, P. 1999. "Utvärdering och samarbete—en analys av utvärderingars roll när stat och näringsliv samarbetar" Evaluation and Collaboration—An Analysis of the Role of Evaluation When Government and Business Collaborate. *Candidate thesis*, School of Business, Stockholm University.

Gray, A. G., W. I. Jenkins, and R. V. Segsworth (eds.). 1993. *Budgeting, Auditing and Evaluation: Foundations and Integration in Seven Governments*. New Brunswick, NJ: Transaction Publishers.

Hernes, G. 1975. *Makt og avmakt.* Bergen, Oslo and Tromsø: Universitetsforlaget.

Klages, H., and E. Löffler. 1998. "New Public Management in Germany: The Implementation ProcesS of the New Steering Model." *International Review of Administrative Sciences*, Vol. 641:41-54.

Le Grand, J., and W. Bartlett. 1993. "The Theory of Quasi-Markets," in J. Le Grand and W. Bartlett (eds.), *Quasi-Markets and Social Policy*. London: Macmillan, pp. 13-34.

Ledningskonsulterna. 1999. *Ex-ante utvärdering av förslag till tillväxtavtal.* Unpublished report.

Nordregio. 1999. *Ex-ante utvärdering av utkasten till tillväxtavtal.* Unpublished report.

Pempel, T. J. 1998. *Regime Shift: Comparative Dynamics of the Japanese Political Economy.* Ithaca, NY: Cornell University Press.

Pollitt, C. 1995. "Justification or Works by Faith? Evaluating the New Public Management." *Evaluation*, Vol. 1 2:133-154.

Rist, R. C. (ed.). 1990. *Program Evaluation and the Management of Government: Patterns and Prospects across Eight Nations.* New Brunswick, NJ: Transaction Publishers.

Robinson, R., and J. Le Grand. 1995. "Contracting and the Purchaser-Provider Split," in R. B. Saltman and C. von Otter (eds.), *Implementing Planned Markets in Health Care: Balancing Social and Economic Responsibility.* Buckingham and Philadelphia: Open University Press, pp. 25-44.

Statskontoret. 2000. "Plan for National Follow-up and Evaluation of Regional Growth Agreements." Paper presented by Ann Dahlberg at the 4th European Evaluation Conference, 12-14 October.

Walsh, K. 1995. *Public Services and Market Mechanisms—Competition, Contracting and the New Public Management.* London: Macmillan Press.

7

Results-Based Governance: Collaborating for Outcomes

John Mayne

It is trite to say, but societies are changing and rapidly so. Globalization, a more educated citizenry, the impact of technology, the ready availability of information, political integration and fragmentation are some of the factors at play. Governments worldwide are struggling to provide leadership and direction in the face of these challenges. They are constantly trying to find better ways to provide goods and services to their citizens to manage their affairs better while the practice of managing those affairs—public management—is striving to keep up, sometimes through innovation, more often through imitation of the private sector (Metcalfe 1993).

One evident trend is towards greater use of measurement in the public sector to determine empirically the results of government activities (Kettl 1997; Mayne and Zapico-Goni 1997; OECD 1997; Wholey 1999). Results-based management, managing for results and performance-based management have become familiar terms in the public administration of many jurisdictions. The success of these initiatives is not always evident but efforts continue and gradual progress is being made in improving performance measurement in the public sector. Whether or not these efforts at measurement are deemed successful, they are usually seen as just an adjunct to public management; hopefully useful, but in the end, not essential to good governance. In this chapter we will argue otherwise.

We suggest that three factors are emerging that will be key characteristics of developed society in the twenty-first century: complexity, collaboration, and citizen engagement.[1] Complexity is seen in the significant increases in the amount of information available,

greater interconnectedness of problems, a more educated population, and rapid feedback through information technology. Collaboration between the public and private sectors, and with citizens is
seen as essential for coping with these complexities. Moreover, citizens are demanding a greater say between elections in how they are
governed. As a result, governments are increasing their efforts to
have citizen-centered service delivery.

It is argued that these factors challenge fundamentally traditional
public sector management practices and paradigms. Even more, they
challenge many of the practices of governance (i.e., how the nation
state is managed). New governance models are emerging to cope
with these trends. They are models that rely heavily on measurement of performance in the public sector. Evaluation and performance measurement, management tools of the 1980s and 1990s,
may become key tools of governance in the twenty-first century.

What do we mean here by the term "governance"? The term is
becoming increasingly popular and contains many meanings (Paquet
1999; Stowe 1992; World Bank 1994). Governance is the manner
in which power is exercised. In our context, we are not talking about
questions of state, but rather at a more micro level of how power
and responsibility with respect to a specific programming area is
managed.

Complexity is Here to Stay

Some argue that societies are complex phenomena that have always been changing and continue to do so. Perhaps it is a matter of
degree, but others argue that societies are becoming fundamentally
different (Michael 1993; Mayne and Zapico-Goni 1997; Strange
1996). For example, Rae argues that "The pace of these changes
and the fact that many of them lie outside the control of politics and
governments is critical to understanding how the world around us is
being transformed" (1998: 48).

There are several factors suggesting an acceleration of the pace
of change and a significant increase in complexity. First, societal
problems exhibit a greater interconnectedness than ever. The links
between economic, social and environmental conditions are increasingly recognized as significant and complex, and the importance of
better understanding these links is seen as critical. After encouraging decentralization of activities, there is renewed interest by governments in the need to be able to deal with issues horizontally across

traditional bureaucratic boundaries (Boyle 1999; Privy Council Office 1997).

Second, there is significantly more information on all matters produced, readily and inexpensively available to society. Information, ideas, debate and discussion are all subject to rapid feedback through available information technology, especially through the Internet. One implication is that extensive and lengthy planning exercises once carried out by governments are often unacceptable to citizens who want quicker responsiveness. The public can indeed plan without their governments. Many current approaches to public management and leadership cannot handle rapid feedback. They require a more orderly and protracted process to function well.

Many societies are becoming increasingly diverse through the influence of factors such as their natural diversity, increased immigration and the free flow of ideas across borders. Interest groups with diverse viewpoints are frequently driving the political agenda with politicians vainly trying to please all sides of any issue. Where once the nation-state was a fairly homogenous entity, many states today are inherently complex and becoming more so. Saul (1997) argues, for example, that with its federated state, several founding "nations," its marginal location and significant immigration, the essence of Canada is its complexity. This might show where other nation-states are heading.

Such increasing complexity poses several challenges to public management:

- *Information everywhere.* Traditional public management requires considerable stability and control of information. That information is power has long been recognized and used as the basis for relationships. In an age where information is readily available to any interested person, and can be used by them, where is the power? How will public management work? How will political parties work?[2]

- *Diversity of views.* The existence of interest groups means that on any issue there will be a multitude of often strongly held views. Agreement on actions and solutions to complex problems becomes increasingly difficult. So how is one to govern in societies dominated by diversity of views?

- *Measurement challenges.* While significant advances have been made in measuring performance in the public sector, there remain many more questions than answers. The measurement of public management—performance measurement, evaluation and audit—is and, given increasing complexity, will remain somewhat more of an art than a science. A different measurement paradigm from that offered by the natural sciences is needed which allows for fuzziness, where accuracy and precision are less important than rough measures of the important things, where some uncertainty in measurement is the norm. A focus on learning not control is needed.

Complexity also results from the recognition that to be able to deal with most social problems, coordination and cooperation is required among the different levels of government and in many cases with the private and voluntary sectors.

Collaborative Arrangements are Here to Stay

Collaboration is a growing phenomenon in many countries. Governments, in particular, realize increasingly that they cannot solve most social problems on their own and are seeking partners to help them (Governor General 1997; Prime Minister and Minister for Cabinet Office 1999). Public-public and public-private partnerships are becoming commonplace as ways of bringing more resources and skills to bear to provide better and less expensive services to citizens.

In many jurisdictions, there are deliberate policies to reduce the size of government and rely on market-type mechanisms to help in governance through the delivery of programs and services that were once delivered directly to citizens. Governments are trying to understand better how effective collaboration can be carried out (see, for example, the Auditor General of Canada 1999a, 1999b). Collaboration is likely to be the norm in the twenty-first century in terms of how governments work.[3] However, with collaboration comes further complexity for public management. The result is a much more diffused governance (Rhodes 1996; Paquet 1999) with many players other than governments involved in governing (Auditor General of Canada 1999b). Many of the norms and practices of established public management fall apart in collaborative arrangements and diffused governance:

- *New forms of accountability are needed.* Accountability is traditionally seen as applying to hierarchical relationships with subordinates accountable to their superiors (e.g., see Segsworth, ch. 9 in this volume). Collaboration, however, often involves a relationship built on non-hierarchical structures. Accountability in parliamentary systems is upward through ministers to parliaments. If governments are in collaborative arrangements with other levels of government or the private/voluntary sector, what kind of accountability is in play? Collaborative arrangements imply that any one partner is not in complete control of the arrangement and its results. Individuals and organizations are often not comfortable with the idea of being accountable for results they do not control. Yet if government partners in such arrangements continue to use funds and authorities they are assumed to remain accountable in some fashion to their respective legislative bodies, at least with regard to their choice of partners and the specific arrangements made. Yet, at the same time, they would appear also to have some form of accountability to those partners, all of which is a far cry from the traditional accountability up through ministers.

- *Leadership challenges.* Traditional leadership qualities in hierarchical structures are well known. However, leadership in a collaborative arrangement requires different skills and approaches, and these skills may differ in different types of arrangements. In some cases, negotiation and compromise may serve better than steadfastness and firm direction. In others, leadership will depend on the expertise available or on the ability to share rather than sell a vision.

- *Models of management.* It is not at all clear how collaborative arrangements can be effectively managed. Good practices have still to be identified and learned. Many of the standard features of management such as planning, control, and evaluation would seem to be needed in collaborative arrangements, but how they can be implemented is uncertain, given the complexity of working with partners and the need to build trust.

Citizen Engagement, Public Reporting and Public Accountability

One constant theme of the public reform initiatives is an increased focus on service to citizens (see Mayne and Rieper, ch. 5), including various efforts both at better informing citizens on what they should expect from their governments and seeking out their views and concerns. While on the surface these citizen-focused efforts can be seen as straightforward attempts to improve the services governments provide, they in fact, either deliberately or as a side effect, challenge the traditional accountability to Parliament through ministers.

Parallel with this focus on citizens is a proliferation of enhanced reporting on the performance of governments both to parliaments and to the public directly. In many countries, governments have adopted a more aggressive reporting strategy, with regard to both the accomplishments of individual departments and agencies (e.g., Canada, Australia, UK, Florida), as well as in many cases, the performance of the government as a whole (e.g., in Alberta and numerous U.S. states). This has come at the same time as the huge growth in the use of the Internet by governments as a convenient and accessible means for communicating and assessing accomplishments.[4]

While there is little evidence on the efficacy of such reporting (Auditor General of Canada 2000a; Tasmanian Audit Office 1996), one cannot dispute the significant increase in readily available information on government performance.

These trends towards more direct involvement of citizens in governance have several implications:

- *Direct accountability.* The many quality service initiatives coupled with the ready availability of information on public services is encouraging a form of direct accountability between public service providers and service users. How this will complement ministerial accountability is not clear but may become an additional or alternative form of accountability demanded by citizens. There is another effect occurring. Those governed are better educated and less willing to be led by elite-based governments. The public is often out ahead of politicians who are increasingly unable to play their traditional leadership role. This would all appear to change the nature of traditional political accountability.

- *A flood of information.* While legislative bodies remain the priority audience of the increased performance reporting, the Internet has made this information very accessible to citizens. Rather than going through their elected representative, citizens and interest groups can increasingly find out for themselves basic information on government activities and information on what has been accomplished with their tax monies. This opens up the possibility of free-form evaluation by citizens. Even for legislatures, traditional hard copy performance reports are likely to be replaced with web-page reporting, allowing users to create their own reports depending on their interests. Governments cannot control this flood of data, analysis and information.

One can see a move, perhaps in addition to traditional ministerial accountability, to a more direct accountability for governments, ministers, departments and agencies directly to those citizens they serve, perhaps bypassing elected legislative bodies. While this phenomena is relatively new, with an increasingly literate, Internet-connected and vocal citizenry, one might anticipate a significant effect on how governance is exercised. The cumulative effects of these various challenges to traditional governance cannot be ignored nor can they be predicted.

New Governance Approaches Needed

The issue, then, is the extent to which organizations and governments will be able to cope with these challenges. The need for learning and adaptability in the face of these challenges is clear (Michael

1993; Metcalfe 1993; Paquet 1999) while the need for new concepts and approaches to governance is evident (OECD 1997: 8). The form of governance that is likely to emerge from these challenges will be based on adaptability. Organizations and societies will have to adopt learning as their predominant culture. Organizations and governments that develop a capacity to learn from experience will develop the resilience needed to deal with complexity and change.

There is need for organizations to be able to live with uncertainty and adopt planning approaches that acknowledge that much will remain unknown. They will need to "embrace errors" (Michael 1993) and encourage the taking of calculated risk, rather than seeking out who to blame when things go wrong. Measurement systems for identifying errors, understanding why things occurred and what was learned as a result, will need to be developed, along with reporting systems for communicating the understanding gained. With complexity and change, there is a need for resilience in organizations. Traditional concepts of what counts as success will need to be modified.

In this learning environment, Michael (1993) argues that the role of government is to act as support for societal learning. This again suggests the need for built-in measurement and reporting systems to support learning and for "learning regulations" or "intelligent systems," *Deliberate learning* needs to planned for and on a societal level would require an active government to move society along this path. In our view, it is not sufficient to simply encourage experimentation, to let a thousand flowers bloom and see in a passive way what works well. Deliberate learning requires more attention, actively trying to learn from experience and experimentation, and then communicating what was learned. It also requires sensible measurement.

Monitoring Outcomes as New Governance

As mentioned in the introduction, there appears to be a world trend towards the measurement of performance of government accomplishments (OECD 1997; Mayne and Zapico 1997, Ch. 1). This has taken different forms in different countries and complete success remains a challenge (Wholey 1999). Most frequently the focus of the measurement involved has been on outputs—the products and service directly provided by government departments and agencies to citizens—rather than outcomes, the impacts and benefits which result from the outputs provided. Some governments such as the UK and New Zealand, have, at least in the past, deliberately emphasized outputs as what the non-elected officials produce for the elected officials and hence for which they can and should be held accountable. Ministers are seen, in this view, as accountable for outcomes. This has led to output-based management being pursued in some countries (OECD 2000). For many local and municipal governments, a focus on outputs results from the direct nature of the services they provide to their citizens rather than from a model of public management.

Increasingly, however, measurement in the public sector is focusing on outcomes, even in countries like the UK which have had a focus in the past on outputs.[5] This focus on outcomes is often seen as a better indication of what government is all about. Managing for outcomes, results-based management and performance management all represent an approach to delivering public services which encourages officials (and ministers) to manage resources and authorities in a manner which maximizes the chance that the outcomes sought will be attained, recognizing that there are a number of factors over which officials do not have complete control (Auditor General of Canada 2000b; OECD 1997). Focusing on outcomes is intended to avoid the problem of short-term success in producing outputs being mistaken for the purpose of public sector programs.

For this approach to management to succeed, learning would appear to be an essential ingredient and accountability regimes will need to be able to deal with the fact that good or bad performance may not be linked directly with the attainment of the outcomes sought, since other factors will also be at play. Whatever the challenges, managing for results (outputs and/or outcomes) has become an accepted approach to public sector management.

Much less accepted is the idea of monitoring outcomes as a means of governance. By this is meant using the setting, agreeing, monitoring and reporting of outcomes especially in collaborative arrangements. Armstrong and Lenihan (1999) argue that:

> ...because the outcomes [sought] are complex, different programs and policies from different departments, governments or sectors can conflict with one another in ways that undermine or significantly weaken their effectiveness. Good government thus requires more than the right policies and programs; it requires a *co-ordinated* approach across levels of government, and even across the private and voluntary sectors. How can this be achieved?... If two governments adopt the same outcomes and performance indicators, a certain level of co-ordination should automatically follow. (p. 53)

In a specific setting, O'Hara (1997) in a report on strengthening federal-provincial relations in Canada suggested that:

> Integrating outcome measures into the social union would increase government's accountability for results and help mobilize governments and citizens around priority outcomes.... Outcomes might also become an alternative way to express social program principles, and reporting to citizens could ultimately become *an alternative to government-to-government enforcement of principles.* (p. 2; italics added).

This idea was echoed by Howse (1997) with respect to labor market training in Canada. One can imagine using outcomes as an alternative way to express constitutional commitments such as, in Canada, mobility and access to national programs delivered at the provincial level. This has, in fact, come about with the signing of the Social Union (Canada 1999) agreement where agreement on and the measurement and reporting of common outcomes has served as a focus for a federal-provincial governance regime.

The reports of the Steering Committee for the Review of Commonwealth/State Service Provision (1997) sees a similar role for performance measurement in Australia while the OECD work on multilevel governance suggests that countries can "apply performance management techniques to improving inter-governmental relations" (1998: 1).

Intended Benefits from Results-Based Governance

Measuring and reporting on outcomes as a form of governance in complex areas is seen by proponents to offer numerous benefits. In general, the expectation is that managing through outcomes builds trust among those involved, allows for flexibility in actions and hence supports empowerment, focuses on what matters to citizens and produces information for accountability. Extending these, results-based governing could be a means to address several problems of governance.

Sort out roles and responsibilities. A key problem in establishing effective collaborative arrangements is sorting out just what each of the partners can and should be doing. Focussing on outcomes allows for a sorting out of roles and responsibilities. It plays down issues of who should deliver what, concentrating more on getting agreement on what outcomes are important and how to track progress towards them (Armstrong and Lenihan 1999: 54). As a result it can reduce the need for operational management by senior levels of government (Steering Committee 1998) and provide for monitoring without meddling. In a jurisdiction such as Canada, with variations in different regions, it allows for asymmetrical programming where local variations are undertaken in light of national goals (Armstrong and Lenihan 1999: 54, Howse 1997).

Coordinate governments and citizens. A commitment to focus on common outcomes would encourage the coordination and cooperation required among governments and private sector to deal with the complex problems being faced today. The set of common outcomes would provide a framework for discussion towards achieving this needed cooperation. Developing a results-based governance model offers a means for different organizations and governments in related program areas to coordinate their efforts towards higher outcomes of significance to citizens, while maintaining and encouraging flexibility and decentralization. In a more traditional setting, governance has meant top-down direction to component parts of a programming area or other levels of government.

Results-based governance should build relationships and trust among governments, citizens, and interest groups by identifying shared values and desired outcomes and working together to achieve them (O'Hara 1997). An example of this could be Canada's Model Forests Program. Established in 1992, this is a national program composed of 12 Model Forest Groups scattered across the country, each created to work in partnerships to enhance forest management based on principles of sustainable development. All 12 model forests work toward the achievement of common objectives, for example, to encourage the demonstration of management approaches that are based on principles of sustainable development, to ensure that the results and knowledge gained through the Model Forest Program are disseminated at local, national and international levels and to encourage the representation of a broad range of forest values in each model forest. The goals of forest planning must consider more than timber production; they must maintain healthy ecosystems and restore damaged ones. These common objectives have brought together diverse interests. The partners range from different levels of government, industry, environmentalists to First Nations. The partners understand that it is in everyone's best interest to manage for forests that are healthy and sustainable in the long term.

In addition to the common program objectives, more specific goals are established at the individual model forest level. Each model forest group has established a results-based performance measurement framework that reflects core program elements, but with the flexibility to be tailored to the specific nature of the forest through the development of local level performance indicators. This allows for ongoing collection of performance information from each individual model forest and the national program as a whole (Natural Resources Canada 1999).

Encourage local and citizen involvement. In providing for flexibility and decentralized program delivery, outcome-based governance encourages community involvement and hence ownership in achieving broad social goals. It mobilizes citizens, communities and governments around priorities by shining a light on outcomes upon which players can "hook" their own activities (O'Hara 1997). It gives groups a direct role in designing and managing services they care about (Armstrong and Lenihan 1999: 54).

Encourage learning. The focus on measuring and reporting outcomes produces information on accomplishments in ways that allow different jurisdictions to learn from the results achieved by different means tailored to their own ways. The process encourages the sharing of a common vocabulary, enabling more productive discussion and debate about the outcomes being sought and the means chosen to achieve them.

Enhance accountability. The whole process could also greatly enhance accountability. It would help to demonstrate to citizens that agreed-upon priorities are reflected in government actions, provide regular reports on outcomes to inform a dialogue among citizens (O'Hara 1997) and allows for interregional comparison on the results being achieved. Such a decentralized process would by its very nature demand a significant level of transparency and thereby further enhance accountability (Armstrong and Lenihan 1999; O'Hara 1997; Steering Committee 1998).

Challenges to Results-Based Governance

Potential is one thing, implementation another. Results-based governance faces all the hurdles results-based management does, and more. We have discussed many of these challenges earlier under the headings of complexity, and the need for collaboration and citizen involvement. Here we wish to highlight several specific challenges dealing with accountability, reporting of performance and measuring performance and how they would have to change to support results-based governance. In particular,

- Can we escape blame-based accountability?

- Can we communicate effectively the information needed for results-based governance?

- Can we move to sensible measurement and avoid the well documented pitfalls of measurement in the public sector?

Implications for Accountability

To support a learning environment, new forms of accountability consistent with the new governance are required. Accountability must be linked with responsible learning not blaming. Accountability must be able to deal with outcomes which cannot be completely controlled and with uncertainty (Kettl 1997; Hatry 1997; Mayne 1997; Shergold 1997; Office of the Auditor General of Canada and Treasury Board of Canada 1998). Traditional accountability, on the other hand, is comfortable with systems and procedures, and certainty.

In the past, accountability for inputs and perhaps outputs was most likely to be the regime in which most public officials worked. As such, there often was a reluctance to accept accountability for results beyond outputs, namely outcomes over which one does not have control. Being accountable for outputs has been much more acceptable than being accountable for outcomes. And it lends itself to the more traditional view of accountability as assigning blame: if the expected outputs are not delivered, then the responsible person can be identified and appropriate action taken since one ought to be in control of the processes used and the outputs produced.

In the case of managing for outcomes, the degree of administrative control and scope for influence a manager has over the outcomes sought will vary considerably in different situations. In some cases, the manager in question is the main player and has a quite significant degree of control over the outcomes. In other cases, the manager might be only one of several players trying, with the resources and authorities available, to best influence the achievement of the intended outcomes. Effective accountability implies that managers understand these considerations, and have the means to deal with these more complex situations.

If the expected outcomes have not been accomplished, there may be several reasons, only one of which may be that the "responsible" manager hasn't done a good job. One might have indeed done all that could be expected, but the results were not achieved due to circumstances beyond one's influence. To encourage and support managing for results, we need a new view of accountability that acknowledges this more complex management world. What is needed is a practical form of "accountability for results/outcomes":

> Accountability for results asks if you have done everything possible with your authorities and resources towards affecting the achievement of the intended results and if you have learned from past experience what works and doesn't work. Accounting for results of this kind means demonstrating that you have made a difference, that through your actions and efforts you have contributed to the results achieved.... In essence, accountability for results means demonstrating that you have been managing for results and accepting responsibility for those actions. (Office of the Auditor General and Treasury Board Secretariat 1998: 6)

Kettl (1997: 456) suggests it is "impossible to underestimate just how radical a transformation democratic accountability [the change from focusing on processes to focusing outside government to outcomes] is." Understanding of and acceptance of accountability for results is essential for results-based governance. It entails demonstrating in a timely manner:

- the extent to which the results (outputs and outcomes) have occurred as intended;

- an assessment of the contribution made by the program or organization to the outcomes observed;

- what has been learned as a result; and

- the strategies used have paid due regard to prudence and probity.

In addition, the collaborative nature of modern governance further challenges accountability based solely on traditional hierarchical relationships. A revised articulation of accountability that provides for collaborative arrangements by not requiring a hierarchical relationship has been suggested:

> Accountability is a relationship based on the obligation to demonstrate and take responsibility for performance in light of agreed expectations. (Office of the Auditor General and Treasury Board Secretariat 1998: 4)

It is perhaps significant that the World Bank (1998b) has started to use this conceptualization for the way it closes the loop between managing, measurement and reporting and allows for shared accountability in collaborative arrangements.

In a collaborative arrangement, the partners involved have several accountabilities (Auditor General of Canada 1999a; OECD 1999). Each is accountable to its own governing body (such as Parliament) for the overall results, each is accountable to the other partners for their own contributions to the arrangement and together they are accountable to the users and stakeholders being served by the arrangement. Thus, an effective practice of shared accountability is required for results-based governance in collaborative delivery.

Implications for Reporting

We have seen that enhanced public reporting on the performance of government activities will be a key element of public management in the next century. But if this is to come about, new approaches to and new understanding of reporting potentials and limitations are needed. Some of these have been mentioned already:

- Electronic reporting will become the norm, giving users a powerful means to "publish" their own reports on subjects and from perspectives they choose, thus creating new information from available data. This may threaten governments who will want to remain in control but cannot.

- Perhaps "reporting" may not be the right term to use any more. Governments will be pushed to making significant amounts of information available to the public through access to their data bases.

- Reporting will allow comparisons to be made across all forms of government outcomes and services, as is now starting to occur in some jurisdictions (Steering Committee 1997, 1998; Audit Commission 1996).

Yet this explosion of information does pose problems since the information produced is not on its own "truth." It is likely to come with significant caveats regarding its reliability and hence open to misinterpretation and misuse. Users will have to become more sophisticated but will also demand that the robustness and limitations of data and information made available are clearly stated. We will have to learn to deal with incomplete, fuzzy yet credible reporting.

The Florida web page mentioned earlier presents one approach to how assurance might be provided on reported performance information. The need for some type of assurance would suggest a role for audit, by providing assurance on the reported information. But audit practice will have to evolve for this to become a useful part of the new governance and a simple extrapolation from the financial assurance model of providing an opinion may not be appropriate nor the most useful approach to adopt. For example, for several years the audit office in Western Australia has been providing a form of assurance with respect to performance indicators published by agencies elsewhere (Auditor General of Western Australia 1997) and the Auditor General of Canada provided his first assessment on a performance report in the 1998 Annual Report of the Canadian Food Inspection Agency. Thus, audit offices continue to explore this new form of assurance.

There may be other or additional ways of enhancing the credibility of public reports (or publicly available information). O'Hara (1997) argues for the need for appropriate reporting principles for users of public reports. These might, for example, require public reporting to include such information as

- Who identified the desired outcomes and measures?
- Do they meet the tests of practicality, relevance and accountability?
- What values lie behind the outcome?
- Who collected the outcome data?
- What is the process for modifying the outcomes?

Finally, the credibility of performance reporting would likely increase if not only the reports were public but the data and information behind the reports were made readily available. To the extent that citizens could evaluate and challenge the information, there would be considerable pressure on governments to report in a fair and balanced manner. That is, increased transparency should lead to enhanced credibility and perhaps less of a need for audit assurance.

The bottom line on all of this is that real transparency of government information is required to support a learning society. Society cannot become a learning society without good information about what is working and what is not. If governments are to help in this move, they will need to seek out transparency not guard against it.

Implications for Measurement, Evaluation, and Audit

Much of the practicality of a new governance of learning rests on the ability to measure sensibly the accomplishments of government programs and policies. Results-based governance challenges not only traditional concepts of public management but also concepts of measurement. We need to view and practice measurement as a tool for learning not for control (Majone 1989; Mayne 1997). Without better sensible measurement, the empirical basis of results-based governance will not be achievable. As a result, we need to reassess what measurement can practically deliver, and what we should measure as success.

Realistic expectations for measurement. Expectations regarding the measurement of the performance in the public sector through either performance measures or program evaluations are often unrealistic. They are set too high a standard that cannot be met. Measurement in this area will often be inconclusive. Given the complexity and horizontal nature of the social and economic problems being dealt with, measuring the magnitude of many outcomes and sorting out the contributions being made by different programs and different factors will not be unambiguous. This is reality and more should not be expected. Expectations that measurement will deliver uncontroversial proof of whether programs or organizations are performing well and what they contribute will not be realized.

On the other hand, in almost all cases measurement can be undertaken to provide some additional useful information on a program and its performance. We can usually reduce uncertainty about the program or organization. We just need to be able to deal with uncertainty in measurement. Measurement as a tool of control has difficulty dealing with this uncertainty. Measurement as a learning tool does not.

> For many, "measurement" means trying to determine the precise magnitude of things. [Rather, one needs to see] "measurement" more broadly, as the gathering of relevant information to enhance understanding about what a program is accomplishing. ...measurement will often suggest rather than prove the level of performance [achieved].... Measurement does not replace judgements on the value of programs; it allows officials, ministers, [and] parliamentarians...to make value judgements on better evidence than would otherwise be available.... Measurement does its job by enlightening—not ending—debate on the issue of the day. (Auditor General of Canada 1996: 21)

A similar idea from a different perspective was developed by Majone (1989) who suggested the concept of measurement as argument rather than technique. Evaluation and outcome measurement should be seen as developing a credible argument to help clarify complex phenomena. This is similar to the idea of developing a credible performance story through logical argument and available evidence (Mayne 1999).

These arguments for new measurement paradigms are further reinforced with the added complexity of collaboration becoming more the norm for government activities. New standards for measurement of the contributions made in these arrangements are required for the arrangements to work and accountability to be effective (Office of the Auditor General and Treasury Board Secretariat 1998; Hatry 1997; Behn 1995). There is a need to be able, for example, to measure the level and nature of trust and cooperation in collaborative arrangements if we are to understand how to better manage such arrangements. There is also a need to be able to measure in a practical way the contributions made by different partners in a collaborative arrangement.

Evaluation. Evaluation of public sector programs is built on several traditions (Hudson, Mayne, and Thomlison 1992). Much of its history is associated with evaluation research that has a direct link to traditional social sciences. In this mode, evaluation is trying to establish truth and seeks to be as definitive as possible. This is often the model assumed when evaluation is seen as part of a control regime. On the other hand, much actual evaluation practice, especially outside the academic environment, is a less sophisticated enterprise and in its better forms makes do with more modest goals and results. While trying to be as robust and rigorous as possible, it does what is possible in a given circumstance. But this approach is quite consistent with a learning approach to management and governance as it can add valid information to the discussion. It can reduce uncertainty concerning how well a program is performing. It is often encumbered with caveats but that is what "fuzzy" measurement is all about. Judgment is still required to use it. Evaluation undertaken from this perspective is useful, is consistent with and indeed essential for a learning public service.

There is an additional challenge for evaluation. Collaboration in the delivery of services and programs implies collaboration in the management of evaluation. Evaluation is further complicated by differences in the views, approaches and underlying purposes of the various partners involved in collaborative arrangements. This speaks to the need for discussion and negotiation at the outset (Auditor General of Canada 1999a) and the need for practical tools to manage evaluation in complex, collaborative situations. Toulemonde et al. (1998) have provided some suggestions on how to deal with such difficulties as getting agreement on expected outcomes (using a concept mapping technique to reconstruct the logic of the collaborative program), developing appropriate measurement tools (using scoring sheets rated by partners), and developing conclusions all partners can support (using multicriteria analysis to identify areas of consensus).

Performance measurement. Fuzzy measurement is also what is needed when dealing with using and reporting performance measures, which by their very nature are only able to describe part of the performance of a program. This is fundamentally so when such measures deal with outcomes rather than just outputs. Mayne (1999) discusses the need to use *contribution analysis* to help tell a credible performance story with performance measures by making the best of the evidence available in a logical and coherent fashion. For both evaluation and performance measurement, modesty is required concerning what can be "proven" about the performance of government programs. Measurement needs to be seen as a learning tool.

Performance audit. Performance and value-for-money audit perhaps faces an even more difficult challenge in a government based on learning which deals with uncertainty and fuzzy measurement. Audit practice has thrived on being able to develop clear criteria and assessing in a definitive and objective manner performance against those criteria (Power 1997). Audit is expected to tell the "truth" in a world of ambiguity and biased views (Gunvaldsen and Karlsen 1999). Governance as learning poses significant challenges to traditional performance audit practice.

Some thought may have to given to the kinds of assurance auditors provide. If the measurers of performance in the public sector are being challenged to deal with uncertainty in their profession, auditors can hardly be expected to fair any better. As an independent source of challenge, auditors can indeed add credibility to the measurement undertaken by government, but cannot provide a guarantee for or against matters in many cases. In dealing with matters of performance, conclusions will often not be a simple yes or no. Auditing may have to develop more complex forms of "conclusions" to deal with the increasingly complex issues it attempts to adjudicate. Similarly, developing truly different levels or types of assurance and educating the clients of audit as to which they are providing would go some way to meeting the challenge of complexity, collaboration and public reporting.[6]

Further, while some regularity audit will always be needed, performance audit primarily based on audit against rules and regulations may be seen as quite inconsistent with a learning public service. Rather than rules-based, audit that focused on the principles behind the rules and regulations, and whether the principles were seriously at risk would be another step in the right direction. It would also be consistent with the general trend of reducing "unnecessary" rules and regulations. Principle-based audit practice would support a learning organization by not only identifying significant performance risks, but also by identifying outmoded and unnecessary rules and regulations.

New things to measure. Measurement of public sector performance has for the most part focused on measuring the traditional three E's of economy, efficiency and effectiveness. As argued earlier, these are not sufficient in the new governance paradigm. We need to develop an ability to measure the capacity of organizations to learn and adapt (Majone 1989; Metcalfe 1993; Mayne and Zapico-Goni 1997).

Majone (1989) suggests that "the rationality of public policy-making depends more on improving the learning capacity of the various organs of public deliberation than on maximizing achievement of particular goals" (p. 183). To that end, Mayne and Zapico-Goni (1997) discuss the need for three new measures of success— the three D's—instead of or at least in addition to the more traditional three E's of economy, efficiency and effectiveness:

- *Diagnosis*—the identification of new problems or the redefinition of current problems, taking into account changes in the environment and the interests of stakeholders, building a common perception of the problem.

- *Design*—the formulation of new solutions, including the incentives to solve new problems identified, and the adaptation of organizational and inter-organizational structures and strategies.

- *Development*—the actual implementation of new solutions as a learning process, coping with resistance to change, redefining problems and solutions during implementation, and learning from experience (p. 264).

They argue that meeting objectives set some time ago—effectiveness—may not be the most important goal for organizations in a complex and changing society. Adaptability and sustainability linked to a goal of deliberate learning is likely to be the hallmark of successful organizations in the future (World Bank 1998a). All of this presents measurement with further challenges since measuring the three D's is, for the most part, still in its infancy.

Evaluation might usefully focus on the unintended effects of moving towards results-based governance, looking at how people and organizations adapt to an evidence-based culture. Many have observed that measurement in organizations can often lead to dysfunctional behavior with organizations pursuing results that are measured rather than results that matter (Smith 1995). There are likely many such concerns that need to be monitored. A component of evaluation has always addressed this issue of unintended effects. If we are indeed fundamentally challenging approaches and paradigms to management and governance, undertaking deliberate studies to better understand and be able to learn from mistakes ought to be a part of all evaluation work in this area.

Conclusions

We have argued that the complexity of societies and their problems, the increase in the use of partners in governing—replacing government in governing—and the demands by citizens to be involved in governing are challenging and changing traditional forms of public management and governance. To survive, governments and public sector organizations will have to become both resilient and adaptable and true learning entities. However, to do so is quite difficult for most. The culture change required is significant. A focus on results can help by supporting and encouraging learning as the essence of public management and governance.

Results-based governance sounds idealistic and naive: "governing by numbers." Governing involves people and rights and politics and difficult decisions; things well beyond counting. Information on results—even good information—will not and should not determine decisions. Rather it should inform decisions and be a key element in the deliberate learning society needs. We have suggested that results-based governance can help meet the challenges to traditional governance.

Traditional governance models based on command and control and paternalistic frameworks cannot work as societies moves towards diffused and market-based governance. Public managing for results, on the other hand, provides an administrative mechanism compatible with this trend. We argue that government and governance cannot work in a complex collaborative citizen-focused society without effective measurement, accountability, evaluation and audit; hence, results-based governance is essential.

We have also discussed the potential benefits from results-based governance but also focused on the challenges. To move to results-based governance will require a number of changes. We discussed three in relation to the themes of this book. Results-based governance will require adopting a learning-based accountability rather than traditional blame-focused accountability. It will require significant improvements in our ability to report of the performance of governments and more realistic and sensible measurement through evaluations, performance measurement and performance audit.

But is all of this likely? Certainly, managing and reporting for results remains a significant trend in public management. This is occurring despite the limited, if growing, evidence that managing for results actually improves public management. Studies have shown that the key for implementing managing for results successfully in an organization is strong and committed leaders (Wholey and Newcomer 1997; Auditor General of Canada 2000b; National Performance Review 1999). Hence, an essential factor in moving towards governance as evidence-based learning is the development and presence of strong public sector leaders supporting results-based governance efforts.

We need politicians who accept the need to learn from empirical experience. Experimentation and deliberate learning need to become the norm in political life. Perhaps this will only come about by a more mature citizenry demanding better governance with politicians catching up. Yet there is some evidence of a changing vision. In Canada, several recent major initiatives discussed earlier have emphasized a results-based culture as of central importance. We would not have seen that ten or even five years ago. So perhaps results-based governance is well on its way to becoming accepted. It is hard to recognize trends when you are in the middle of the stream.

Notes

1.   John et al. (1994) discuss a similar set of characteristics.
2.   Information available on the internet (www.E-Democarcy.org) has been influential in the election of Jesse Ventura in Minnesota, bypassing the power of the traditional political parties (Tapscott 1998).
3.   The one counter to this trend could be the increasing evidence that collaboration does not work in some or many cases. Although the evidence is not in, some

problems have been identified, particularly where the private sector is used to provide public services (Walsh 1995; Kirkpatrick 1999).
4.   One of the more useful such web sites has been developed by the state of Florida, where an agency of the legislature provides an assessment of the performance of the state's programs and services: http://www.oppaga.state.fl.us/government/.
5.   See the new Public Service Agreements being put in place (Cm 4181, 1998).
6.   Even the assurance provided by traditional attest financial audit is being challenged. See, for example, Chigbo 1998.

References

Armstrong, J., and D. Lenihan. 1999. *From Controlling to Collaborating: When Governments Want to be Partners: A Report on the Collaborative Partnerships Project*. New Directions Number 3, Institute of Public Administration, Toronto.

Audit Commission. 1996. *Local Authorities Performance Indicators 1994/95*. London: HMSO.

Auditor General of Canada. 1996. *Report to the House of Commons: Matters of Special Importance—1996*. Ottawa.

Auditor General of Canada. 1998. "Auditor General's Assessment," in The Canadian Food Inspection Agency. *Annual Report*. Ottawa.

Auditor General of Canada. 1999a. *Report to the House of Commons: Chapter 5: Collaborative Arrangements: Issues for the Federal Government*. Ottawa.

Auditor General of Canada. 1999b. *Report to the House of Commons: Chapter 23: Involving Others in Governing: Accountability at Risk*. Ottawa.

Auditor General of Canada. 2000a. *Report to the House of Commons: Chapter 19: Reporting Performance to Parliment: Progress Too Slow*. Ottawa.

Auditor General of Canada. 2000b. *Report to the House of Commons: Chapter 20: Managing Departments for Results and Managing Horizontal Issues for Results*. Ottawa.

Auditor General of Western Australia. 1997. *Public Sector Performance Report 1997*. Perth.

Behn, R. D. 1995. The Big Questions of Public Management. *Public Administration Review,* 55/4 July/August: 313-324.

Boyle, R. 1999. *The Management of Cross-Cutting Issues*. Committee for Public Management Research and Institute of Public Administration. Dublin.

Canada. 1999. *A Framework to Improve the Social Union for Canadians*. An agreement between the Government of Canada and the Governments of the Provinces and Territories. February 4. http://socialunion.gc.ca.

Chigbo, O. 1998. "GAAP under fire." *Camagazine*, January/February.

Cm 4181. 1998. *Public Services for the Future: Modernisation, Reform, Accountability*. Chief Secretary to the Treasury. London: The Stationery Office.

Governor General. 1997. Speech from the Throne to Open the First Session Thirty-Sixth Parliament of Canada. Privy Council Office. Ottawa. *http://www.pco-bcp.gc.ca*.

Gunvaldsen, J., and R. Karlsen. 1999. "The Auditor as an Evaluator—How to Remain an Influential Force in the Political Landscape." *Evaluation* 5 (4): 458-467.

Hatry, H. 1997. "We Need a New Concept of Accountability." *The Public Manager,* 263: 37-38.

Howse, R. 1997. "Outcome-based National Standards as an Instrument of Federalism: The Case of the Labour Market Agreements." *The Alternatives Network*, 23.

Hudson, J., J. Mayne, and R. Thomlison. 1992. *Action-Oriented Evaluation in Organizations: Canadian Practices*. Toronto: Wall and Emerson.

John, D., D. Kettl, B. Dyer and B. Lovan. 1994. "What Will New Governance Mean for the Federal Government?" *Public Administration Review,* 542: 170-175.

Kettl, D. F. 1997. "The Global Revolution in Public Management: Driving Themes, Missing Links." *Policy Analysis and Management,* 163: 446-462.

Kirkpatrick, I. 1999. "The Worst of Both Worlds? Public Services Without Markets or Bureaucracy." *Public Money and Management.* October/December, 19/4: 7-14.

Majone, G. 1989. *Evidence, Arguments and Persuasion in the Policy Process.* London: Yale University Press.

Mayne, J. 1997. "Accountability for Program Performance: A Key to Effective Performance Monitoring and Reporting," in J. Mayne and E. Zapico-Goni (eds.), *Monitoring Performance in the Public Sector: Future Directions from International Experience.* New Brunswick, NJ: Transaction Publishers.

Mayne, J., and E. Zapico-Goni (eds.). 1997. *Performance Monitoring: Implications for the Future. Monitoring Performance in the Public Sector: Future Directions from International Experience.* New Brunswick, NJ: Transaction Publishers.

Mayne, J. 1999. *Addressing Attribution with Performance Measurement: Using Performance Measures Sensibly.* Office of the Auditor General of Canada. http://www.oagbug.gc.ca/domino/other.nsf/html/99dpl_e.html.

Metcalfe, L. 1993. "Public Management: From Imitation to Innovation," in J. Kooiman (ed.), *Modern Governance.* London: Sage, 173-189.

Michael, D. 1993. "Governing by Learning: Boundaries, Myths and Metaphors. *Futures,* January/February: 81-89.

National Performance Review. 1999. Balancing Measures: Best Practices in Performance Management. Washington, DC.

Natural Resources Canada 1999. *Final Evaluation Framework for Canada's Model Forest Program.* Audit and Review branch. Ottawa.

OECD. 1997. *In Search of Results: Performance Management Practices.* Paris.

OECD. 1998. Managing Across Levels of Government: Part One, Overview. Paris. *http://www.oecd.org/pdf/M00004000/M00004170.pdf.*

OECD. 2000. *The OECD Outputs Manual.* 21st Annual Meeting of Senior Budget Officials. Paris, May 29-30.

Office of the Auditor General and Treasury Board Secretariat. 1998. Modernizing Accountability Practices. Ottawa. *http://www.tbs-sct.gc.ca/rma/account/OAGTBS_E.html.*

O'Hara, K. 1997. *Securing the Social Union.* Canadian Policy Research Network.

Paquet, G. 1999. *Governance Through Social Learning.* Ottawa: University of Ottawa.

Power, M. 1997. *The Audit Society: Rituals of Verification.* Oxford: Oxford University Press.

Prime Minister and Minister for the Cabinet Office. 1999. *Modernising Government.* London: Stationery Office

Privy Council Office 1997. *Fourth Annual Report to the Prime Minister on The Public Service of Canada.* Ottawa.

Rae, B. 1998. *The Three Questions: Prosperity and the Public Good.* Toronto: Penguin Books.

Rhodes, R. A. W. 1996. "The New Governance: Governing without Government." *Political Studies* XLIV, 652-667.

Saul, J. S. 1997. *Reflections of a Siamese Twin: Canada at the End of the Twentieth Century.* Toronto: Viking Penguin.

Shergold, P. 1997. "The Colour Purple: Perceptions of Accountability across the Tasman." *Public Administration and Development,* 172: 293-306.

Smith, P. 1995. "On the Unintended Consequences of Publishing Performance Data in the Public Sector." *International Journal of Public Administration,* 18 (2 & 3): 277-310.

Steering Committee for the Review of Commonwealth/State Service Provision. 1997. *1997 Report on Government Services.* Australia.

Steering Committee for the Review of Commonwealth/State Service Provision. 1998. *1998 Report on Government Services*. Australia.

Stowe, K. 1992. "Good Piano Won't Play Bad Music: Administrative Reform and Good Governance." *Public Administration*, 70: 387-394.

Strange, S. 1996. *The Retreat of the State*. New York: Cambridge University Press.

Tapscott, D. 1998. "The Brave New World of E-Domocracy: Debate Must Mow Begin on the Parameters of Digital Liberty. *Financial Post*, December 16.

Tasmanian Audit Office. 1996. *Review of Performance Indicators of Government Departments*. Special Report No. 24.

Toulemonde, J., C. Fontaine, E. Laudren, and P. Vincke. 1998. "Evaluation in Partnership." *Evaluation*, 42: 171-188.

Walsh, K. 1995. *Public Services and Market Mechanisms: Competition, Contracting and the New Public Management*. Basingstoke: Macmillan.

Wholey, J. S., and K. Newcomer. 1997. "Clarifying Goals, Reporting Results." *New Directions for Evaluation*, No. 75, Fall: 91-98.

Wholey, J. S. 1999. "Performance-Based Management: Responding to the Challenges." *Public Productivity and Management Review*, 223; 288-307.

World Bank. 1994. *Governance: The World Bank's Experience*. Washington, DC.

World Bank. 1998a. *Partnerships for Development: Proposed Actions for the World Bank*. Discussion Paper, Partnerships Group, Strategic and Resource Management. Washington, DC.

World Bank. 1998b. *1998 Annual Report on Operations Evaluation*. Operations Evaluation Department. Washington, DC.

8

Auditing and Evaluating Collaborative Government: The Role of Supreme Audit Institutions

Marie-Louise Bemelmans-Videc

In this volume characteristics of collaboration in public services are discussed partly as a product of and partly as a counter-movement to the supposedly competitive nature of New Public Management. In this chapter, we concentrate on the methods and standards by which national Supreme Audit Institutions (SAIs) have judged these developing collaborative arrangements. On the basis of case studies of Canadian[1] and Netherlands SAIs, we shall also discuss whether audit judgments are supportive or corrective of the effects of collaborative government.

The political re-appreciation of the concept of collaboration restates an idea that government needs to find its legitimacy in consensus and binding social values. New public management, as a collection of instruments representing a distinct approach of public management and involving new patterns of relationships, and hence policy, did not seem to offer such legitimacy (Bemelmans-Videc 1999). Its market-oriented values provided incoherent direction, granting a dominant role to the values of efficiency and effectiveness to the neglect of legal order and, to a degree, democracy as leading values for governmental structures and action in a *Rechtsstaat*. This orientation has also been exemplified by the emerging codes of accountability in new public management reforms which "have (also) altered financial codes of accountability by placing more emphasis on technical and economic rationalities at the expense of legal" (Gray and Jenkins 1993: 63).

The alternatives to these new markets and traditional hierarchies as coordinators of social life are being re-appreciated (e.g., Touraine

1992; Thompson et al. 1998). Streeck and Schmitter (1998) go further and identify a distinctive additional "basis of order which is more than a transient and expedient amalgam of the three others [community, market and state] and is capable of making a lasting and autonomous contribution to rendering the behavior of social actors reciprocally adjustive and predictable" (p. 227). This association is identified by its "guiding principle of interaction and allocation: organizational concertation" (p. 228) and, they claim, offers a better understanding of today's "bargained economies and societies." Streeck and Schmitter present the idea as drawing on Hegel's *Korporationen* and subsidiarity (as elaborated in *Rerum Novarum* [1891] and *Quadragesimo Anno* [1931] within Roman Catholic social philosophy). Subsidiarity holds that higher echelons of state should not execute tasks that may as well be executed by lower echelons. It expresses an appreciation of the social functions of organizations and institutions between state and individual. In this sense the "delegation of public policy functions to private interest governments represents an attempt to utilize the collective self-interest of social groups to create and maintain a generally acceptable social order, and it is based on assumptions about the behavior of organizations as transforming agents of individual interests" (Streek and Schmitter 1998: 234).

The ideological counter-wave that we are witnessing also revalues government as a "business in its own right." A growing empirical literature on restructured governmental services and agencies (Pollitt 1995; Kirkpatrick and Martinez 1996) has revealed disappointing outcomes in effectiveness and efficiency and especially in the democratic quality and legality. All four of these evaluation criteria represent values of good governance that provide the legitimacy for government action (McSwite 1997). The values of regularity and legality find a renewed emphasis in recent legislation aiming at complementing the new freedom of quangos and similar constructions by rules of the game that re-emphasize the public nature of their functions. These values are also reflected in persuasive arguments in support of public service, showing how bureaucrats do a difficult job well (Holzer and Callahan 1998).

This re-appreciation of *Res Publica* and its institutions, in line with the discussion on legitimacy, is illustrated by an extensive literature on supervisory control and the accountability question (Gray and Jenkins 1993; Stone 1995; Gates and Hill 1995; Jenkins 1996;

Woodhouse 1994). It is on this theme of control in order to effect accountability that we shall now focus on exploring the vital role of Supreme Audit Institutions in the emerging collaborative government. We shall, first, describe the main roles of SAIs in general and give some thought to their role in promoting the cause of evaluation, second, explore emerging audit methodologies, third, investigate cases of auditees in collaborative arrangements, fourth, discuss judgment standards and, finally, reflect on the effects of the audit of collaboration by SAIs.

Audit and Evaluation in Collaborative Government: The Challenges

Audit Institutions: Roles and Responsibilities

Supreme Audit Institutions (SAIs) have an external controlling function over the Executive, usually assisting the Legislature. In the European context (NAO 1996), but in the Americas as well, they are the most prominent external controlling bodies. SAIs have an effective measure of independence and play an important role in formulating the general standards against which government performance is to be evaluated. Although the legislation stipulating the SAIs' functions may vary, most SAIs have the right to undertake some form of performance audit as well as more traditional financial (or regularity) audit. The International Organization of Supreme Audit Institutions (INTOSAI) states that the full scope of government auditing ("comprehensive/integrated audit") includes both types of audit. The standards in financial audits relate to regularity (i.e., conformity to relevant authorization) while those in performance audits relate to value for money, specifically economy, efficiency and effectiveness.

The European Implementing Guidelines, issued by the European Court of Auditors (ECA 1998) and applied in the context of European Union activity, provide a similar methodological thread for both regularity and performance audits that runs through the diverse public audit traditions of the EU Member States. Although these and other SAI audit manuals and guidelines set out their formal audit methodology and standards, the actual application of audit standards and their synthesis in SAI judgments are much less publicized. Frey and Serna (1994) and Power (1994, 1997), for example, emphasize the procedural and formal information that SAIs produce. However, Barzelay (1996), Bemelmans-Videc (1998),

Leeuw (1998), and Pollitt and Summa (1997) have begun to explore the empirical application. We shall say more about this later.

SAI external supervisory functions are often described as "control" in the restricted sense of supervision or checking "is" (*ist*) against "ought" (*soll*). However, given the directive nature of SAIs' standards, the resulting judgments will, in actual practice, have broader "steering" consequences. Holding the executive accountable is, of course, the ultimate rationale of SAIs. The degree and nature of accountability is dictated by the (delimitations of an) actor's authority, as expressed in the direct relation between the concepts of authority, responsibility and accountability:

- authority is the right to act; (delegated) authority presupposes the allocation of commensurate responsibility;

- responsibility is the obligation to perform delegated duties and tasks; while

- accountability is the obligation to present an account of and answer for the execution of responsibilities to those who entrusted those responsibilities (Gray and Jenkins 1993: 55).

The hierarchical relation implicit in the accountability concept has created a problem in the audit of new configurations where more or less "horizontal" relations are involved. Discussions of any new arrangement in relation to accountability tend to focus on traditional hierarchical relations. Thus, the Auditor General of Canada, in his report on *Collaborative Arrangements* (1999), identified the key need for "strong accountability" in keeping with the principle of ministerial responsibility and accountability to Parliament. This implied "clear roles and responsibilities...clear and agreed expectations, balanced expectations and capacities, credible reporting and reasonable review, program evaluation and audit" (pp. 5-13).

Of old, audit functions were executed by accountants. Their profession used to dominate the staff of SAIs. With the increasing role of performance audit and its social science related methodology, however, accountants have given way to economists, social and policy scientists. This trend is notable in both the Anglo-Saxon tradition (e.g., Canada, UK, and the United States) and those with a predominantly judicial audit tradition (e.g., Belgium, France, and the Mediterranean nations). Possibly also induced by the growth of public and private sector requests for performance audits, accountancy has of late been adopting ambitions and methods earlier associated with social science evaluation. Thus, new specialisms like management audit and operational audit have emerged (Power 1994, 1997).

Such role-conceptions have strengthened accountants' participation in the definition of the process and contents of audit functions including in the corporate and wider governance discussion in the United States, UK, and elsewhere (COSO 1992; CIPFA 1994, 1995; Cadbury Report 1992; CICA 1995). This discussion of governance has had consequences for the audit of collaborative government: it has put internal control systems in the center of a regulatory policy, which connects internal control with quality assurance ambitions (Power 1997: 55-57). As Gray and Jenkins (1993) point out, this can lead to the development of the accounting system as apparently the only co-ordinative mechanism. However, "Accounting is not itself a system of management, but an information system. Thus attempts to enforce centralized accounting regimes as though they were systems of management will serve only to reinforce the co-ordinative vacuum. The systems should be judged on their contribution to management effectiveness and this in turn on its contributions to the quality and efficiency of public services" (p. 64).

SAIs: Promoters of Good Evaluation Practice

SAIs are often crucial to the promotion of the philosophy and theory of evaluation, the establishment of evaluation functions in government and the determination of relevant indicators of good performance (Rist 1990; Gray, Jenkins and Segsworth 1993; Furubo et al. 2002). In 1990, the Algemene Rekenkamer (The Netherlands Court of Audit) provided an exemplar in its government-wide study of evaluation practices in the executive branch of central government (Algemene Rekenkamer 1990). The recommendations pointed at the need for systematic and periodic evaluation activities in order to regularly cover all policy fields. In its response, the government declared its intention to issue legislation (which was realized in 1992) on the systematic and periodic program evaluation that it deemed an integral part of the policy process. It was to be a standard function within departmental structures, a prime responsibility of political and administrative leaders of the ministerial departments, with the results of evaluations considered in budgetary decision-making. Ministries are now also obliged to inform Parliament and the Court of Audit on the state of affairs regarding their self-evaluations and their results. This enables the Algemene Rekenkamer to practice a form of meta-evaluation of which we shall say more when discussing audit methodology.

The Court's endeavors to improve transparency of the budgetary process have also played a major role in the government's recent initiative to put new life into the old Planning-Programming-Budgeting approach. Linking money to policy (-effects) is the objective in both budget-preparation and financial reporting of the reformed accountability process, called *Van beleidsbegroting tot beleidsverantwoording* (From Program Budget to Program Accountability). The methodology required will need to rest on performance indicators based on systematic evaluation (Bemelmans-Videc 2001).

The Office of the Auditor General of Canada (OAG) has also been a strong external proponent of evaluation (OAG 1996b; Segsworth 2001). In 1997, the Treasury obligated departments and agencies to evaluate their programs systematically. In 1978, the Auditor General's criticism of the limited number and poor quality of program-evaluations led to the creation of the Office of the Comptroller General (OCG) within the Treasury Board, with the task of reforming program evaluation. Evaluation units were formed in each department and by the early 1990s the evaluation function was well embedded throughout government institutions. However, the evaluation function has become amalgamated with other functions, most prominently with auditing and performance and quality measurement (OAG 1996b; Segsworth 2001).

The European Union: New Evaluation Challenges

The European Union provides an illustration of the resulting evaluation challenge. Its revenues and expenditures are huge. Perhaps as a result, European regulations increasingly dominate national regulations and increase the complexity of national evaluation and control. European law stipulates that the proper spending of European money is the responsibility of national governments, even if this money is being transferred directly to subsidiary governments or other bodies involved in the execution of public tasks. These characteristics of subsidiarity, decentralization and collaboration between the Union and member states in effecting and controlling European law are perhaps unusual in that accountability arrangements are often provided not through a formal regulation but through so-called "decentralization letters" that have the character of a covenant. This implies an agreement between a central government and another party in exercising financial responsibilities and public tasks to realize government policy (Comijs 1998: 69-71).

The principle of subsidiarity was added to the Single European Act of 1987 and formalized in the Maastricht Treaty. It was designed to provide the means of deciding what policies should fall within the competence of the European Union and what should be the role of national governments. Paradoxically, subsidiarity has a centralizing tendency as it presupposes a common framework of general policy aims. If in being applied to the entirety of the European Union action this principle was intended to allow national bodies as great a part in executing Union policies as possible, its practice has not provided the desired clarity (Barnes and Barnes 1995: 19-21).

Subsidiarity also provides for an increase in the tasks of national SAIs with regard to European revenue and expenditure. Indeed, the European Union Treaty implies the obligation of national SAIs to co-operate—on a voluntary basis—with the European Court of Auditors in their audits in national states (Art. 188 C3, European Union Treaty). The signing of the Maastricht Treaty, giving the European Court of Auditors the status of a full EU institution, also led to the new requirement for a so-called Statement of Assurance (*Déclaration d'Assurance/DAS*) on the activities financed by the European Community Budget. The European Court of Auditors here needs to co-operate closely with national SAIs. It has taken on a leading role in devising audit and evaluation standards and methodology that should harmonize these material and procedural instructions across different administrative cultures (ECA 1998).

Power (1997) evaluates the functioning of the European Court of Auditors as problematic, referring to imperfect links with national audit bodies, ambivalent relations with the budgeting arm of the European Parliament, an uneasy operational mixture of regularity and value-for-money auditing and the absence of an internal audit function in the Commission. However, the Commission has recently set up a central unit to coordinate the fight against fraudulent use of EC money, currently estimated at 1 or 2 percent of the EC budget. If this suggests that within the Commission there is political resolve, there may be still a long way to go. In 1995, the actual "practice of evaluation...(was) still unevenly spread across Commission services.... [The] quantity of evaluation reports produced yearly is rising but is not matched sufficiently by measures assuring quality control; [there are] insufficient organization units specializing in evaluation...and feedback is the weakest link" (Vanheukelen 1995). A 1997 study analyzing the lessons from policy evaluation and advice of the EU Structural Funds concludes: "The potentiality of policy evaluation and policy advice to stimulate learning through feedback, cognitive stimuli, or 'true' dialogue and argumentation seems limited" (van der Knaap 1997: 337).

Audit Methodology

As described earlier, SAI tasks include financial and regularity audit and performance or value-for-money audit. Even in countries where the constitution or legislation does not require the SAI to carry out value for money audits, there is a tendency to include these in an audit of "sound financial management." Such performance audits often require system-based judgments that are founded on premises relating to the economy, efficiency and effectiveness of organizational structures and procedures. These premises are often implicitly or explicitly based on organization and management theories.

Since this book focuses on the role of *evaluation* in collaborative government, it is necessary to examine the relationship between performance audit and program evaluation. *Performance audit* may be understood:

1.   in a restricted sense, as part of financial audit, concentrating on the examination of the "soundness" of financial management; in this case, it examines only internal policies and processes and may result in findings and judgments on the *output* of policies and processes;

2.   in a broader sense, where both internal and external policies and processes are subject of the audit, and which may result in findings and judgments on both *output and outcome* of policies or processes. In this sense, performance audit is equivalent to program evaluation.

In many countries (e.g., Canada, Denmark, the Netherlands, Sweden, the UK and the United States), actual performance audit practice seeks to correspond with the broader interpretation of performance audit as program evaluation. In performance auditing, the general concepts of economy, efficiency and effectiveness need to be interpreted in relation to the subject audited. However, the resulting criteria often vary in corresponding with the administrative and management theories underpinning them.

The growing need to discuss these criteria (audit standards) with auditees both in advance and when concluding an audit, underlines this development (and is discussed below). The INTOSAI audit standard (1992, para. 183) which indicates that as a consequence, performance audit reports are varied and contain more discussion and reasoned argument, also points to an important difference between the two kinds of audit. The financial auditor is obliged to operate within the strict framework of the standards and guidelines of an accountancy discipline or institute. In performance audit, consensus on standards and methods is growing, although the related discipline of policy evaluation does not yet have the full professional status or codified methods of the accountancy profession.

Auditees in Collaborative Arrangements

Recent pubic sector reform has resulted in governmental structures of growing differentiation and complexity where authority and ensuing accountability relations have become more diffuse. As a consequence, checks on government are sought via new procedures and evidence to make complexity transparent, for example, through performance indicators, citizen charters, etc. Reforms, especially perhaps those under new public management (NPM), have also encouraged more autonomous agencies to practice self-evaluation on a regular basis. This practice has taken root in the two countries that we shall now discuss further: the Netherlands and Canada.

The academic literature suggests problems with democratic accountability under NPM. Gates and Hill (1995), for example, discuss the duties formerly discharged by government and now by nonprofit organizations. They show that governments are unwilling and, in some ways, unable to control such organizations completely. Moreover, they demonstrate how the innovative features of nonprofit organizations can undercut democratic accountability. They conclude that while the loss of accountability can be lessened, some loss of public control will be inevitable. This must be weighed against any improvement in service delivery.

Most Western SAIs are involved in auditing and evaluating private-public partnerships. Such partnerships include crown corporations (Canada), ventures to bring private-sector finance and operational know-how to public service delivery (United Kingdom), financial links through issuing guarantees or subsidies (the Netherlands, Germany, and Norway), and joint service provision through multiple agencies (the Netherlands, Sweden, Denmark). In the audit of these arrangements the SAIs face difficulties of methodology and standards and will often emphasize performance agreements between partners and self-evaluation as a basis for their judgments.

Dutch Auditees

It may be typical in a country such as the Netherlands, which identifies itself with the seemingly contradictory characteristic of a decentralized unitary state, that forms of collaboration with both public and private sector partners have become a dominant way to realize effective government. Long-standing examples are *medebewind* (co-governance with provincial and local government) and *complementair bestuur* (complementary administration with these same partners and with other functionally decentralized public bodies) as well as with private partners, the so-called *polder model* (where central government respects self-regulation by private bodies, seeks consensus with these partners on the general policy framework, and provides facilitating conditions like subsidies and infrastructure) for the execution of public tasks. The Netherlands also has a large nonprofit sector (12.4 percent of the Dutch professional population), which is financially dependent on government for about 60 percent of its income (compared to 30 percent in the United States) (Salamon et al. 1998). *Covenant* is the present day term for a tradition of gentlemen's agreements between governments and public or private sector parties, which regulate these various forms of collaboration and their supervision.

The creation of semi-autonomous authorities, especially those external to government, is a tradition going back to the sixteenth century (see chapter 3 of this volume). Their relative numerical growth from the 1980s and the development of new forms of contracting-out and decentralization induced the Algemene Rekenkamer to investigate them. Such authorities include a wide range of organizations (e.g., the Manpower Services Organization, industrial insurance boards, state universities and the Radio and Television License Fee Agency). Their tasks range from providing benefits and subsidies and collecting levies to supervisory duties and issuing approval certificates. They vary as to their history, legal form, financing and accountability formulas.

The Algemene Rekenkamer's government-wide audit (1995a) focused on the manner in which ministerial responsibility for these bodies is regulated and the form this takes in practice. The study looked at 162 of the 189 then existing clusters of such authorities that in 1993 received almost 38 billion DFL of public funds (18 percent of total state expenditure) and spent about 160 billion DFL, the majority on social security and statutory health insurance programs. Previously, in 1990, the government prepared a position paper on functional decentralization that dealt with the regulation of the new semi-autonomous authorities. In 1991, the Lower House called for all such bodies to be reviewed in the light of this government framework. In 1993, the Algemene Rekenkamer reported that the points referred to in the government position paper were insufficiently regulated in respect of any of the bodies studied and that in many cases ministers had insufficient powers to fulfill their general responsibility for the policy areas in which the authorities operated. It recommended specifying the defining characteristics of semi-autonomous authorities, clarifying their tasks, funding, composition and organization and incorporating into their regulatory framework the supervisory powers for ministers/supervisory bodies deemed necessary by the Court. It also stressed that the operation, performance and effectiveness of these authorities should be evaluated regularly.

The official response to the audit was that the recommendations were in keeping with the government's objective of restoring political primacy in this area. In 1996, the Minister of Internal Affairs published a report providing more detail of the composition, tasks and responsibilities of these bodies. He also met the concerns and recommendations of the Court in issuing instructions for the creation of new authorities that weighed the advantages of a decrease in ministerial responsibility for the public task involved against the disadvantages of a decrease of parliamentary control. Since then a law on Autonomous Administrative Authorities has been under parliamentary discussion. This law may be anchored in the Constitution indicating that autonomous authorities may only be created by legislation that will stipulate their organization and responsibilities and their regulatory supervision. This should force Parliament to decide on the degree to which the ministerial responsibility involved is to be limited, which is the logical consequence of the creation of such an authority.

The Algemene Rekenkamer's Audit of *Covenants* (1995b) presents an overview of these contractual arrangements between governmental actors and private industries and institutions. Central government increasingly seeks cooperation from industries and organizations/institutions to realize its policy via covenants. By the mid-1990s, over 150 covenants were in force. Of these nearly 60 percent related to environmental policy and 20 percent to educational policy. The main findings of the audit, which had both regularity and performance audit characteristics, related to the obscurity as regards the use of government money involved in the implementation of the covenants; the fact that the majority of the covenants contained agreements that were not or hardly enforceable and the absence or vagueness of objectives and instruments to realize them. The recommendations of the Court related to the choice and legal status of the instrument of the covenant, the clear stipulation of its objectives and its financial consequences, and the degree to which parties are bound by the agreement. It also recommended regular evaluation of covenants' terms and objectives. The Court concluded that if parties involved in a covenant only wished to present a declaration of intent, without enforceable obligations, this needed to be made explicit in the covenant.

The Algemene Rekenkamer then presented an overview of 24 regularity and performance audits carried out in the years 1995-1997, including the audit of autonomous administrative authorities and the supervision of corporate bodies (*rechtspersonen*) engaged in public tasks (1998). The Court focused on the emergence of corporate bodies who combined the execution of public tasks with commercial activities (hybrid organizations) as well as the increasing influence of the European Union in fields such as social security, (health) care, higher education, the financial sector, and transport.

Central to the audit standards employed was the principle of continuing ministerial accountability to Parliament for the execution of a legal or public task and for the collection, management and spending of public money. This principle also applies when public tasks are executed by an organization outside central government. Hence, the minister needs to ensure the supervision of tasks or spending through associated corporate bodies.

The report explicitly stated the Court's intention to communicate with all parties involved (auditees) in order to realize an adequate set of generally accepted standards. The central concept of *toezicht* (supervision) was defined with reference to the collection of information in an effort to establish a degree of correspondence between requirements and actual action, with intervention as a possible outcome. The analysis resulted in an overview of failings and the presentation of an analysis of the standards applied in the audits of corporate bodies. Starting from premises relating to ministerial responsibilities and accountability before Parliament, the Court specified requirements regarding the hierarchy of supervision (*toezichtsketen*) and the outcome of this. The structure of this supervision should be such that it results in the product required, guarantees that the subsequent elements in the hierarchy have been coordinated and no elements are missing, that the management of supervisory tasks is in order and that the design and execution of the actual supervision is correct. In addition, the outcome of this supervision should result in the reasonable assurance that the execution of public tasks by the corporate body is up to standards and that it employs public resources in a legal, efficient, and orderly manner so that its actions are auditable. In operational terms this means that the minister and the supervisory body should publish a yearly report on their findings and judgments to be presented to Parliament. If more than one supervisor is involved, their judgments should be integrated into these reports. The judgments of various supervisory bodies in a particular sector (e.g., higher education) should also be presented in an aggregated fashion so as to represent an overall and balanced judgment for the sector as a whole.

So what are the effects of this audit? Current political and academic discussions on ministerial responsibility in general, and on the form and nature of supervision and control in particular, are still inconclusive. In general, there is a growing sense that more order is required in face of the growing complexity of collaborative or competitive partners in the public's business. Recent legislation shows some developments towards this end.

Canadian Auditees

The *Canada Infrastructure Works Program*, audited by the Office of the Auditor General (OAG 1996a) is a cost-shared initiative, involving the federal, provincial, and municipal governments. Program objectives include economic recovery, upgrading of infrastructure, employment creation, enhanced economic competitiveness and improved environmental quality. The federal government's involvement in, and control over, day-to-day implementation and delivery of the program is limited, with federal funding conditional on performance and on compliance with program requirements.

As the program involves five federal government departments, twelve provincial/territorial governments and numerous local governments, it is both inter- and intra-governmental. Nongovernmental organizations are beneficiaries, not collaborators and the program is voluntary. Following an invitation from the prime minister, federal, provincial, and territorial officials met to define the program, and to set out a general framework for its implementation. The mode of governance here is contractual. Federal-provincial agreements establish implementation, financing and governance provisions, as well as Management Committees (MCs) that are the main mechanism of coordination. MCs generally have four members representing equally the federal and provincial governments, each of which provides a co-chair. Only co-chairs can vote on project approvals and only the provincial co-chair can nominate projects for approval. These agreements are complemented by a series of arrangements between provincial governments and project proponents (mainly municipal governments).

The approach to the audit of these arrangements evolved over time. The flow of information between the parties and the provinces assured that eligibility for contributions became a matter of significance. Criteria included the adequacy of the framework of responsibilities, financial and management controls, and the funding allocation. The clearance process was expanded to include the Management Committee of each province's program, given political sensitivities. This involvement of the provincial level constituted the biggest change in audit roles and responsibilities. The audit also examined the compatibility of the parties and the suitability of the collaborative structure and procedures to achieve the program objectives. As a consequence, the audit findings pointed to changes needed in the collaborative arrangement, such as tightening up the definition of infrastructure, clarifying project selection guidelines and the inclusion of clear requirements for compliance auditing. The audit was not designed specifically to facilitate knowledge building within the arrangement, but appears to have had that effect and to have influenced the redesign of the agreements for Phase II of the program.

A contrasting collaboration involved *The Atlantic Groundfish Fisheries* (OAG 1997a). Due to a serious decline of groundfish stocks off Atlantic Canada, the Atlantic Groundfish Strategy (TAGS) was launched in April 1994. Program objectives were to restructure the fishery industry to make it economically viable and environmentally sustainable through resource renewal, labor market adjustment and community economic development. Implementing TAGS involved four federal government organizations working with provincial and municipal governments, educational institutions and the private sector. Hence, the collaboration was primarily of the intra-government level type (federal), though there were elements of working with other levels of government and the nongovernmental sector.

The federal departments of Fisheries and Oceans (DFO) and Human Resources Development Canada (HRDC) were to be held equally responsible for managing TAGS, with DFO leading the restructuring of the fishing industry and HRDC the income support program. In addition, two other federal government departments were involved—Atlantic Canada Opportunities Agency and Federal Office of Regional Development, Quebec—responsible for community and regional economic development. These organizations were to work with provincial and municipal governments, educational institutions and the private sector. There were few formal mechanisms for defining roles and responsibilities or for coordinating activities. There were no integrated strategic plan or performance indicators. Each organization conducted its own audit and evaluation activities and results were not consolidated. Governance was based on "communion" (as defined in chapter 1 of this volume), regulated by covenants of shared values.

The fact that the OAG tabled two chapters on DFO and one on HRDC, with respect to the TAGS program could be viewed as indicative of the type of audit conducted. The program was not looked at as an integrated entity, but rather as related sub-programs of the key departments. The nature of audit work was not really affected. There was no overall program management structure in place, communications among departments was poor and they did not understand the strategy in the same way. Since there were no real collaborative structures and procedures accountability was through existing departmental arrangements. The audit did not look at this type of arrangement compared to privatization or disposal, nor at the compatibility of the partners, nor did it use any new methodologies. Observations related primarily to the lack of strategic planning, coordination and collaboration in program decision-making, planning and implementation, pointing to the need to define clearly and formalize roles and responsibilities, particularly relating to governance and accountability. As the situation was then, there was no assurance of obtaining value for money.

In its response to the OAG's conclusions regarding the need to institute formal measures to ensure accountability for the strategy as a whole, the department agreed that this should be in place and refers to its presence in newly initiated programs.

The final Canadian experience relates to a 1997 audit on *Ozone Layer Protection* (OAG 1997b). In an effort to address ozone depletion, Canada has linked with other countries, United Nations agencies and other international organizations to develop a domestic and international control regime to address ozone depletion, while accommodating a range of competing interests. In September 1987, 24 countries signed the *Montreal Protocol on Substances That Deplete the Ozone Layer* and more than 160 countries have since ratified it. The 1992 National Action Plan (NAP), a political and jurisdictional compromise between federal and provincial governments, is based on shared responsibilities, with each governmental level to take action in specific areas. Environment Canada (EC) is the lead federal department, engaging in international negotiations, implementing and enforcing environmental protection regulations and public education. EC works in partnership with other federal departments and levels of government in Canada, industry, academia, nongovernment environmental and health organizations, and the public. As custodian of the NAP, EC is also responsible for managing the harmonization process.

Some of the achievements of the NAP have been a Code of Practice, implementation of provincial regulations, and technician training. In its report, the Office of the Auditor General (OAG 1997b) recommended that the NAP needed to articulate clearly roles and responsibilities of the respective levels of government, measure and report on objectives, and expected outcomes and establish mechanisms to provide for redress and necessary program adjustments. The way that this audit reviewed the nationally coordinated program with the provinces had a large impact on how the audit was carried out. It sought to acknowledge the problems inherent in a collaborative arrangement that evolved from a political undertaking. This impacted on the scope and evidence gathering which had to revolve around the federal entities, given the limitations of the OAG's jurisdiction.

The key focus of auditing accountability arrangements was on the accountability of the federal government for the nature and management of the NAP. The accountability framework lacked measurable or quantifiable objectives and targets and was imprecise. Audit roles, responsibilities and methodologies did not really change. The compatibility of the parties was not an issue, nor was the suitability of collaborative structures and procedures, given the political nature of the arrangement. No specific implications were evident for high-level government decision-making as to alternative use of collaborative arrangements vs. privatization. The audit indicated that there has been some progress on parts of the NAP and the overall thrust of arrangements, but recommended a number of changes be made during revision of the NAP-related primarily to clarifying roles and responsibilities, accountabilities, and redress. For its part, EC responded to the audit findings and recommendations by agreeing with the need to clearly assign responsibilities and authorities and indicated that this was being done in regulations and draft plans.

Audit Standards and Judgments

The audits by the Algemene Rekenkamer and the OAG offer descriptive overviews of the variety present in the audited phenomenon while subsequently testing their correspondence with stated policy objectives and existing laws. The Algemene Rekenkamer has, in presenting these overviews, greatly influenced political discussion in developing and using relevant concepts and standards in audits and evaluations

Dutch Experience of Standards and Judgments

The audits discussed here relate to vertical, inter-governmental collaboration as well as vertical and horizontal collaboration between government and nongovernmental organizations. The modes of governance are mixed. Hence, we find characteristics of command, where the minister remains responsible and accountable to Parliament, and contract and communion, expressed in agreements with public and private bodies and resting on moral commitment to the public interest in general and to specific covenants' terms in particular. These modes confirm that, in its choice of management instruments, governments face combinations of the "stick," the "carrot" and the "sermon" as sources of control (Bemelmans-Videc, Rist and Vedung 1998).

In its audits the Algemene Rekenkamer explicitly relates decreasing transparency to decreasing auditability of the delegation and decentralization used to make the constructs work. The following key audit standards may also be discerned:

1.   clear and controllable goals to justify moves towards greater independence by semi-independent bodies, either in- or outside of government;

2.   sufficient authority and information for the minister to supervise the implementation of the public tasks involved; authority and monitoring are necessary since the minister will remain accountable to Parliament for the functioning of these bodies and will need to inform Parliament on the administrative and financial consequences of the developments;

3.   clear consequences of the creation of these new bodies and arrangements for the Budget, implying adequate regulation of supervision and financial control.

In its 1995 Annual Report (Algemene Rekenkamer 1996), the Court expressed its intention to continue its focus on "arms-length" agencies within and outside government. In its view, the increasing number of autonomous bodies, funds and other constructions make the auditability of public tasks more problematic. In its strategic program for 1999-2004, the Court again reflects on the increased complexity of public administration given the involvement of a variety of actors. Consequently, policy processes and their financial implications are more complex, which complicates insight into the relation between money and policy. This requires greater transparency, hence a request for more objective audits. The Court accords itself a role in pressing for greater transparency and in tracking actual policy practices. It also wishes to increase the transparency of its own judgments and underlying standards.

As illustrated by the political response to the Court's audits and recommendations, the Netherlands government starts from the same premises in its regulation of autonomous administrative bodies and hybrid organizations. It wants to see an explicit commitment in terms of increased efficiency weighed against the possible loss of democratic supervision and control (van Montfort and Andeweg 1998).

Canadian Experience of Standards and Judgments

In Canada, the OAG audits discussed above represent a variety of governance and collaboration modes. For example, the *Canada Infrastructure Works Program* (OAG 1996a) was voluntary and of the horizontal intra- and inter-governmental type, its mode of collaboration contractual. The audit focused on some of the program's collaborative characteristics, using audit criteria that included the adequacy of the framework of roles and responsibilities, financial and management controls, and funding allocation. The *Atlantic Groundfish Fisheries* strategy (OAG 1997a) implied equal, though task-specific responsibilities for a number of central government actors as well as collaboration with provincial and municipal governments, educational institutions and the private sector. Governance was basically of the communion-type, regulated by covenants of shared values. In the audit the emphasis was on standards requiring management tools like strategic planning, coordination and collaboration in decision-making. At the same time there was the often articulated request for clearly defined roles and responsibilities, particularly relating to governance and accountability, coupled with the need to obtain value-for-money.

The Ozone Layer Protection program (OAG 1997b) clearly most represents a collaborative construct with many different actors. The relationships of Environment Canada with other federal departments, levels of government, industry, academia, private environmental and health organizations, and the public is branded as "partnership" and implies "horizontality." The intra- and inter-governmental relations within the 1992 National Action Plan are based on "shared responsibilities." The collaboration modes preferred seem to be communion and contract. The audit sought to acknowledge the problems inherent in collaborative arrangements that evolved from a political undertaking. The key focus was on auditing accountability, specifically the accountability of the federal government for the nature and management of the program. The accountability framework lacked measurable objects and targets and clarity with regard to roles, responsibilities and accountabilities, while program adjustment mechanisms needed further revision.

In the OAG's report on *Collaborative Arrangements: Issues for the Federal Government* (April 1999), the Office defines collaborative arrangements as:

> an alternative way—a potentially more innovative, cost-effective and efficient way—to deliver programs and services that traditionally have been provided by the federal government departments and Crown corporations. In collaborative arrangements, the federal government, other levels of government and organizations in the private and voluntary sectors agree to share power and authority in decisions on program and service delivery. (p. 9)

The risks of these arrangements are then identified as "poorly set up arrangements among the partners...; partners not meeting commitments; insufficient attention to protecting the public interest; insufficient transparency; and inadequate accountability." The report then takes a firm stand stating that to serve the public interest, effective *accountability* and greater *transparency* should be basic elements of a framework for these arrangements. Here partners are collectively accountable, in terms of three kinds of accountability relationships: among the partners, between each partner and its own governing body, and to the public. The transparency requirement (which should be greater than in the case of traditional delivery by government departments) is directly related to the involvement of several different partners, which makes it difficult for citizens to know who is responsible.

Following Pollitt and Summa (1997), we may conclude from the nature of the audit-standards discussed, that the OAG's role-conception is both constitutionalist and managerialist. The same can be said of the Algemene Rekenkamer's. In both cases we find the classic law-compliance criteria as well as the request for transparency with regard to actual program effectiveness and efficiency. The Canadian and Dutch SAIs also clearly agree on the diagnosis as formulated by Peters (1996: 133) that the move toward myriad and often conflicting reform models in recent years has been driven by ideology rather than by thoughtful, impartial evaluation of the models. The audits discussed illustrate the SAIs' response to this development in pressing for empirical validation of the assumptions underlying the reforms.

Changes in Audit Standards, Methodology, and Judgments?

The starting point in the development of standards and judgments will—of necessity—be the existing rules of the political game which will induce the SAI to ask questions about tasks, responsibilities and authorities to get a clear picture of accountability relations. Next, the SAI will audit the actual performance against the stated objectives and to do so will ask for valid performance indicators. Given the complexity of the new constructions, the request for greater transparency here is only logical. In line with classic accountability practice the audit approach will first request factual information regarding the (non-) actions of the auditee ("answerability"), and then request a justification for those (non-) actions ("amenability"), whereby the stated policy objectives and existing laws form the natural frame of reference. Policy objectives should also indicate the added value of collaborative arrangements. As a third phase, the SAI could develop its own view on how collaborative arrangements are to be set up in order to be effective, efficient, and accountable. The OAG report on Collaborative Arrangements (1999) summarizes the framework for assessing these arrangements starting from the normative premises of "serving the public interest," "effective accountability arrangements," and "greater transparency." This framework is operationalized in terms of factors such as effectiveness, added value of collaborative arrangements, maintenance of public service values, agreed and clear objectives, clear authorities, roles and responsibilities and democratic accountability to Parliament.

The methodologies of the audits by both SAIs are not fundamentally different from those used in traditional auditing. However, the collaborative constructions require an increased amount of self-evaluation by the partners, given their more complex accountability relationships. Consequently, SAIs need to rely more heavily on the results of self-evaluations in their audits. The Algemene Rekenkamer has therefore developed a new guideline for *meta-evaluation*. This development will put greater strain on the external-internal controller relationship by focusing on scientific (epistemological) criteria of the quality of primary research (self-evaluation/internal audit) and on criteria of usefulness of evaluation and audit research for policy and management practice. This development is intensified by the formation of more supervisory layers in collaborative arrangements and of supranational bodies like the European Union. This growing complexity will induce evaluators and auditors in the respective layers of government to rely increasingly on audit and evaluation of the lower layer. The upper layer will therefore have an interest in instructing the lower layer in standards and guidelines for its required (self-) evaluation.

Interestingly, classic financial and regularity audits already imply reviewing techniques and judgments, based on the internal accountant's statements. In performance audit, present developments within the departments—now obliged to self-evaluate their programs on a regular basis—will also enhance the new meta-evaluative role. What may be needed in the longer term is a form of coordination of both types of audit (performance and financial/regularity audit), a form of evaluation synthesis in which results on all these criteria need to be made comparable and compatible. Therein lies an even greater methodological and also political challenge (Bemelmans-Videc and Fenger 1999).

Auditing Collaborative Developments: Results and Effects

What are the prospects for and the results of the audit and evaluation of collaborative developments? Do SAI activities correct the positive and negative effects of the collaborative arrangements in public management? Are SAIs themselves involved in "collaboration" in their control-relations with the auditee?

We described above the political and technical challenges SAIs face when dealing with collaborative arrangements. Analysis of auditees' primary reactions to SAIs' standards and judgments points to more tension than usual. The SAIs' lasting defense of the classic values of good governance may clash with modern or even postmodern views on public management. Reference to clear roles, responsibilities and accountabilities is understood as hierarchy while collaboration in delayered relationships is preferred. Such factors have induced the Canadian OAG to present a modernized view of accountability to accommodate partnering by not requiring a hierarchical relationship (Mayne, Ch. 7). What then are the effects of SAIs' judgments given this response and how do they fit in with the propositions developed in this volume's introductory chapter?

The effects of the audits described indicate that their primary function was that of enlightenment: the audits and evaluations often presented an initial and thorough description of the phenomenon in question. Second, the phenomenon is tested by its correspondence to the law and/or stated program objectives. The audits thus offer reference points for further discussion. This resulting structuring of the debate may be typified as conceptual utilization.

As amply illustrated, the SAIs' classic "constitutionalist" approach will request clarity with regard to authorities, responsibilities and accountabilities, especially in these often complex arrangements where political aspirations may outweigh the clarity required by constitutional-judicial considerations. SAIs will, of necessity, request this transparency; it is a *conditio sine qua non* for the auditability of the arrangements in question. This auditability again is a prerequisite for parliamentary control, the state institution served by SAIs. Next comes the managerialist emphasis on proof for claimed or expected performance. Often—and again for political reasons—

objectives as reference points for performance indicators, will be articulated in inconclusive ways when collaborative arrangements need to be set up. The analysis and recommendations by the SAIs have found fertile ground in parliamentary scrutiny of new legislation and regulations to "discipline" the new arrangements in accordance with the rules of the "*Rechtsstaat*'. In this sense, there is clearly impressive proof of instrumental utilization.

Our findings most clearly relate to *Proposition 3* of the introductory chapter, which hypothesizes that collaboration will limit the need for formal control and reduce transaction costs. The audits discussed indicate that for this proposition to be validated, transparency needs to be established regarding the subjects of potential formal control. If partners are not clear about intentions, standards or created expectations, then also informal control will have difficulty in anchoring the partnership.

Moreover, as we saw earlier, the hierarchical dimension of accountability is undeniable and is confirmed by the politically independent position granted to most SAIs. So, do the "delayering" tendencies of modern collaborative arrangements have consequences for the relation between auditor and auditee? What are the SAIs' views in this respect? In the Netherlands, the Algemene Rekenkamer has aimed at optimizing the effectiveness of its audits by taking an explicit stand in line with principles of proper administrative process. Thus, it seeks to find optimal consensus on standards, conclusions and recommendations of its audit reports, within a clearly defined relation to the auditee. To realize that optimal consensus, it seeks to communicate with Parliament and its auditees on a regular basis. Parliament, in particular the Public Accounts Committee, is regularly briefed on upcoming and concluded audits. The audit's objectives and standards are discussed with auditees at the start of an audit and in the concluding phase in clearance procedures with both ministers and administrative officials.

The Algemene Rekenkamer has also deliberately "opened up" recently by publishing its methods and standards, and discussing these subjects with interested parties. By this act the Court declares its wish to broaden the support and legitimacy of its judgments. At the same time, the Court's independent position remains a vital asset, demonstrated in the conclusions and recommendations of audit reports. The Court does not represent a special interest but the interest of the common good.

Yet this is not a position unique to the relations of the Algemene Rekenkamer with Parliament and its auditees. The cases above, especially as they relate to standards for assurance engagements and its audit practice, also show how it applies to the Canadian Office of the Auditor General. Indeed, in its recent report to the Canadian Parliament on Collaborative Arrangements, the OAG takes on a central issue in both the management and audit of collaborative arrangements: "The essence of collaboration is mutual trust and confidence among the parties to the arrangement" (1999: 11). Discussions of the sorts of hybrid entities often involved in collaborative service provision focus on their perceived structural and cultural complexity: the diversity of participants and their non-specified power-relations as well as the possibly conflicting market-sector and public-sector values and interests.

SAIs may prefer complexity to be tackled by clarity (transparency) and by a less tangible quality, that of trust. Lenin's dictum, *Dawierjaj, no prawierjaj* (trust is good, control is better), might be reformulated for SAI purposes as "trust is fine, auditability is better." One could argue that for SAIs there is an existential need for their auditees to be auditable. Some may view such a preoccupation as leading to an overemphasis on standards relating to procedural and structural prerequisites for auditability. However, the preference for certain formal regulations and transparent responsibilities and accountabilities, which may be considered to reflect a preoccupation with procedural ethics, at the same time expresses concern about values of regularity, legality and democracy and hence about substantive ethics.

Partly induced by increased organizational complexity, a (historically) prominent role has emerged for audit expressed by Power (1994) as an "audit explosion." Power argues that the main function of modern audit is to offer "a way of reconciling contradictory forces: on the one hand the need to extend a traditional hierarchical command conception of control in order to maintain existing structures of authorities; on the other, the need to cope with the failure of this style of control, as it generates risks that are increasingly hard to specify and control" (1994: 6). This reconciling function is induced by the "reinvention of government" with, on the one hand, the "centrifugal pressures for the decentralization and devolution of services and for turning government into enterprises" and the "equally powerful pressures to retain control over functions that have been made autonomous" (1994: 15).

Power also asserts that in practice the energies of many auditors have recently been devoted to rendering institutions and their activities auditable rather than to assessing effectiveness. Influenced by the difficulties of measuring effectiveness and efficiency from a central point in organizations, control-activities, including evaluation, concentrate more on setting up control-systems themselves, instead of checking "first order activities." "What is audited is whether there is a system which embodies standards and the standards of performance themselves are shaped by the need to be auditable" (1994: 19). Thus, auditing becomes a formal loop by which the systems observes itself; a control of control. Again, one may interpret this phenomenon as the undeniable necessity for auditors to have their audited objects transparent in order to make auditing possible. Power believes that this request for transparency clashes with the need for trust and confidence in the New Public Management age: "Audit has spread as much because of its power as an idea and, contrary to the assumptions of the story of lost trust, its spread actually creates the very distrust it is meant to address" (1994:13).

Thus, the final question is one that Power later poses: "What we need to decide...is how to combine checking and trusting..." (1997: 2). Checking implies being explicit about things; trust, however, presupposes implicit agreement. In this chapter we have seen how two SAIs have found a balance to this dilemma when judging the perceived complexity of collaborative government. It probably is a wise choice where it seeks to combine present-day appreciation of flexibility, creativity and trust with the lasting values of the democratic *Rechtsstaat*.

Note

1. For the description and analysis of the Canadian case studies in this chapter, I am greatly indebted to D. Allison Fader and J. Mayne of the Office of the Auditor General of Canada.

References

Algemene Rekenkamer. 1990. *Verslag van de Algemene Rekenkamer over 1989*. Tweede Kamer, Vergaderjaar 1989-1990, 21 481, nrs. 1-2.

Algemene Rekenkamer. 1995a. *Zelfstandige bestuursorganen en ministeriële verantwoordelijkheid* (Autonomous Administrative Authorities and Ministerial Responsibility). Den Haag, Verslag van de Algemene Rekenkamer over 1994 (deel 3), Tweede Kamer, Vergaderjaar 1994-1995, 24 130, nr. 3.

Algemene Rekenkamer. 1995b. *Convenanten van het Rijk met bedrijven en instellingen* (Covenants of Central Government with Private Industries and Institutions). Tweede Kamer, Verslagjaar 1994-1995, 24 480, nrs. 1-2.

Algemene Rekenkamer. 1996. *Verslag van de Algemene Rekenkamer over 1995.* Tweede Kamer, Verslagjaar 1995-1996, nr. 24 658, nrs. 1-2.

Algemene Rekenkamer. 1998. *Toezicht op uitvoering publieke taken* (Supervising the Execution of Public Tasks). Tweede Kamer, Vergaderjaar 1997-1998, 25 956, nrs. 1-2.

Barnes, I., and P. M. Barnes. 1995. *The Enlarged European Union.* London: Longmann.

Barzelay, M. 1996. "Performance Auditing and the New Public Management: Changing Roles and Strategies of Central Audit Institutions." OECD-PUMA, *Performance Auditing and the Modernization of Government.* Paris: OECD, pp. 15-56.

Bemelmans-Videc, M. L. 1998. "De Algemene Rekenkamer: controlenormen en -stijlen in een veranderende bestuurlijke context," in N.J.H. Hils et al. (eds.), *Omgaan met de onderhandelende overheid; Rechtsstaat, onderhandelend bestuur en controle.* Amsterdam University Press, pp. 89-117.

Bemelmans-Videc, M. L., R. C. Rist, and E. Vedung (eds.). 1998. *Carrots, Sticks and Sermons; Policy Instruments and Their Evaluation.* New Brunswick, NJ: Transaction Publishers.

Bemelmans-Videc, M. L. 1999. "Renewing Government: A Tale for all Times," in N. Nelissen, M. L. Bemelmans-Videc, A. Godfroij, and P. de Goede (eds.), *Renewing Government: Innovative and Inspiring Visions.* Utrecht: International Books, pp. 13-33.

Bemelmans-Videc, M. L., and H. J. M. Fenger. 1999. "Standards of Good Governance: Harmonizing Competing Rationalities." *Knowledge, Technology and Policy,* Vol. 12/ 2, summer: 38-51.

Bemelmans-Videc, M. L. 2001. "Evaluation in the Netherlands 1990-2000: Consolidation and Expansion," in J-E. Furubo, R. C. Rist, and R. Sandahl (eds.), *International Atlas of Evaluation.* New Brunswick and London: Transaction Publishers.

Cadbury Report. 1992. *Report of the Committee on the Financial Aspects of Corporate Government.* London.

Canadian Institute of Chartered Accountants (CICA). 1995. *Guidance on Control.* Toronto.

Canadian Institute of Chartered Accountants (CICA). 1995. *Guidance for Directors— Governance Process for Control.* Toronto.

Chartered Institute of Public Finance and Accountancy (CIPFA). 1994. *Effective Internal Control: A Framework for Public Service Bodies.* London.

Chartered Institute of Public Finance and Accountancy (CIPFA). 1995. *Corporate Governance: A Framework for Public Service Bodies.* London.

Comijs, D. E. 1998. "The Word That Says Maastricht? The Principle of Subsidiarity and the Division of Powers within the European Community." *Common Market Law Review,* 29, 1107-1136.

COSO (Committee of Sponsoring Organizations of the Threadway Commission). 1992/4. *Internal Control; Integrated Framework.* New York: AICPA.

European Court of Auditors (ECA). 1998. *Implementing Guidelines for the INTOSAI Auditing Standards.* Luxembourg.

Furubo, J-E, R. C. Rist, and R. Sandahl (eds.). 2002. *International Atlas of Evaluation.* New Brunswick and London: Transaction Publishers.

Frey, B., and Serna, A. 1994. "Eine politisch-ökonomische Betrachtung des Rechnungshofs." *Finanzarchiv,* Vol. 48, 244-270.

Gates, S., and J. Hill. 1995. "Accountability and Government Innovation in the Use of Non-profit Organizations." *Policy Studies Review,* 14:1/2, 137-148.

Gray, A., and W. I. Jenkins. 1993. "Codes of Accountability in the New Public Sector." *Accounting, Auditing and Accountability Journal,* Vol. 6/3, 1993, 52-67.

Gray, A., W. I. Jenkins, and R. V. Segsworth. 1993. *Budgeting, Auditing and Evaluation; Functions and Integration in Seven Governments.* New Brunswick and London: Transaction Publishers.

Holzer, M., and K. Callahan. 1998. *Government at Work; Best Practices and Model Programs*. Thousand Oaks, London and New Delhi: Sage.

INTOSAI (International Organization of Supreme Audit Institutions) Auditing Standards Committee. 1992. *Auditing Standards*.

Jenkins, S. 1996. *Accountable to None: The Tory Nationalisation of Britain*. Harmondsworth: Penguin Books.

Kirkpatrick, I., and M. Martínez. (eds.). 1996. "The Contract State and the Future of Public Management." *Public Administration*, Vol. 74/1.

Knaap, P. van der. 1997. *"Lerende" overheid, intelligent beleid; De lessen van beleidsevaluatie en beleidsadvisering voor de structuurfondsen van de Europese Unie* ("Learning" Government, Intelligent Policies: The Lessons of Policy Evaluation and Policy Advice for the European Union Structural Funds). The Hague: Phaedrus.

Leeuw, F. L. 1998. "Doelmatigheidsonderzoek van de Rekenkamer als regelgeleide organisatiekunde met een rechtssociologisch tintje?" *Tijdschrift voor de sociaal-wetenschappelijke bestudering van het recht*, 2: 35-69.

McSwite, O. C. 1997. *Legitimacy in Public Administration. A Discourse Analysis*. Thousand Oaks, London and New Delhi: Sage.

Montfort, C. J. van, and A. M. Andeweg. 1998. "Toetspunten voor hybride organisaties en een toepassing op de terreinen van zorg en zekerheid." *Beleidsanalyse*, 1998/1: 5-13.

National Audit Office of the United Kingdom (NAO). 1996. *State Audit in the European Union*. London: Stationery Office.

Office of the Auditor General of Canada (OAG). 1996. *Canada Infrastructure Works Program—Lessons Learned*. Ottawa.

Office of the Auditor General of Canada (OAG). 1996b. *Report of the Auditor General of Canada to the House of Commons, Chapter 3: Evaluation in the Federal Government*. Ottawa: Public Works and Government Services Canada.

Office of the Auditor General of Canada (OAG). 1997a. *Atlantic Groundfish Fisheries*. Ottawa.

Office of the Auditor General of Canada (OAG). 1997b. *Ozone Layer Protection: The Unfinished Journey*. Ottawa.

Office of the Auditor General of Canada (OAG). 1999. *Collaborative Arrangements: Issues for the Federal Government*. Ottawa.

Peters, B. G. 1996. *The Future of Governing: Four Emerging Models*. Lawrence: University Press of Kansas.

Pollitt, C. 1995. "Justification by Works or by Faith? Evaluating the New Public Management." *Evaluation*, pp. 133-154.

Pollitt, C., and H. Summa. 1997. "Reflexive Watchdogs? How Supreme Audit Institutions Account for Themselves." *Public Administration*, Vol. 75/2: 313-336.

Power, M. 1994. *The Audit Explosion*. London: Demos.

Power, M. 1997. *The Audit Society: Rituals of Verification*. Oxford: Oxford University Press.

Rist, R. C. (ed.). 1990. *Program Evaluation and the Management of Government: Patterns and Prospects across Eight Nations*. New Brunswick and London: Transaction Publishers.

Salamon, L., H. Anheier, and Associates. 1998. *The Emerging Sector Revisited*. Center for Civil Society Studies, Baltimore, MD: John Hopkins University.

Segsworth, R. V. 2001. "Evaluation in the 21st Century: Two Perspectives on Canadian Experience," in J-E Furubo, R. C. Rist, and R. Sandahl (eds.), *International Atlas of Evaluation*. New Brunswick and London: Transaction Publishers.

Stone, B. 1995. "Administrative Accountability in the 'Westminster' Democracies: Towards a New Conceptual Framework." *Governance*, Vol. 8/4: 505-526.

Streeck W. and P. C. Schmitter. 1998. "Community, Market, State—and Associations?," in G. Thompson, J. Frances, R. Levacic, and J. Mitchell. 1998. *Markets, Hierarchies and Networks; The Co-ordination of Social Life*. London, Newbury Park and New Delhi: Sage, pp. 227-41.

Touraine, A. 1992. *Critique de la modernité*. Paris: Fayard.

Vanheukelen, M. 1995. "The Evaluation of European Expenditure." *Knowledge and Policy,* Vol. 8/3: 34-42.

Woodhouse, D. 1994. *Ministers and Parliament: Accountability in Theory and Practice*. Oxford: Clarendon Press.

9

Evaluation, Accountability, and Collaboration

Bob Segsworth

This chapter examines the relationships between evaluation and accountability in collaborative arrangements. Over the past fifteen years observers raised concerns over both the traditional notions of accountability in Westminster systems (primarily, ministerial responsibility) as well as the more recent forms of results-based accountabilities that emerged under the influence of New Public Management and the separation of policy and service delivery functions.

Collaborative agreements pose interesting accountability problems for governments. One of them involves the notion of dual accountability—to Parliament and also to the collaborative entity itself. There is also the risk of partial accountability wherein governments are held to account only for the use of their public funds and their specific responsibilities and not for the entire range of collaborative objectives and activities.

Evaluation provides a variety of tools and analytic approaches that can enhance the accountability of officials and their political masters to their legislatures and other relevant parties. The contributions of evaluation can extend the understanding of evaluation beyond the performance management systems and program monitoring initiatives of New Public Management reporting practices. In doing so, evaluation can also expand the range of functions for which officials and politicians may be held accountable.

At the same time, collaborative arrangements may pose challenges for evaluators and evaluation processes. Collaborative agreements involve more complex decision-making, communication and reporting processes than direct delivery arrangements. In addition, the choice of a collaborative agreement rather than some other form of governing instrument involves an accountability concern: could the government have chosen a better way of achieving particular public policy objectives? For the evaluator, then, considerations directly linked to the choice, operation and results of the collaborative arrangement become issues in the design and conduct of the variety of evaluation activities that may be employed.

In this chapter, we examine the notion of accountability and its evolution over the past several decades.[1] Collaborative arrangements may complicate traditional understandings of accountability and the chapter outlines Canadian governmental responses to this concern. The chapter describes a number of roles that the evaluator may play to enhance the accountability of collaborative arrangements. It concludes by arguing that the focus of evaluations must become broader to consider the unique characteristics of the collaborative and by suggesting that, in practice, Canadian experience does not demonstrate the effective use of evaluation to enhance accountability. Rather, Canadian experience suggests that the obstacles to effective evaluation created by "so-called" collaborative agreements have limited the role of evaluation significantly.

The Notion of Accountability

Accountability has had a particular importance in discussions of responsible government and in public administration generally. Kernaghan and Langford (1990: 162) suggest that "a persuasive argument could be made that accountability has been the dominant administrative value over the past fifteen years and is likely to remain so for the foreseeable future."

Discussions of accountability often are contained in broader analyses of the concept of responsibility. The classic debate on the subject of political responsibility is found in the work of Finer (1941) and Friedrich (1940). Finer argued that because of the growth of government power in the modern state, external controls over bureaucratic behavior by the legislature, judiciary and the hierarchy of the public service were necessary. Without external controls, he claimed (p. 377) "sooner or later, there is abuse of power." Friedrich suggested (p. 10) that "parliamentary responsibility is largely inoperative and certainly ineffectual." He believed that political responsibility could be achieved if the appropriate norms and values were internalized by public servants and the public was informed of the views of public servants on key issues.

Mosher (1968) develops these ideas in his treatment of objective and subjective responsibility. Objective responsibility (p. 7) "connotes the responsibility of a person or of an organization to someone else, outside of self, for some thing or some kind of performance." Subjective responsibility concerns itself with (p. 7) "to whom and for what one feels responsible and behaves responsibly." Kernaghan and Langford (1990) argue that accountability has the same meaning as objective responsibility only.

In British parliamentary systems, the principles and application of ministerial responsibility are the traditional mechanisms providing accountability in governance. In its study of accountability of third-party arrangements, a steering committee of Canadian deputy ministers defined (1994: 6) the fundamental underpinnings of this form of accountability as:

1.   The formal accountability link with Parliament is the responsible minister;

2.   The accountability of the minister to Parliament includes the obligation to report on the manner in which responsibility has been discharged;

3.   Effective accountability to Parliament requires that public servants support their minister through their actions, advice and information;

4.   Public servants appearing before parliamentary committees do so at the discretion of their minister and under his or her direction.

In terms of minister-public servant relationships, the notion of individual ministerial responsibility includes conventions of public service anonymity, political neutrality by a merit-based career public service enjoying security of tenure subject to good behavior, confidential advice to ministers and zealous implementation of government decisions by public servants regardless of their personal views.

The application of New Public Management approaches over the past fifteen years has had significant consequences for this traditional notion of accountability in British parliamentary systems. The first is the separation of policy and management evident in the creation of Executive Agencies in the U.K. and contractual arrangements in New Zealand. The second is the increased emphasis on accountability for "results" rather than simply compliance with process (Kernaghan and Siegel 1995).

The concerns resulting from the first issue have been summarized neatly by Hodgetts (1991: 13)

If the inevitable drift of public management into the political realm of governance itself…is to be the path of the future, then we must be prepared to see senior managers assume the role of scapegoats for the failure of others who, in our system of responsible cabinet government, have hitherto been elected to bear that direct responsibility.

The Al-Mashat Affair in Canada and British experience with HM Prisons provide examples of the veracity of Hodgetts' argument. In the first case, the former Iraq ambassador to the U.S. was admitted to Canada as a landed immigrant. The public controversy that followed led federal cabinet ministers to blame publicly a senior public servant (Sutherland 1991). In the second case, the home secretary refused to accept responsibility for a number of prison breakouts and prison suicides and sacked the director-general of HM Prison Service, an executive agency. The minister, Michael Howard, argued that the appointed official should be held accountable for short-term operational matters while he, as minister, should be held responsible for longer-term policy (Barker 1998).

Jenkins and Gray (1993) raised concerns about the second issue. "At issue is what mechanisms and powers Parliament has to scrutinise the agencies" (p. 88). They note that in practice "results reporting" rarely deal with the product or service itself or with the impact of the activities of agencies. As they describe it (p. 92), "the good delivery of bad policy is hardly the measure of a healthy state."

Some contemporary observers argue that the separation of policy and service delivery and the emphasis on results have, in fact, enhanced ministerial responsibility. Aucoin (1995), for example, argues that these developments in Britain and New Zealand encouraged (p. 247) "those responsible for operations to serve ministers well by doing what ministers want done." He concludes (p. 253) that "accountability—of ministers to Parliament, public servants to ministers, and through them to Parliament—has been enhanced in the three other Westminster systems. Armstrong (1998) supports this conclusion, but adds that Parliament has an obligation to ensure that rigorous discipline is applied within the public service to protect the public interest.

Critics of this view suggest that reliance on ministerial responsibility is no longer appropriate in the light of recent changes. The OECD (1997), for example, notes a distinction between the public accountability of politicians and the managerial accountability of officials. Cooper (1995) argues that public officials now face an increased emphasis on legal, individual and market mechanisms of accountability. Farrell and Law (1999) remind us of notions of professional accountability and public accountability, in addition to those already mentioned. Barberis (1998) attempts to develop a model of accountabilities for public officials that responds to the fundamental questions of who is accountable to whom, for what, by what means and with what outcomes. He argues that a clearer specification of what civil servants are accountable for is essential. Paquet (1999) argues that "360-degree accountability" must become a central feature of the new governance arrangements that have emerged and that will develop in the future.

In Canada, the Office of the Auditor General and Treasury Board Secretariat (1998) responded to the perceived need to clarify and update the understanding of accountability in a contemporary setting. They defined it as a relationship based upon the obligation to demonstrate and take responsibility for performance in light of agreed expectations. In the context of NPM, this definition fits well with the situation that Aucoin has described (1997) and the emergence of results reporting as an important management tool. It suggests that government is responsible for achieving results that are clearly defined. It responds to one citizen who argued in a recent letter to the editor of the *Sudbury Star* (18 April 2000) that "The government should be setting an example. They should be able to show how efficiently and correctly things are being done. After all, we elected them because we believed that they could do the job properly."

In essence, the notion of accountability remains hierarchical. Public servants remain accountable to their superiors and through them to the minister. The minister is responsible to Parliament and parliamentarians are accountable ultimately to the electorate.

Public servants are fundamentally accountable for the management of public policy. In the New Zealand case, this means the economic, efficient and effective provision of specified (contracted) outputs. Politicians retain responsibility for policy outcomes. There is, of course, the nexus of minister-public servant relations, which involves the provision of policy advice by public servants, but with the clear understanding that the final decision on policy rests with the elected politicians.

The development of results reporting enhances, at least in theory, and closes the accountability loop by providing both policy and managerial information to Parliament and the public. As the president of the Treasury Board put it (1999), "Parliamentarians have a vital role to play in this process. Indeed, managing for results can succeed only if parliamentarians are actively and fully engaged" (president's message). Delacourt and Lenihan (1999) go even further and suggest that results reporting could "re-energize" parliamentary committees by providing "an integrated and complete picture of departmental planning and evaluation...assigning committees the significant role of providing bottom-up feedback on the plan, permitting members to situate specific initiatives, such as legislative bills in a broader departmental context and perhaps by allowing for a more collegial and less adversarial relationship between ministers, departmental officials and parliamentary committees" (p. 117).

At this point, one can envisage at least three accountability relationships at work in collaborative arrangements. The first, reflecting traditional practice, is to one's superiors. The second is to the various partners in the collaborative arrangement. The third is to the collaborative itself.

Collaborative Agreements, and Accountability

In this chapter, we use a rather common understanding of a collaborative arrangement (partnership) as the bringing of previously separated organizations into a new structure with full commitment to a common mission (Mattessich and Monsey 1992). What distinguishes collaborative arrangements from other forms of partnership is the sharing of decision-making authority among the members of the collaborative. Risks, resources and benefits of the arrangement are also shared.

Such arrangements lead to shared accountability for the attainment of the desired outcomes and create potential problems for the traditional notions of accountability in Westminster systems. In such agreements "the needs of the partnership come first and the role of government and any other funder comes second" (Frank and Smith 1997: 27). Clearly, there is an accountability relationship to the partners and to the collaborative itself.

This accountability relationship is different from service delivery by contractors or specialized government agencies where accountability is hierarchical. It is different from departmental cooperative arrangements where the verticality of accountability (albeit through more than one minister) also applies. Accountability becomes particularly complex in federal systems where two "sovereign" levels of government enter into collaborative agreements. There danger here is that of "partial accountability" wherein for example, federal officials and the federal government could only be held accountable for their particular responsibilities in the collaborative. A second potential problem is that of verifying the extent to which other partners are fulfilling their obligations. The Auditor General of Canada cannot audit the provincial or local government's use of public resources. Simply put, "the partnership creates accountability arrangements among the partners. In addition, each partner retains accountability obligations to its governing body such as Parliament in the case of federal partners" (Office of the Auditor General and Treasury Board Secretariat 1998: 8). To some extent, the Government of Ontario, as illustrated by Table 9.1, shares this view.

A good deal of the literature on collaborative arrangements recognizes this potential dilemma and outlines a mechanism whereby these dual obligations can be met. Mattessich and Monsey (1992) indicate that comprehensive planning and well-defined communication channels operating on many levels are essential. Weber and Khademian (1998) argue that a set of formal binding rules is essential to a successful collaborative agreement.

The notion is that formal agreements between the partners must be developed and put in place. In the Oregon Option, these are referred to as partnership agreements (Dyer 1996). Frank and Smith (1997) support the need to formalize matters in action plans. Taylor-Powell, Rossing and Geran (1998) discuss the formalization of structure, decision-making procedures and action plans including desired results and specific indicators.

Table 9.1
Service Delivery Mechanisms and Accountability

Delivery Mechanism	Example	Ministerial Accountability Arrangement
Privatisation	Ontario Hydro	Market
Franchising	Canada Post	Market
Self-Management	Safety Regulations	Set and Enforce Standards
Agencies	Liquor Control Board of Ontario	Supervision
Service Contracting	Garbage Collection	Results
Partnership	Labour Management Development Agreements	Results
Devolution	Hospitals	Results
Direct Delivery	Canada Pension Plan	Results

Source: Adapted from Corporate Policy Branch, Management Board Secretariat (1999). Alternative Service Delivery Framework. Toronto: Queen's Printer for Ontario.

In addition, there appears to be general agreement that the accountability concerns of government partners legitimately should be recognized in the formal agreements. Taylor-Powell, Rossing and Geran point out (1998) that the particular accountability concerns of funders and public officials must be recognized in the formal agreements. Not only does this include monitoring and evaluation provisions, but also recognition of particular audit requirements.

Governments have refined their requirements for participation in collaborative arrangements. Their notions of accountability emphasize a results management orientation. The UK government's policy document, *Modernising Government* (1999), outlines (p. 12) a need to "establish common targets, financial frameworks, IT links, management controls and accountability mechanisms that support such arrangements." The Treasury Board Secretariat and Office of the Auditor General joint paper on *Modernising Accountability Practices in the Public Sector* suggests that collaborative agreements should ensure that (1998: 5-6):

1. The roles and responsibilities of the parties in the accountability relationship should be well understood and agreed upon;

2. The objectives being pursued, the accomplishments expected and the constraints to be respected should be explicit, understood and agreed upon;

3. The performance expectations need to be clearly linked to and in balance with the capacity (authorities, skills and resources) of each party to deliver;

4. Credible and timely information should be reported to demonstrate the performance achieved and what has been learned;

5. Enlightened and informed review and feedback on the performance achieved should be carried out by the accountable parties, whose achievements and difficulties are recognized and necessary corrections made.

In similar vein, the Treasury Board Secretariat, in its *Six Steps to Successful Partnership* (1995) outlines the following regime:

a. ensure that a workable arrangement can be made by assessing four elements in advance—propriety, value to Canadians, accountability of the parties, and the ability to provide sound management;

b. check definitions that include a true legal partnership and a collaborative arrangement and determine appropriate funding;

c. consult a range of departmental and central agency specialists on legal, financial, contracting, risk and project management, human resources, official languages and communications issues;

d. ensure the accountability of all partners for legal financial and operational arrangements;

e. apply sound management techniques necessary to achieve the best results from a partnering environment.

The OAG addressed the issue of accountability directly in its chapter on *Collaborative Arrangements: Issues for the Federal Government* (1999). It argued that there were five key elements required for strong accountability in a collaborative agreement—clear and agreed expectations, clear roles and responsibilities, balanced expectations and capacities, credible reporting and reasonable review, program evaluation and audit (pp. 5-13). Reporting on her experience, Dyer (1996) notes that in their partnership agreement, the Oregon Workforce Cluster members refer to accountability as the responsibility accepted by each individual for promised results. They call accountability the glue that holds the system together.

Evaluating Collaboratives and Accountability

Increasingly, even governments are recognizing the need to engage more actively in evaluation research as part of the accountability arrangements of collaborative agreements. The Treasury Board Secretariat of Canada (1995) includes agreement on measures for determining results, accountability, and audit and evaluation procedures as part of its basic checklist. The Blair government in the United Kingdom has committed itself to more evaluation of policy and program, the modernization of evaluation standards and tools and the establishment of public service agreements with targets, measures and a focus on outcomes as part of its modernizing government initiative (Cabinet Office 1999). Seidle's (1995) discussion of collaborative efforts in Canada illustrates the importance and value of both performance measurement and summative evaluation in successful collaborative initiatives.

There is, then, a good deal of evidence that evaluation has a major role to play in successful collaborative arrangements and that contemporary governments recognize this. Of particular interest is that the notion of evaluation in this context is broader than the results (or performance measurement) notions of New Public Management. It corresponds more closely to the definition of evaluation outlined in the introduction of this volume. Further, there is recognition that the particular accountability requirements of funders and the public sector must be accommodated in collaborative arrangements through appropriate monitoring and evaluation systems and products.

Evaluation can play a significant role in collaboratives in support of accountability as well as other functions. In this section we suggest that there are six evaluation activities of value to the collaborative process. There are feasibility evaluation, process/implementation evaluation, the development of logic models, the development of output/outcome (performance) measures, outcome/impact evaluation and evaluation of the collaborative instrument itself. It is important to note that, in the application of these evaluation activities, the focus of evaluation must be broadened to take into consideration the unique characteristics of collaboratives.

Feasibility Evaluation

A collaborative arrangement is one of many mechanisms or policy instruments available to government. It may not always be the best choice and in specific circumstances, the partners may not have the requisite skills and resources to achieve the desired public policy objectives. Bemelmans-Videc, Rist and Vedung (1998) point out that evaluation can play a major role in the governing instruments choice process. Front-end work of this nature may determine that a collaborative agreement is not an appropriate mechanism. Taylor-Powell, Rossing and Geran (1998) suggest that a feasibility evaluation be undertaken. They describe a case in which a local Health and Human Services department was preparing a grant application that required community collaboration. "There were some indications that the department's real motivation for the grant was to gain funds and that they expected to control the resources they received pretty tightly" (p. 69). As a result of this evaluation, at least one potential partner decided not to participate. This analysis responds to questions such as, is a collaborative needed, what is likely to be the most appropriate approach, what exists in the context that presents opportunities and/or barriers and are the requisite resources and capacities available within the potential collaborative. Dyer (1996) notes that a series of "readiness factors" were required before the federal, state and local partnership known as the Oregon

Option could proceed with reasonable expectations of success. The Treasury Board Secretariat of Canada (1995) claims that the first step (p. 2) is to "collaborate by choice, not by chance" and that the values of propriety, value, accountability and sound management must be used to assess prospective collaborative arrangements.

Monitoring and Implementation Evaluation

Once the collaborative agreement has been struck, ongoing monitoring and implementation evaluation are essential. Monitoring provides a means to respond to typical accountability concerns such as the number and types of outputs and it provides some data regarding the results of the activities undertaken by the collaborative. Implementation evaluation responds to the question of whether the activities undertaken and the services and/or products delivered are those envisaged in the action plans of the collaborative. The implementation literature (Pressman and Wildavsky 1979; Mazmanian and Sabatier 1983) demonstrates that what was actually done and what was delivered to beneficiaries may bear little resemblance to what officials and politicians had intended. Implementation evaluation also provides data essential to impact/outcome evaluation to establish any causal attribution of outcomes and impacts to the interventions of the collaborative. In the case of the Canada-New Brunswick Agreement on Labour Market Development,[2] a formative evaluation to assist in improving the design, delivery and supporting infrastructure of the activities has been completed.

Logic Models

Frequently collaboratives develop action plans to guide their work. As part of this process, the development of logic models can be extremely helpful in developing shared agreement on the means to achieve desired ends. They provide a means to visualize what the collaborative wishes to achieve, the activities it is employing to attain those goals and the specific results expected. Logic models also provide a means to assess the logical consistency of the plans. Evaluators have a long history of using logic models to assist groups to work through issues and to enhance the probability of achieving desired results (Rush and Ogborne 1991).

Taylor-Powell, Rossing and Geran (1998) argue that developing a logic model provides six benefits to collaboration partners (p. 28).

1. Develops understanding. It helps build understanding, if not consensus, among collaborative members about what the collaborative is, what it expects to do, and what measures of success it will use.

2. Monitors progress. It provides a plan against which you can keep track of changes so that successes can be replicated and mistakes avoided.

3. Serves as an evaluation framework. It makes it possible to identify appropriate evaluation questions and data that are needed.

4. Bares assumptions. It helps members be more deliberate about what they are doing and identifies assumptions that may need validating.

5. Restrains overpromising. It helps members and others realize the limits and potential of any one collaborative.

6. Promotes communication. It creates a simple communication piece useful in portraying and marketing your collaboration to others.

Performance Measurement

If, increasingly, governments are concerned about results rather than process as NPM observers suggest (Public Policy Forum 1998) then, appropriate performance management systems are required. As Dyer (1996) points out (p. 24) "accountability for results begins with all parties understanding and agreeing to a set of results." Seidle (1995: 20) argues that "internal performance monitoring, although not devoid of problems, can lead to improvements in productivity and provide useful data when targets are being set. In this context, it is important to underline that performance measurement facilitates greater visibility of the activities of managers and staff."

The work of experts like Wholey (1983) demonstrates the added value that evaluators can bring to the design, development and operation of performance measurement systems in a wide variety of collaborative arrangements. Indeed, it is fundamental to the Oregon Option's results-based accountability system that results are compared with planned benchmarks (targets) (Dyer 1996). The Canada-New Brunswick Labour Market Development Agreement requires the regular reporting of key indicators such as the number of active Employment Insurance (EI) claimants that have access to provincial benefits, returns to employment of EI claimants, savings to the EI account, the number and unit costs of clients becoming employed/self-employed and the number and unit costs of clients becoming self-sufficient.

Summative Evaluation

As Taylor-Powell, Rossing and Geran point out (1998), outcome/impact evaluation assists in closing the accountability loop. It demonstrates that the results obtained can (or cannot) be attributed to the activities undertaken by the collaborative. It allows us to obtain data regarding coverage, intangibles and impact that are not typically obtained by performance measurement systems. Outcome evaluation also provides a mechanism, which responds to the concern expressed by Jenkins and Gray (1993) regarding the possibility that this is bad policy being delivered well. The Canada-New Brunswick LMDA requires that a summative evaluation be completed by the end of 2000. This evaluation must address the issues of outcomes, impacts and the cost-effectiveness of the various initiatives undertaken as a result of the agreement.

Evaluating the Collaborative Itself

Evaluation has a role to play in assessing the collaborative arrangement. In essence the question to be answered is whether the arrangement functions as a collaborative or more like a command or contract arrangement. Mattessich and Monsey (1992), for example, suggest that there are 19 factors on which to assess collaboration. These include considerations of the environment, membership characteristics, process and structure, communication, purpose and resources. Many of these relate clearly to front-end (feasibility) evaluation and implementation evaluation; however, impact evaluation questions are also applicable. For example, what differences resulted from working as a collaborative, that is, could we have achieved the same results by choosing a different instrument? A second question asks whether the collaborative effort was worth the time and other costs expended to achieve these results, that is, was the choice of collaboration cost-effective. Such an approach responds to Pollitt's (1995) concerns that claims about techniques and governing instruments reflect "faith" rather than hard evidence.

Much of the literature on collaborative arrangements required the development of agreement on targets (specific objectives to be attained in a specified time frame) (Dyer 1996; Frank and Smith 1997; Office of the Auditor General of Canada 1999). The Canada-New Brunswick Labour Market Development Agreement (1996), for example, required the annual creation of results targets for (para.7.1):

1. The number of active Employment Insurance (EI) claimants that have access to provincial benefits;

2. Returns to employment of EI clients, with an emphasis on active EI claimants; and

3. Savings to the EI account.

This emphasis on accountability by meeting performance targets poses a potential problem. As Blau (1963) demonstrated, results accountability of this type may lead to activities facilitating creaming. For example, it is easier to remove relatively well-educated individuals with work experience from the EI rolls than those with little education and no work experience. To increase the probability of meeting the targets, one can organize activities in such a way that the focus is on the former category of claimants rather than on the latter. Process/Implementation evaluation can bring such issues to light and remove this important "equality" concern from the managerial agenda to the political, where it properly belongs.

A Note of Caution

There are at least two issues involving collaborative arrangements that impact on evaluation and accountability. The first involves the growing use of the term "collaborative" to cover arrangements that do not meet the definition provided by Mattessich and Monsey (1992). The second deals with responses to perceived "crises" in collaborative arrangements.

The Social Union

On February 14, 1999, the Social Union Framework Agreement codified new rules governing intergovernmental relations in all areas of social policy in Canada. It ushered in what the Minister of Intergovernmental Relations (April 22, 1999) described as greater cooperation and consensus building between the federal and provincial governments. The notion was that Canada had entered an era of collaborative federalism. The key idea of this new arrangement is that " the two orders of government should relate to one another on a non-hierarchical basis" (Lazar 1998: 24).

By applying New Public Management principles to the analysis of the Social Union Agreement, Alain Noel (2000) comes to quite a different conclusion. He argues that it (p. 7) "associates democratically accountable provincial governments to private or voluntary sector service providers that are in a principal-agent relationship with the federal government. Like other agents, provinces row for the federal government, which steers and sees that they row in the right direction, at the appropriate rhythm and with sufficient energy." In other words, the relationship is hierarchical and does not respect the "equality of partners" that characterizes collaboratives.

Some federal officials reflect Noel's analysis in their comments. They see many of the current arrangements as transfers to the provinces over which federal officials have no control and little information regarding the ongoing activities and results of these new arrangements. Some federal evaluators indicated that they have had very severe problems in obtaining data and that they had no way to determine the reliability and validity of the data they did receive. They claimed that they would have to limit the scope of their evaluation work to federal government responsibilities and activities only. For them, partial accountability results in partial evaluation.

A Political Crisis

In the fall of 1999, an internal audit in Human Resources Development Canada (HRDC) revealed several administrative shortcomings in the grants and contributions of the department. Members of the Opposition and the media portrayed the findings as an example of a $1.6 billion boondoggle and demanded the resignation of the minister. An intensive examination of all of the files revealed that only $6,500 was missing. For our purposes, what is more interesting is the reaction of the department to the "crisis" in terms of its regional operations. The center responded with increased controls, reduced discretion for field managers and requirements for greater formality in agreements with partners. The level of trust with partners declined considerably. The response to the "crisis" has been to replace collaborative management with a command and control approach.

The HRDC experience demonstrates that accountability requirements can be an impediment to successful collaboration. Consulting and Audit Canada (1998: 17) found that "partnering arrangements do not always fit easily with the established machinery of government and its associated system of accountability." It concludes that since the existing accountability system is unlikely to change, the issue becomes one of how best to adapt partnering arrangements to the existing system. As the HRDC example illustrates, it is highly unlikely that a collaborative agreement that becomes embroiled in political controversy is likely to retain all of its collaborative characteristics regardless of how extensive the adaptations to ensure accountability might be. In addition, such experiences are likely to make public officials even more risk-averse and to prefer arrangements in which they have greater control of all aspects of policy and program delivery.

Conclusion

Evaluation can enhance the accountability issues involved in collaborative arrangements. As Taylor-Powell, Rossing and Geran point out (1998: 16) "it has multiple purposes allowing partners in collaboratives to answer critical questions, build capacities and assist the relationship in achieving its objectives. It can assist policy makers to decide if a collaborative approach is the most appropriate means by which to achieve public policy objectives. It can assist the partners to develop logically coherent action plans. It provides ongoing information on both results and activities to provide feedback to the partners and allow them to take corrective action where appropriate. It can provide evidence that the collaborative activities are, in fact, making a difference in the designated target population and it can also provide an assessment of the extent to which the partners functioned in a collaborative manner.

In order to achieve such lofty goals, there must be formal agreement among the parties to engage collectively in evaluation activity. The Canadian Labour Market Development Agreements, for example, require both formative and summative evaluations to be undertaken. They require the ongoing information of adequate performance measurement systems. They also allow the federal and provincial partners to undertake independent evaluations that address questions of interest to only one of the partners. They require that the partners in this evaluation activity share information.

Evaluation, then, can respond to the four concerns expressed by Treasury Board Secretariat (1995) as fundamental issues in collaborative arrangements. It provides assessments on the feasibility of a proposed collaboration being successful. It can tell us if the collaboration has added value. Evaluation reporting responds to the typical demands of auditors and others for results-based accountability information and by providing assistance in the design of programs and in monitoring their implementation, it provides valuable information to support sound management. By doing so, evaluation broadens the notion of accountability as simply one of the four elements of a collaborative arrangement to include accountability for all of them.

Despite this, in many cases in Canada, the role of evaluation in collaborative arrangements has been limited severely. In part, this results from the fact that some alleged collaborative arrangements are not real collaboratives. Ironically, evaluation has the capability to determine if the governing instrument used is, in fact, a collaborative one. In part, the difficulty results from the failure to develop written agreements that meet the requirements described by the Office of the Auditor General, Treasury Board Secretariat and/or Consulting and Audit Canada. A third problem is the view, adopted especially by provincial governments, that performance measures are sufficient to respond to all of the relevant concerns about collaborative arrangements. A final difficulty is that partisan political pressures provide little incentive for public servants to engage zealously in higher-risk systems like collaboratives. To a considerable extent, the potential of evaluation research to enhance the accountability concerns related to collaborative agreements is unfulfilled.

Notes

1.   Much of the material used in the preparation of this chapter is primary and secondary literature that is readily available. Interviews with officials in Treasury Board Secretariat and the Office of the Auditor General in the Government of Canada and with officials in eight ministries in the Government of Ontario provided clarification of many issues and allowed the author to pursue some issues in greater depth. A version of the chapter, presented at the May 2000 Conference of the Canadian Evaluation Society, generated helpful comments from both federal and provincial officials.

2.   In response to pressure from provincial governments, the Government of Canada promised to establish a new relationship with the provinces and the territories to strengthen national and local labor markets. This resulted in a series of agreements between the federal government and the provincial governments that reflect regional priorities and interests with a focus in getting unemployed people back to work. These agreements allow the provinces a significant role in the design and delivery of employment benefits provided under the federal Employment Insurance Act.

References

Armstrong, J. 1998. "Some Thoughts on Alternative Service Delivery." *Optimum*, 28 1:1-10.

Aucoin, P. 1997. "The Design of Public Organizations for the 21st Century. Why Bureaucracy Will Survive in Public Management." *Canadian Public Administration*, 40 2: 290-306.

Aucoin, P. 1995. *The New Public Management: Canada in Comparative Perspective.* Montreal: Institute for Research in Public Policy.

Barberis, P. 1998. "The New Public Management and a New Accountability." *Public Administration*, 76 3: 451-70.

Barker, A. 1998. "Political Responsibility for U. K. Prison Security—Ministers Escape Again." *Public Administration*, 76 1: 1-24.

Bemelmans-Videc, M. L., R. C. Rist, and E. Vedung (eds.). 1998. *Carrots, Sticks and Sermons: Policy Instruments and Their Evaluation.* New Brunswick, NJ: Transaction Publishers.

Blau, P. 1963. *The Dynamics of Bureaucracy.* Chicago: University of Chicago Press.

Cabinet Office. 1999. *Modernising Government*, Cm. 4310. London: Stationery Office.

Consulting and Audit Canada. 1998. *Impediments to Partnering and the Role of Treasury Board.* Ottawa: Treasury Board Secretariat.

Cooper, P. J. 1995. "Accountability and Administrative Reforms: Towards Convergence and Beyond," in B. G. Peters and D. J. Savoie (eds.). *Governance in a Changing Environment.* Montreal: Queen's-McGill Press.

Delacourt, S., and D. G. Lenihan. 1999. *Collaborative Government: Is There a Canadian Way.* New Directions #6. Toronto, Ontario: Institute of Public Administration of Canada.

Dwivedi, O. P. and J. I. Gow. 1999. *From Bureaucracy to Public Management: The Administrative Culture of the Government of Canada.* Toronto: Broadview Press.

Dyer, B. 1996. *The Oregon Option: Early Lessons from a Performance Partnership in Building Results-Driven Accountability.* Washington, DC: National Academy of Public Administration.

Farrell, C. M., and J. Law. 1999. "Changing Forms of Accountability in Education? A Case Study of LEAs in Wales." *Public Administration*, 77 2: 293-310.

Frank, F., and A. Smith. 1997. *The Partnership Handbook.* Ottawa: Human Resources Development Canada.

Friedrich, C. J. 1940. "Public Policy and the Nature of Administrative Responsibility," in C. J. Friedrich and E. S. Mason (eds.). *Public Policy.* Cambridge: Harvard University Press, pp. 3-24.

Finer, H. 1941. "Administrative Responsibility in Democratic Government." *Public Administration Review*, 1: 335-350.

Hodgetts, J. E. 1991. *Public Management: Emblem of Reform for the Canadian Public Service.* Ottawa, ON: Canadian Centre for Management Development.

Jenkins, B., and A. G. Gray. 1993. "Reshaping the Management of Government: The Next Steps Initiative in the U.K.," in L. Seidle (ed.), *Rethinking Government: Reform or Reinvention?* Montreal: Institute for Research on Public Policy, pp. 71-118.

Kernaghan, K., and j. Langford. 1990. *The Responsible Public Servant.* Halifax: Institute for Research on Public Policy.

Kernaghan, K., and D. Siegel. 1995. *Public Administration in Canada.* 3rd edition. Toronto, ON: Nelson.

Lazar, H. (ed.). 1998. *Canada: The State of the Federation 1997: Non-Constitutional Renewal.* Kingston: Institute of Intergovernmental Relations.

Mattessich P., and B. Monsey. 1992. *Collaboration: what Makes it Work—A Review of Research Literature on Factors Influencing Successful Collaboration.* St. Paul, MN: Amherst Wilder Foundation.

Mazmanian, D., and P. Sabatier. 1983. *Implementation and Public Policy.* Glenview, IL: Scott, Foresman.

Mosher, F. 1968. *Democracy and the Public Service.* New York: Oxford University Press.

Noel, A. 2000. *Without Quebec: Collaborative Federalism with a Footnote?* Institute for Research on Public Policy, Vol. 1, no. 2.

OECD. 1997. *Managing Across Levels of Government*. Paris: OECD.

Office of the Auditor General and Treasury Board Secretariat. 1998. Modernizing Accountability Practices in the Public Sector: Discussion Draft. Available at *www.tbs-sct.gc.ca/rma/account*.

Office of the Auditor General. 1999 *Report for 1999*. Chapter on *Collaborative Arrangements: Issues for the Federal Government*. Ottawa, ON: Minister of Supply and Services.

Pacquet, G. 1999. "Tectonic Changes in Canadian Governance," in L. Pal (ed.), *How Ottawa Spends 1999-2000*. Toronto, ON: Oxford University Press.

Pollitt, C. 1995. "Management Techniques for the Public Sector: Pulpit and Practice," in B. G. Peters and D. J. Savoie (eds.), *Governance in a Changing Environment*. Montreal: McGill Press, pp. 203-238.

Pressman, J., and A. Wildavsky. 1979. *Implementation*. 2nd ed. Berkeley: University of California Press.

Public Policy Forum. 1998. Performance Management: Linking Results to Public Debate. Available at *www.tbs-sct.gc.ca/rma/account*.

Rush, B., and A. Ogborne. 1991. "Program Logic Models: Expanding Their Role and Structure for Program Planning and Evaluation." *Canadian Journal of Program Evaluation*, 6 1: 95-106.

Seidle, F. L. 1995. *Rethinking the Delivery of Public Services to Citizens*. Montreal: Institute for Research on Public Policy.

Steering Committee of Deputy Ministers. 1994. *Study on Accountability for Grant, Contribution and Other Transfer Payments Delivered Through Third Parties: Final Report*. Available at www.tbs-sct.gc.ca/rma/account.

Sutherland, S. 1991. "The Al-Mashat Affair: Administrative Accountability in Parliamentary Institutions." *Canadian Public Administration*, 34 4: 573-603.

Taylor-Powell, E., B. Rossing, and J. Geran. 1998. *Evaluating Collaboratives: Reaching the Potential*. Madison: University of Wisconsin-Extension.

Treasury Board Secretariat. 1995. *The Federal Government as Partner: Six Steps to Successful Collaboration*. Ottawa: Treasury Board Secretariat.

Treasury Board President. 1999. *Managing for Results Annual Report for 1999*. Ottawa, ON: Treasury Board

Weber, E., and A. Khademian. 1997. "From Agitation to Collaboration: Clearing the Air through Negotiation." *Public Administration Review*, 57/5, 396-410.

Wholey, J. 1983. *Evaluation and Effective Public Management*. Boston, MA: Little Brown.

10

Evaluation and Collaborative Government: Lessons and Challenges

Andrew Gray and Bill Jenkins

The years immediately after the Second World War brought both judicial and extra-legal retribution for many who had collaborated with now defeated powers. In those days collaboration had a distinctly pejorative, even sinister meaning. In contrast, the chapters of this volume have provided a distinctly more positive view of the aims and benefits of collaboration with the agencies of the state. Indeed, in some countries the pursuit of collaboration has constituted both a positive value of a democratic political system and a hallmark of a civil society (Putnam 2000).

In this chapter we will reflect on this more positive view by first summarizing what the earlier chapters have discovered about the emergence of collaboration in public service delivery and its evaluation. We shall then discuss the implications of the developments chronicled and revisit the rationale for collaboration.

Evaluating Collaborative Arrangements: Coping with New Contexts

Previous chapters provide a varied chronicle of the manifestations of collaboration in a number of systems of government and the emerging challenge for policy and program evaluation within them. Mayne, Wileman, and Leeuw (chapter 2) examine the development of *partnering and networks*. They paint a picture of government departments seeking out partners in local government, voluntary organizations and pressures groups in order to develop policy and build delivery capacity both within a policy area and across boundaries (e.g., the Waterfowl case). Partnerships and networks appear in some ways driven by performance outcomes, but importantly also by the values brought by collaboration itself. The attendant blurring of accountabilities and diffusion of objectives towards capacity building and away from rational outcome frameworks present difficulties for traditional evaluation approaches and methodologies. In particular, evaluation has to consider the relative emphasis in evaluation on economic or social factors and the need to assess process (e.g., partnering) as well as results.

Jenkins, Leeuw, and Van Thiel (chapter 3) explore the peculiar world of *Quangos as collaboratives*. That the British Labour government can argue that in spite of past sins Quangos may be a way of enhancing collaboration suggests they may be a transferable policy technology. It also reveals the Quango as both an end in itself and a means to an end. Thus, in both the UK and the Netherlands it has been used for a variety of different political purposes. However, the authors provide examples (such as the British Health Action Zones) of Quangos that have been designed and developed as collaborative agencies. They also reveal something of a paradox in this development. While the dysfunctions of the fragmented hierarchy and market regimes have led to a need for alliances and networks to address intractable cross-cutting issues (such as social exclusion), the new agencies have been simply added to existing arrangements and have thus aggravated the fragmentation of the state at the same time as addressing it. Moreover, the authors point out the value of collaboration as less a means for delivering discrete policy outputs than as a mechanism in itself. British work in the evaluation of the Health Action Zones has shown this feature shaping novel evaluation approaches incorporating "realistic evaluation" (Pawson and Tilley 1997) and models of social change (Connell et al. 1995). The suggestion here is that models of evaluation designed for hierarchical program delivery of outcomes might not be appropriate for collaborative organizational systems.

Schwartz's contribution (chapter 4) discusses a push by governments in different countries to enhance policy development *via collaboration with voluntary organizations*. The latter range from altruistic informal groups to professionalized charities with powerful political connections and are known collectively as the "third sector." A more restricted steering role for government has looked increasingly favorably on collaboration with this sector as a way to lessen the burden of policy delivery, energize outside groups and gain legitimacy. Schwartz suggests that in Israel the major advantage of such collaboration might be to "provide services in a complementary or supplementary fashion." But he draws attention to a number of complicating issues. These include (a) the sometimes dubious political agenda (nepotism and beyond) that may shape collaboration, (b) the resistance of many sector groups to formal evaluative mechanisms (as they prefer ambiguity for both for political and fund raising reasons) and (c) the sensitivity of collaboration that values organization (and the sustainability of this) above truth. It is thus not difficult to appreciate that formal evaluative mechanisms might be counterproductive here and that a dominant communion mode of governance might require more bottom-up or realistic evaluation. But even this will require a management of the particular politics of evaluation that characterizes working with this sector.

Voluntary organizations are often cited by users as providing more attention than their public sector counterparts to *consumer need and quality of service*. Mayne and Rieper (chapter 5) show that (a) service quality is of general and increasing importance to governments in a variety of contexts, (b) the search for quality leads to the creation of collaborative arrangements and (c) these factors in turn challenge the design and operation of evaluative mechanisms. Collaboration is seen as a mode necessary to the development of service quality arrangements in their single window or one-stop shop Canadian and Danish examples. However, the partnering leads to problems for accountability as the different parties involved in these activities and their differing perspectives (values) affect the way collaboration mechanisms are established and evaluated. The authors thus speculate on what should happen to the evaluation of these arrangements. They propose what they see as three foci for evaluation in public service quality: (1) the implementation process of quality initiatives, (2) the success of the same and (3) the success of the programs and institutions that are engaged with this. Thus they argue that implementing evaluation for quality in collaborative systems may be highly problematic.

In a discussion drawing on the experience of Nordic countries Arvidsson (chapter 6) sees waves of public management from traditional hierarchies through markets to the *collaboration or pooling of resources*. Government efforts to create markets and contracts to achieve greater efficiency and effectiveness in service delivery have not been totally successful; hence the move to pooling resources. Arvidsson notes that collaboration has a distinguished history as a tool of public policy and shows in cases of contracting out in Danish national government and Stockholm health care that even the competition involved in securing contracts may involve collaboration. But he also observes that such possible negative effects of collaboration as elite collusion and monopoly over policy areas may lead in turn to control problems. From his examination of the operation of contracting out and pooling resources he argues that evaluation may need to develop its traditional functions of control, validation and innovation to accommodate a new role, that is, trust building in quasi markets. He is aware, however, of the challenges of involving multiple stakeholders and recognizes that the complexities of evaluating collaborative arrangements may, at best, be poorly understood.

Results-based governance is revisited by Mayne (chapter 7). He concurs with other contributors to this volume that the architecture of state is changing and with it various sets of relationships. In particular, he sees traditional values and practices, such as trust and parliamentary accountability, under challenge from new complexity, collaboration and citizen engagement. Much of the pressure in Canada, for example, lies in a failure to employ rational and empirically grounded measurement systems. Such a regime of results-based governance would increase trust, flexibility, and empowerment, clarify roles and responsibilities and assist coordination. Yet there are problems even here. Drawing on examples in a range of OECD countries and work by the World Bank, Mayne suggests that the pressures for this outcome orientation will in turn put collaborative relationships under pressure to deliver both policy results and involvement (including by citizens through information technologies). However, results-based governance can at the same time help to deal with uncertainties and develop learning government. Results-based governance can thus go beyond output measures to assess effectiveness and provide a framework through which collaboration can be achieved. This will require new forms of evaluation.

But what of the *role of the audit institutions* in this and the implications for the fundamental accountability relationships? The message from Bemelmans-Videc (chapter 8) is quite simple: that Supreme Audit Institutions (SAIs) have come under pressure as new public management appears to be failing to deliver as promised. Drawing on Dutch and Canadian experiences that involve actors across several layers of government, she demonstrates how SAIs are faced by novel situations to which they are attempting to adjust. However, they are showing signs of overlooking their traditional roles as guardians of accountability and representatives of parliament. Indeed, in the manner of Power (1997), a central issue may be the appropriate checking role in a system where performance of service delivery is being built on the collaboration of multiple actors and where trust may be a central value and objective.

The message here is perhaps that such collaborative mechanisms are not so much new as now more numerous and made more complex by including supra-national issues (e.g., European dimension). As such they throw up evaluative challenges for the approach and methods of SAIs (including its accommodation with the traditional regularity audit role), the relationships with their auditees and even the traditional independence as agents of parliaments. Particularly striking is the question of the appropriate function (constitutional, managerial, and enlightening) of evaluating a world of delegation and decentralization. In the past SAIs have tended to respond to challenges by marginally adjusting the status quo rather than constructing new and different methodologies and approaches. The main question for Bemelmans-Videc is whether this will be sufficient to meet the methodological challenge without threatening some of the fundamental values that underpin traditional functions.

The *accountability* issue central to both the SAI role and the developing collaboratives is examined by Segsworth (chapter 9). The Canadian response to an experience of programs involving multiple partners (including in provincial and local governments) seems to have been a series of official guidelines on collaboration and partnering that seeks to formalize accountability mechanisms often through the development of results-based systems for the collaborative. Segsworth is not sure of the efficacy of such a formal response and notes that evaluation has the potential to "enhance the accountability issues involved in collaborative arrangements." However, for various reasons (illustrated by Canadian examples) this potential is not realized. Indeed, he finds that "Canadian experience suggests that collaboration inhibits evaluation." In support of this thesis Segsworth characterizes accountability relationships in collaboration and examines how the various accountabilities in col-

laborative relationships have been officially conceptualized in results-based terms in the Canadian context. He concludes that the
identified potential of evaluation may be realized only by "new"
modes of evaluation to enhance accountability and other collaborative functions and include an evaluation of the collaborative itself
which should not be taken as a self-evident good.

Patterns of Collaboration

As the preceding paragraphs suggest, the earlier chapters have
revealed some emerging patterns of collaboration in the state at the
beginning of the twenty-first century. They have indicated, for example, at least four *objectives of collaboration*. First, *improving policy
delivery* may be seen in networks seeking to integrate policy interests to gain effects (chapter 2), Quangos circumnavigating block-
ages in existing political organizations (chapter 3), and service quality being defined more in terms of consumer need (chapter 5) and
other outcomes (chapter 7). Second, policy delivery has been seen
as hindered by institutional and processual weaknesses: thus the
need for *development of policy capacity* by joining up mechanisms.
Partnering and networks (chapter 2) and working with the voluntary and private sectors to pool resources (chapters 4 and 6) are thus
parts of a strategy for governmental redesign of policy delivery that
collectivizes policy skill, experience and learning. Third, the argument for developing networks and partnering is based on the objective of *developing social capital* through collaboration (chapter 2).
Similarly, the rationales for working with and through the third sector (chapter 4) and with service consumers (chapter 5) are based
heavily on a communion mode of governance in which "active communities" of policy delivery are encouraged. And, fourth, we may
see in collaboration the *development of alternative policy instruments*, in some cases to outflank established interests (chapter 3)
and in other cases to co-opt or incorporate them (chapter 4).

The chapters have also shown something of the architecture of
collaborative government. Departments of State are shown to be
principal architects of many of the networks (chapter 2), Quangos
(chapter 3) and collaborations with the third and private sectors
(chapters 4 and 6). Despite the homogeneity of parentage, the new
architecture of collaboration is strikingly varied. It comprises local
authorities, Quangos, third sector, private sector organizations in
almost every conceivable combination of public-private-third sec-

tor collaboration. Indeed, the manifestations of collaboration suggest co-working by government agencies and co-government. Such
a distinction suggests that we may characterize collaboratives by
the status of the collaborators or types of organization. Thus, intergovernmental collaboration is that between sovereign national authorities as in the European Union. In contrast intra-governmental
collaboration is that within a government and may be vertical as
between levels such as federal, provincial and local authorities, or
horizontal as between central departments or agencies at the same
level. A third variant is extra-government collaboration, in which
government agencies work with external partners from the private
and voluntary sectors (see Box 10.1).

A third set of observed patterns portrays the relationships under
collaborative change. The history of commissioning and providing
services, for example, has been traditionally dominated by the command economy. More recently, especially in the last twenty years of
the twentieth century, this pattern has been significantly altered in
a number of countries with quite distinct regimes by various ad-
ventures in the creation of internal markets. They are now being
further influenced by new collaboratives seeking to pool resources
across and within command and contract arrangements (chapter 6).
The shift involves Quangos, for long instruments of the command

Box 10.1
Collaboration Classified by Status of Partners

1. Inter governmental collaboration
e.g., security collaboration between nation states

2. Intra governmental collaboration
(a) Vertical collaboration
e.g., federal-state-local;
(b) Horizontal collaboration
e.g., department-department;
department-non departmental agency

3. Extra governmental collaboration
(a) Government - voluntary sector
(b) Government - private sector
(c) Government - citizen

and contract state, which are now seen also as ways of replacing contract either through their regulatory potential or by re-bridging the commissioning and providing functions and incorporating the interests of service users (chapter 3).

The relationship of *service and consumer* is also clearly being reformed through collaboratives that focus on integrating user needs and thereby enhancing quality of service (chapter 5). Indeed, a principal rationale of collaboration is the joining up of government to meet user need, especially in tackling social deprivation. But, we have seen some tension between this relationship and the emphasis on the now more visible discrete service outcomes in part a product of results-based performance allocation (chapter 7). And the *auditing relationship*, under much pressure as Supreme Audit Institutions are accused of being part of the overemphasis in our systems of government on checking at the expense of doing, is further challenged by the complexity of tracking responsibilities in collaborative ventures (chapter 8). This in turn creates tensions within *accountability*. Quangos, for example, now even more established under collaboration, are seen by many as part of the democratic deficit with obscure processes and criteria (chapter 3). Moreover, while we observe a recognition that collaboration has made more complex the liabilities to give accounts, the recorded tendency has been to codify and thus formalize a results-based governance that brings its own problems (chapters 9 and 7).

A final set of relationships represents modes of governance. In the introduction to this volume (chapter 1) we suggested that governance was in essence not a form of government but the relationship through which authority and function are allocated and rights and obligations established and maintained. We suggested there were three ideal types or modes of relationship—command, contract and communion—whose emphases in the practice of government give the latter its characteristics. The explorations of subsequent chapters reveal that despite the essential communion of collaboration, much of the collaborative development identified has, perhaps paradoxically, come from command and contract. The statutory imposition in the United Kingdom of the Health Action Zones (Quangos described in chapter 3) and, more recently, Primary Care Trusts (new Quangos bringing together and commissioning local clinical, nursing and social services) are illustrations of the former and the joining of interests within market arrangements in Stockholm's health care (described in chapter 6) an example of the latter. Nevertheless, the consequent collaborations have altered the modes of governance distinctively with the result that new relationships emphasize trust and common purpose and may well offer a challenge to subsequent government attempts to impose direction through command. Thus, if primary care trusts, although creatures of statute, integrate strongly and develop distinctive communion and shared purpose in alliance with service users, they could be powerfully resistant to future central direction. Similarly, compacts between local governments and the voluntary sector could develop a sense of common purpose that form new establishments of vested interests. Thus today's enabling and empowering collaborations may come to be seen by tomorrow's central governments as wreckers and forces of conservatism.

Evaluating Collaboratives:
Challenges to Traditional Organizations and Processes

In the introduction we presented alternative sets of implications for evaluation brought by this developing collaboration in government. We speculated, first, that there was nothing new in collaboration, so evaluators might need only their usual toolkits, second, in contrast, that the changing nature of relationships between corporate actors in the collaborative society was so pervasive and complex that evaluators might require completely new methodologies, and finally that evaluators might after all not need to worry about all this because in the world of collaboration evaluation is not necessary: trust, commitment and reputation were all around and evaluation would only risk undermining the trust itself.

Even if collaboration with the third sector identifies something of the latter, in that shared political agendas might resist the function of formal evaluation and thus seek its substitution by trust and other shared understandings (chapter 4), the chapters in this volume have revealed a more complex world than that presented by these alternatives. Moreover, they confirm that evaluation is required to check that the collaborative mechanisms are working to provide the intended service and process values and even to assess the collaborative relationship itself. Evaluation can also bring understanding of the complex networks of relationships of collaborative ventures and thus may facilitate knowledge building in the collaborative development and inform debates and choices about collaborative alternatives to the problems of the effectiveness of the public sector. As

Mayne et al. argue in relation to their examples of waterfowl and labor movement partnerships (chapter 2), "there is not a priori evidence that the network or collaborative government approach is more efficient and effective [than hierarchies and markets and] evaluation and audit are clearly needed to determine how well these approaches to public sector management actually work."

Yet the greatest functional challenge is presented less by these variants of traditional evaluative tasks than by the intensification of the governance dilemma of checking (evaluation and audit) and doing (delivering goods and services). As Bemelmans-Videc shows (chapter 8), the checking functions of supreme audit institutions are not simply traditional but have developed from a distinct separation of principals and stewards in the delivery of policy and programs. Hierarchies and markets bring their own reasons for checking that stewards discharge their obligations to principals as intended. The expansion of state activities through these mechanisms has been matched (some such as Power 1997 would say more than matched) by the growth of the checking industry to such an extent that it is a burden on the very capacity of the state itself. Collaborations built on common purpose and trust may be seen, therefore, and not only by themselves but also by state architects, as mechanisms that will reduce this checking burden and release capacity for service delivery itself. If so, we may expect greater emphasis on self and even meta evaluation (trust building) and more rather than less distinction between the regularity and performance audit functions of supreme audit institutions and their like (chapter 8).

The chapters suggest, however, some limitations of traditional evaluation methodology in responding to such shifts of function. The limitation appears to be partly the result of limited capacity and experience in self-evaluation and a product of reliance by external evaluators on institutional approaches to service delivery and an only gradual recognition of the need for systemic and contingent approaches to the changes to the structures, processes and behavior of delivering public goods and services (chapters 8 and 9). Yet there is a clear change in evaluands. Collaboration with the third sector, for example, may be more appreciative of evaluations of the sustainability of organizational values than the traditional performance truths (chapter 4). Similarly, it appears that traditional evaluation mechanisms may have little experience in dealing with cross-cutting issues, the organizational systems of networks and Quangos and the need to assess their integrative capacity (chapters 2 and 3). Such limitations may limit evaluation's performance of the functions described above and lead it to under- or over-state the properties brought by collaboration.

Perhaps at the heart of the functional and methodological challenge is the necessary shift in evaluative criteria. Mayne et al. (chapter 2) stress the criteria that make for a successful collaboration: development of social capital, differentiation of goals from outcomes, appropriateness of the mix of partners and their patterns of interactions, levels of financial and human resources available, and formalization of structures and stability of partnering. The other chapters confirm that many collaboratives are designed not only to improve economy, efficiency and effectiveness but also democratic quality and legitimacy (chapter 8), social learning, adaptability and developmental capacity (chapters 3 and 7), political integration and nation building (chapter 4), and common purpose and trust (chapter 6).

It can be argued that these current discussions of the interactions between collaboration and evaluation might be limited by the narrow range of political and organizational contexts which the respective chapters draw on (further, see below). However, the evidence emerging from them tends to support both our original hypotheses: that is, that evaluation is being offered new functions, evaluators, evaluands, criteria and methodologies by collaborative reform, and that evaluation is being both substituted and complemented by collaborative and associated mechanisms. We wish to elaborate some of the principal implications and place these within the context of current discussions of the developing architecture of the state and rebuilding of civil society. We do this in the final section of this chapter. First, however, we return briefly to the wider context examined initially in chapter 1.

Collaboration and Evaluation: The Centrality of Context

The examples discussed in this book reflect experiences in a variety of political and institutional contexts but most notably in Canada, the UK, the Netherlands, Scandinaavia and Israel. As such they offer a set of illustrations drawn from well-established political systems (parliamentary and federal) with a long institutional history and well developed public policy structures. It is within these developed contexts that the collaborative histories recounted here are rooted. Even if evaluative mechanisms are less well developed they are often well-established bodies, such as Supreme Audit Institutions (SAIs), with several decades (if not longer) of experience at developing systematic evaluative mechanisms most frequently from a top-down, rationalistic perspective.

Some might suggest that these limitations should circumscribe the applicability of any findings to other settings. Certainly we would offer caution here but reinforce an observation made in chapter 1 that collaborative mechanisms can be found in a much wider variety of political contexts, including Latin America, post-Communist Europe and the emerging nations of Africa and Asia. As we have seen, the emergence of collaboratives in different and varying forms is often a product of particular circumstances and political history. However, there is also evidence that the perceived failings of policy delivery associated with traditional state bureaucracies or new market-led mechanisms have driven different political actors to share an engagement with collaborative arrangements as a strategic response, sometimes more rediscovered than discovered, to enhance service delivery and civic capacity.

In all this, collaborative mechanisms should be seen as policy instruments, often long established, that are subject to political forces and which almost certainly redefine inter-organizational politics between and within sectors (e.g., governmental, nongovernmental, markets). Evidence of this emerges clearly from the work of Agranoff and McGuire (2001), Mandell (1999, 2001) and others. Thus, while collaboratives are often advocated as ways of empowering lower tiers of government, civic groups and nongovernmental organizations it would appear, unsurprisingly, that powerful political actors (in particular governments) may and do use collaboration for their own purposes and hence the effectiveness of such arrangements cannot be assumed (Brinkerhoff 2000; Mandel 2001). Further, at a lower level, stakeholders drawn into collaboratives rarely relinquish their own organizational agendas for the collective good but rather battle to impose their own values on the overall goals of the enterprise. These and other issues inform a recent paper by Mandell and Steelman (2001) that highlights the need to set collaboratives in context in order to assess the effectiveness of such arrangements. In particular, it is argued that the operations of collaboratives may be influenced by a variety of factors including the history of relationships (the importance of adopting an institutional focus), the relative power of participants, the political and cultural context in which collaboration takes place and the policy issue and context around which activities are focused.

It is clearly impossible to apply this framework in detail here. Yet the chapters of this book do provide supportive evidence of, for example, the importance of historical and institutional contexts (Netherlands, chapter 3; Scandinavia, chapter 6), the interplay of internal politics (Israel, chapter 4), and the tensions within parliamentary systems in particular with regard to accountability relationships (chapters 3 and 9). Hence, any assessment of the effectiveness of collaborative arrangements demands a contingency approach that embraces internal organizational and political as well as socioeconomic environmental variables. In brief there is no "one best way."

Such factors also relate to the problems of evaluating collaboratives. As Jennifer Brinkerhoff (2000) argues, it is sometimes unclear what the function of collaboratives is intended to be (means or end?). This point is also emphasized by Provan and Milward (2001) who point out that the difficulty of evaluating collaborative arrangements or networks may be directly linked to the plurality of goals and objectives associated with collaboratives. They note that dealing with multiple organizations involves multiple sets of constituencies, in turn raising "substantial problems regarding resource sharing, political turf battles and the like" (2001: 416). For Provan and Milward, then, tensions arise from the differing expectations of distinct levels of stakeholders, ranging from the macro political or community level (political actors, funders and pressure groups) through the network level (intermediate administrative organizations, members of collaborative arrangements) to the organizational/participant level (e.g., street-level bureaucrats, grassroots organizations, client groups). The effect of all this is often (though not always) a set of tensions between levels arising from different agendas and priorities that feed disputes over evaluative approaches and measures as evaluative criteria are valued differently by differing groups. Hence, a macro-level concern with capacity building and the development of social capital may carry little weight with grassroots organizations seeking to maximize particular goals since, as the authors note, "individual organisations have constituency groups but networks do not" (2001: 422). Thus, the problems of evaluating collaborative arrangements may not be so much technical as organizational and political both in a macro and micro sense since the development of collaboratives and networks may, if these are not simply symbolic, alter or threaten the organizational context and power balances of governance systems.

Implications: Evaluation and Collaborative Mechanisms

We have already observed that the extension of collaborative government agencies promotes a more fragmented machinery of government while one of its principal rationales is to redress it. In part, this paradox may be explained by the use of collaboration as a means (a mechanism for addressing failures in policy delivery) and an end (a desired value in the civil society). In any event, the very significant development of collaborative ventures in the late twentieth and early twenty-first centuries has provided not only institutional innovation but also a changing architecture and governance of the state.

Much of the recent usage of architecture applied to organizations has followed Kay's seminal work (1995) on the factors contributing to corporate success in the private sector. For Kay, architecture is "a distinctive collection of relational contracts. The benefits of architecture typically rest in the development of organisational knowledge, flexibility in response, and information exchange within or between organisations" (p. 371). Jackson (2001) draws on this notion in his account of bureaucracy's contribution of added value to the public sector. In identifying modes of governance that are consistent with our usage of command, contract and communion, he expresses the architectural challenge for public services as finding "that architecture which will deliver operational efficiency, effectiveness and also *dynamic* efficiency" (p. 17, emphasis added). Dynamic efficiency embraces "a capacity to enhance information flows, to respond to external change and to be innovative over time [and]co-operation between the different elements within the system" (ibid.).

The success of attempts to meet this challenge, at least in the United Kingdom, has been well captured by Skelcher (2000). He depicts the state in the 1960s and 1970s as "overloaded," in the 1980s and early 1990s as "hollowed out" (after Milward and Provan 1993; Rhodes 1997) and in the period since as "congested." The congested state, says Skelcher, "denotes an environment in which high levels of organisational fragmentation combined with plural modes of governance require the application of significant resources

to negotiate the development and delivery of public programmes...
[through] mediating partnerships" (p. 12). Echoing the findings of
our earlier chapters, he points to the problems the new congestion
brings for legitimacy and capacity for providing goods and services.
The problem of legitimacy he attributes to the ill defined and less
visible authorities and accountabilities of partnerships; that of capacity to the demands of their mediating and negotiating dynamics.

Jackson and Skelcher both draw attention in their otherwise distinctive discussions to the values of collaboration and their impact
on the design and functioning of the delivery of public goods and
services. They are keen to assess the capacities within and demanded
by collaborative arrangements. This requires an elucidation of the
values to be promoted by collaboration and brings us back discur-
sively to social capital and its development. As a concept, social
capital may not be as clear as our account in the introduction (chapter 1) may have conveyed. There are, after all, different interpretations of its elements and prescriptions of its benefits; these range
from collaboration as joined up program delivery to viewing it as a
means of democratic enhancement (community empowerment) or
less state intervention through building up voluntary activity (Social Exclusion Unit 2000). There have also been criticisms of the
broader Putnam thesis (2000) that we outlined in our introduction.
These have questioned both its accuracy in analyzing societal developments and in its prescriptions for rebuilding society in the
United States and elsewhere (Lowndes and Wilson 2001).

We will not engage with this debate here but recognize Putnam's
work as evidence of a decline in civic engagement, a feature of
social and political life that may be associated with the difficulties
that governments face in policy delivery. In particular, the enhancement of a *contract* mode of governance (see chapter 1) has led to
fragmentation and individualization while the language and cur-
rency of markets have eroded organizations and practices based on
more socially cohesive mechanisms and values. One typical response
to the ensuing delivery problems has been to impose or reimpose
command styles of governance leading to further implementation
failures and difficulties together with a continuing decline in such
values as trust. This has contributed to a cycle of more delivery
problems, continued fragmentation and further erosion of legitimacy.
Hence, the case for the Putnam solution, in terms of creating political capacity by developing social capital, gathers strength and stimu-

lates increased interest in collaboration and collaboratives as a manifestation of a *communion* mode of governance.

Here we may link up the Putnam concern with civil society (shared
by communitarian writers such as Tam 1998) with our earlier attention to architecture. As Lowndes and Wilson note (2001), the Putnam
argument tends to treat the architecture as a given or constant whereas
it is very much one of the variables. Recognizing the latter allows
questions to be asked by evaluation that are important to those who
value the development of social capital. Such questions might include
"how far do institutional arrangements promote or hinder the development of policy capacity and social capital?" and "are program goals
and targets consistent or inconsistent with collaborative values?"

If the previous discussion provides few certainties, we may observe, first, that the current debate on collaboration is part of a general concern for state capacity, legitimacy and relations with society, second, collaborative institutions are dynamic organizational
and political relationships and, third, efforts to evaluate collaboratives
risk aggravating tensions arising from the complexity of relationships and call into question some fundamental assumptions regarding the form and function of evaluation itself. However, these observations suggest that our initial reflections (chapter 1) on (a) the
analytical typology of collaboration, (b) the discussion of the rationale for collaboration in the provision of public goods and services,
and (c) the preliminary assessment of the functions of evaluation
may require modification. For example, the typologies of collaboration sketched out earlier and which argued that an examination of
collaboration would be enhanced by an examination of *the status of
collaborators* (or type of organizations involved) and *the modes of
governance* (i.e., command, contract or communion relationships),
have been confirmed as at least diagnostically functional. But it is
now clearly necessary to widen the construct to embrace the *context* in which collaboratives emerge. The interaction between actors
and organizations needs to be located within a developmental and
environmental setting that allows the history of the collaborative
relationship to be charted and interpreted.

Such a widening of the analytical framework is also required to
explain the emergence of collaboration as a preferred political strategy. It was argued in the introduction that three key reasons for
advancing down the collaborative road were (a) to share information, solutions and learning, (b) to build social capital, and (c) to

limit the need for formal control and to reduce transaction costs. Yet, on further reflection, it now appears that such explanations account for some of rather than this entire story. For example, collaboration may widen rather than limit formal control (the mechanism of capture) and the social capital thesis embraces more diffuse and complex themes than those initially examined. Further, and more crucially, the politics of collaboration often expose competing agendas from above (political executives) and below (collaborative actors), characterized by a variety of differing goals and objectives that are only sometimes reconciled in the collaborative operations.

While the functions (and limits) of evaluation are clearly crucial it is also important to recognize the ideological underpinnings of different evaluative mechanisms (e.g., rationalistic and realistic) and that different evaluative functions may compete and thus aggravate tensions within the collaborative system. The function to check and control, for example, may run counter to efforts to develop collaborative relationships and facilitate the development of social learning and capacity building. Thus, the macro and micro functions are not only different but also arise from competing agendas, interpretations and ideologies reflecting the very essence of a partnership.

Thus, in conclusion we note (a) the effects and impact of differing modes of collaboration, (b) the consequences for collaboration and evaluation of moving into quality and results-based government and (c) the inherent tensions between traditional methods of auditing and evaluating state activities in their application to the world of collaboratives. Collaborative ventures have their own contexts in which they are functional and dysfunctional. They demand a management of contingent relations in which dilemmas are inherent. They are not only means for delivering results but enhance a distinct mode of governance with its own values and emphasis on capacity development. Thus, their evaluation faces the task of addressing the values of outcomes and of processes.

References

Agranoff, R., and M. McGuire. 2001. "American Federalism and the Search for Models of Management." *Public Administration Review*, 61/6, 671-81.

Ashby, E. 2000. "Bowling Alone." *Politics Review*, 10/1, 30-3, September.

Brinkeroff, J. 2000. "Conceptual Overview." Comments in Seminar on *Intersectoral Partnering: Tools for Implementation and Evaluation*. Dialogue Notes, April 12.

Connell, J. P., A. C. Kubisch, L. B. Schorr, and C. H. Weiss (eds.). 1995. *New Approaches for Evaluating Community Initiatives: Concepts, Methods and Contexts*. Washington, DC: The Aspen Institute.

Jackson, P. M. 2001. "Public Sector Added Value: Can Bureaucracy Deliver?" *Public Administration*, 79/1, 5-28.

Kay, J. 1995. *Foundations of Corporate Success*. Oxford: Oxford University Press.

Lowndes, V., and D. Wilson. 2001. "Social Capital and Local Governance: Exploring the Institutional Design Variable." *Political Studies*, 49/4, 629-47.

Mandell, M. 1999. "The Impact of Collaborative Effects: Changing the Face of Public Policy through Networks and Network Dtructures." *Policy Studies Review*, 16/1, 4-17.

Mandell, M. (ed). 2001. *Getting Results through Collaboration: Networks and Network Structures for Public policy and Management*. Westport, CT: Quorum Books.

Mandell, M., and T. Steelman. 2001. "The Impact of Networks on Issues of Governance: Developing Strategies for the Future." Paper presented to International Institute for Administrative Sciences (IIAS) Conference, *Government and Administration for the 21st Century*, Athens, Greece.

Milward, H. B., and K. G. Provan. 1993. "The Hollow State: Private Provision of Public Services," in H. Ingram and S. R. Smith (eds), *Public Policy for Democracy*. Washington, DC: Brookings Institution.

Pawson, R., and N. Tilley. 1997. *Realistic Evaluation*. London: Sage Publications.

Power, M. 1997. *The Audit Society: Rituals of Verification*. Oxford: Oxford University Press.

Provan, K. G., and H. B. Milward. 2001. "Do Networks Really Work? A Framework for Evaluating Public Sector Organizational Networks." *Public Administration Review* 6/4, 414-23.

Putnam, R. 2000. *Bowling Alone*. New York: Simon and Schuster 2000.

Rhodes, R.A.W. 1997. *Understanding Governance: Policy Networks, Governance, Reflexity and Accountability*. Buckingham: Open University Press.

Skelcher, C. 2000. "Changing Images of the State: Overloaded, Hollowed-Out and Congested." *Public Policy and Administration*, 15/3, 3-19.

Social Exclusion Unit. 2000, *Policy Action Team 17: Joining Up Locally: The Evidence Base*. London: Cabinet Office.

Tam, H. B. 1998. *Communitarianism: A New Agenda for Politics and Citizenship*. Basingstoke: Macmillan Press.

Contributors

Göran Arvidsson is research director of the Swedish Center for Business and Policy Research (SNS), Stockholm. He is also a part-time associate professor at the School of Business, Stockholm University. He has previously been head of Secretariat of the Expert Group on Public Finance at the Swedish Ministry of Finance and director of the Methods Development Division of the predecessor to the Swedish National Financial Management Authority. He has been a consultant to the OECD, the Swedish Parliament, national, regional, and local government agencies, as well as to private corporations. His research interests include management and financial control in the private and public sectors.

Marie-Louise Bemelmans-Videc is professor of Public Administration, Faculty of Management Sciences, at the Catholic University of Nijmegen, and a Senator in the Netherlands Parliament. Her previous appointments include Leiden University and the Netherlands Court of Audit. She is co-founder of the European Evaluation Society and has co-edited several books on evaluation, auditing, policy instrument choice, and public administration theory.

Denis Desautels, OC, FCA, was auditor general of Canada from 1991 to 2001 and is currently the executive director of the Centre on Governance, an interdisciplinary research and teaching unit of the University of Ottawa. The focal point of the Centre's expertise is collaborative governance systems that underpin complex patterns of decision making—both in and across the public, private and civic sectors. Desautels is currently a member of the Accounting Standards Oversight Council of the Canadian Institute of Chartered Accountants and of the International Auditing and Assurance Standards Board of the International Federation of Accountants. He is also a member of the board of directors of a number of companies and not-for-profit organizations.

Andrew Gray is emeritus professor of Public Sector Management (formerly University of Durham, UK) and now a freelance academic. He is editor of *Public Money and Management*, and from 1999 to 2002 was chairman of the UK Public Administration Committee, the Learned Society for Public Policy and Administration. His research and teaching interests are in the management of mixed economies in the provision of public services. His publications (most with Bill Jenkins) include *Budgeting, Auditing and Evaluation*, Transaction Publishers, 1993.

Bill Jenkins is professor of Public Policy and Management at the University of Kent at Canterbury, UK. His main research interests are in public sector management, public administration, modern British politics and public policy evaluation. He has published widely with Andrew Gray in these areas. Recent work includes a contribution to J-E. Furubo, R. C. Rist, and R. Sandahl (eds.), *International Atlas of Evaluation*, Transaction Publishers, 2002. He is also deputy editor of the journal *Public Administration*.

Frans Leeuw is chief review officer, the Netherlands' Inspectorate for Education, Utrecht, where he is responsible for higher education, knowledge management, evaluation studies, and international affairs. He also is professor of Sociology, Evaluation Studies, Faculty of Social Sciences, Utrecht University. Previous appointments include dean, Netherlands Open University and director of Performance Auditing and Evaluation at the Netherlands Court of Audit. He has also been a Fullbright Scholar with the University of North Carolina at Chapel Hill and president of the European Evaluation Society (1999-2002). He has authored numerous articles, reports, and books in the areas of policy and program evaluation and performance monitoring.

John Mayne is a principal with the Office of the Auditor General of Canada, where he is responsible for the audit areas of accountability and governance practices, managing for results, alternative service delivery, and performance measurement and reporting. He worked previously in the Treasury Board Secretariat and the Office of the Comptroller General, where he was instrumental in the development of the government of Canada's approach to evaluating programs. In recent years, he has been leading efforts at developing effective performance reporting and related auditing practices. He has authored a wide range of articles, reports, and books in the areas of program evaluation, public administration, and performance monitoring.

Olaf Rieper has an MA in sociology (1974) and a Ph.D.in Organization Theory from the Copenhagen Business School, and is an associate professor at the Institute of Local Government Studies, Denmark (AKF), since 1985. Prior to that he was an associate professor at the Copenhagen Business School, Department of Organization and Sociology of Work. He has been visiting scholar at the School of Social Work, University of Michigan, and expert at the European Center for Evaluation Expertise, Lyon 1995-96. He has been teaching organization theory and research methods and is part-time lecturer in evaluation methods at the Department of Sociology at the University of Copenhagen. He is the first president of the Danish Evaluation Society.

Robert Schwartz is lecturer in the Political Science Department of the University of Haifa, Israel. He has published widely on issues of accountability, evaluation, auditing and government—third sector collaboration. Recent publications appear in the *Journal of Public Policy*, *Financial Accountability and Management*, and *International Public Management Journal*. Schwartz has also served as editor of a symposium issue of the *International Journal of Public Administration*, titled "Collaborating with the Third Sector–Problem or Solution: Lessons from the Israeli Experience."

Bob Segsworth is professor of political science and director, Centre for Local Government, at Laurentian University in Sudbury, Canada. He served as editor of the *Canadian Journal of Program Evaluation* from 1994 to 2002. His work has appeared in journals such as *The International Review of Administrative Sciences*, *Knowledge and Society*, *Canadian Public Administration*, and the *Canadian Journal of Progam Evaluation*. He has been a member of INTEVAL since its inception.

Sandra Van Thiel is assistant professor in Public Administration, Erasmus University Rotterdam, the Netherlands. Her publications include *Quangocatization: Trends, Causes and Consequences*, ICS University of Utrecht.

Tom Wileman is director, Office of the Auditor General of Canada, where he manages audit projects in the areas of accountability and governance practices, alternative service delivery, managing for results, and First Nations governance. He worked previously in the Library of Parliament, Research Branch, as research officer seconded to the Standing Committee on Public Accounts of the House of Commons.

Index